PROGRAMS, RECURSION AND UNBOUNDED CHOICE

Cambridge Tracts in Theoretical Computer Science

Titles in the series

1. G. Chaitin *Algorithmic Information Theory*
2. L.C. Paulson *Logic and Computation*
3. M. Spivey *Understanding Z*
4. G. Revesz *Lambda Calculus, Combinators and Functional Programming*
5. A. Ramsay *Formal Methods in Artificial Intelligence*
6. S. Vickers *Topology via Logic*
7. J-Y. Girard, Y. Lafont & P. Taylor *Proofs and Types*
8. J. Clifford *Formal Semantics & Pragmatics for Natural Language Processing*
9. M. Winslett *Updating Logical Databases*
10. K. McEvoy & J.V. Tucker (eds) *Theoretical Foundations of VLSI Design*
11. T.H. Tse *A Unifying Framework for Stuctured Analysis and Design Models*
12. G. Brewka *Nonmonotonic Reasoning*
13. G. Smolka *Logic Programming over Polymorphically Order–Sorted Types*
15. S. Dasgupta *Design Theory and Computer Science*
17. J.C.M. Baeten (ed) *Applications of Process Algebra*
18. J.C.M. Baeten & W. P. Weijland *Process Algebra*
23. E.-R. Olderog *Nets, Terms and Formulas*
27. W.H. Hesselink *Programs, Recursion and Unbounded Choice*
29. P. Gärdenfors (ed) *Belief Revision*
30. M. Anthony & N. Biggs *Computational Learning Theory*

PROGRAMS, RECURSION AND UNBOUNDED CHOICE

Predicate-Transformation Semantics and Transformation Rules

WIM H. HESSELINK
Department of Computer Science
University of Groningen

CAMBRIDGE
UNIVERSITY PRESS

CAMBRIDGE UNIVERSITY PRESS
Cambridge, New York, Melbourne, Madrid, Cape Town, Singapore, São Paulo

Cambridge University Press
The Edinburgh Building, Cambridge CB2 2RU, UK

Published in the United States of America by Cambridge University Press, New York

www.cambridge.org
Information on this title: www.cambridge.org/9780521404365

First published 1992
This digitally printed first paperback version 2005

A catalogue record for this publication is available from the British Library

ISBN-13 978-0-521-40436-5 hardback
ISBN-10 0-521-40436-3 hardback

ISBN-13 978-0-521-01829-6 paperback
ISBN-10 0-521-01829-3 paperback

CONTENTS

PREFACE

This book is about programs as mathematical objects. We focus on one of the aspects of programs, namely their functionality, their meaning or semantics. Following Dijkstra we express the semantics of a program by the weakest precondition of the program as a function of the postcondition. Of course, programs have other aspects, like syntactic structure, executability and (if they are executable) efficiency. In fact, perhaps surprisingly, for programming methodology it is useful to allow a large class of programs, many of which are not executable but serve as partially implemented specifications.

Weakest preconditions are used to define the meanings of programs in a clean and uniform way, without the need to introduce operational arguments. This formalism allows an effortless incorporation of unbounded nondeterminacy. Now programming methodology poses two questions. The first question is, given a specification, to design a general program that is proved to meet the specification but need not be executable or efficient, and the second question is to transform such a program into a more suitable one that also meets the specification.

We do not address the methodological question how to design, but we concentrate on the mathematical questions concerning semantic properties of programs, semantic equality of programs and the refinement relation between programs. We provide a single formal theory that supports a number of different extensions of the basic theory of computation.

The correctness of a program with respect to a specification is for us only one of its semantic properties. We are equally interested in its incorrectness or its equivalence to other programs. For example, we provide formal rules to prove that a recursive procedure does not meet its specification.

The book can be used for courses on predicate–transformation semantics of various sizes. For an introductory course, I prefer to use Chapters 1, 2, 3 and 4, but Chapter 4 can be replaced by subjects from Chapter 5 or by Chapter 6, possibly followed by 7. The more powerful methods of program transformation are contained in Chapters 10, 11 and 12; these chapters should be accessible after 4, 6 and 7 have been covered. Chapter 14 on temporal predicate transformers can be treated directly after Chapter 4.

Some of the material grew out of courses of lectures on programming or programming theory delivered at the University of Groningen. Other parts of the book grew out of my need for a non–operational understanding of standard implementation techniques like the use of stacks for the implementation of recursive procedures. Chapters 14 and 15 were directly inspired by [Morris 1990].

I offer sincere thanks to A. de Bruin, J.J. Lukkien, J. Morris, R. Reinds, J.C.S.P. van der Woude and J. von Wright for critically reading drafts of the book. I also want to express here my deepest gratitude to the three persons who have stimulated and guided my transition from mathematics to computer science: J.W. de Bakker, E.W. Dijkstra and J.L.A. van de Snepscheut. Van de Snepscheut was for five years the inspiring leader of our department. Under his direction I got the opportunity to spend a sabbatical year at the University of Texas at Austin, in 1986/1987. There I worked with Dijkstra, who converted me to a new mathematical discipline, ten years after I had obtained my doctorate in mathematics. Finally, De Bakker showed continuous interest in my computer science papers and encouraged me to write this book. Of course, there were many more persons who stimulated my development but no enumeration can do justice to all of them.

Wim H. Hesselink

Groningen, the Netherlands
June 1991

LIST OF SYMBOLS

Symbols are listed by section number.

Postfix operators

$-^*$ 4.3

$-^{\odot}$ 4.3, 10.1

$-^e$ (where $e = 0$ or 1) 4.4

$\heartsuit$ 0.0

Special parentheses

[ ] 0.0, 1.1

[/] 10.1

{ } 0.6, 2.1

$[\![\ ]\!]$ 6.4

Programming operators

! 1.3

? 1.3

; 1.4, 4.7, 6.2

$[\!]$ 1.4, 4.7, 6.2

$[\!]_f$ 15.2

Relational operators

$\cong$ 0.3, 1.3

$=_V$ 1.6

$\neq_V$ 1.6

$\vdash$ 2.7

$\leq$ 4.1

$\sqsubseteq$ 5.1

$<$ 5.6

$\approx$ 11.3, 12.3

$\ll$ 12.2, 13.3

CHAPTER 0

INTRODUCTION

0.0. The purpose of this book is to develop the semantics of imperative sequential programs. One prerequisite for reading is some familiarity with the use of predicates in programming, as exposed for instance in the books [Backhouse 1986], [Dijkstra 1976], or [Gries 1981]. Some mathematical maturity is another prerequisite: we freely use sets, functions, relations, orders, etc. We strive for providing complete proofs. This requires many backward references but, of course, the reader may sometimes prefer to ignore them. Actually, at every assertion the reader is invited to join the game and provide a proof himself.

In every chapter, the formulae are numbered consecutively. For reference to formulae of other chapters we use the convention that $i(j)$ denotes formula (j) of Chapter i.

At the end of almost every chapter we give a number of exercises, grouped according to the latest relevant section. When referring to exercise $i.j.k$, we mean exercise k of Section $i.j$. Some exercises are simple tests of the reader's apprehension, while other exercises contain applications and extensions of the main text. For (parts of) exercises marked with ♡ we provide solutions in Chapter 16.

References to the literature are given in the form [X n], for author X and year n, possibly followed by a letter.

0.1 Semantics of imperative sequential programs

The word 'semantics' means 'meaning'. In the title of this book, it announces two central themes. The meaning of a program is given by its specification. This leads to the correctness issue: does the program meet its specification? The other theme is program transformation. In fact, when we have separated the meaning from the program, we can ask whether there exist more than one program with that meaning, so that it can be useful to transform the program into a more suitable one of the same class.

We restrict ourselves to imperative sequential programs. Such a program is a command to change the internal state of the computer – and part of the internal state may be visible for output. The easiest way to formalize the meaning of a command is by means of the relation between initial and final states. This method of formalization is called relational semantics. It is theoretically attractive but not well–suited for correctness proofs or derivations of interesting programs. In fact, in the relation between initial and final state, every program variable can have two rôles: it may refer to the initial value or to the final value of the variable. Therefore, in relational semantics, the sequential composition of commands may require extensive renaming. Nevertheless, relational semantics is used rather convincingly in [Hehner 1992].

In actual programming we prefer to use the Floyd–Hoare method, which is based on the following idea. One associates state predicates to points in the program text and uses inductive reasoning to prove that the predicate of a point holds whenever execution of the program reaches that point. This method is formalized in various ways that are known under a number of different names: axiomatic semantics, Hoare logic, dynamic logic, weakest precondition semantics, etc. We use the term predicate–transformation semantics.

Thus, our choice of semantics is motivated by its applicability to programming methodology. Indeed, the important properties of programs are easily expressed in terms of predicate transformers. Predicate–transformation semantics has good modularity properties. It allows an elegant definition of the meaning of recursive procedures that is compatible with the operational semantics but not itself operational.

Finally, predicate–transformation semantics can effortless be combined with nondeterminacy (even unbounded nondeterminacy). Indeed, one of the issues of programming methodology is to avoid over–specification and premature design decisions. Thus, if we require that program variable x gets a positive value, it is important to specify just that, and to postpone a specific choice to a later design phase or perhaps to the compiler. Therefore we want our programming language to contain a construct for unbounded nondeterminate choice, compare [Back 1988].

The realization of this requirement is a distinctive feature of the present book. It is absent from the classical treatises [de Bakker 1980] and [Dijkstra 1976]. The treatment of unbounded nondeterminacy for the repetition is due to [Dijkstra-

Scholten 1990] and, independently, [Apt-Plotkin 1986]. Inspired by Dijkstra's notes, I treated unbounded nondeterminacy for recursive procedures in [Hesselink 1988], essentially by means of relational semantics. The present combination of predicate transformation semantics, recursion and unbounded choice seems to be new.

0.2 Predicate–transformation semantics

We concentrate on control rather than data. So, in the formal theory, the state space is a set without structure and the programs are program schemas built in terms of unspecified simple commands. The semantics are expressed by means of weakest precondition functions *wp* and *wlp*, cf. [Dijkstra 1976]. Roughly speaking, *wp.c.p* is the weakest precondition such that command c terminates and establishes postcondition p, whereas *wlp.c.p* is similar but does not guarantee termination of c.

The basic constructors of commands are the operators for sequential composition and unbounded nondeterminate choice. This yields a powerful foundation. If the set of simple commands contains guards to test for interesting conditions, it is possible to model conditional statements, bounded repetitions and nonrecursive procedures with parameters.

The next step is to introduce recursive procedures. In order to extend the functions *wp* and *wlp* to these commands, we use the condition that every procedure be semantically equivalent to its body. This yields recurrence equations for *wp* and *wlp*. The extended function *wp* is defined as the strongest solution of its equation. The extended function *wlp* is defined as the weakest solution of its equation. This definition agrees with the operational semantics, even in the presence of unbounded nondeterminacy.

A central concept is semantic equality of commands. Since we admit nondeterminacy and nontermination, it is important to decide how to deal with commands that have both finite and infinite execution sequences. In such cases, one may choose to neglect the finite execution sequences. From the point of view of program correctness, this may be a harmless simplification, cf. [Hehner 1984]. Theoretically, it is more attractive to neglect the infinite execution sequences, cf. [de Bakker-de Roever 1973], [Harel 1984]. We follow [Nelson 1989], [Dijkstra-Scholten 1990] and others in using both functions *wp* and *wlp*. In this way, we incorporate both the possibility of nontermination and the results of all finite execution sequences into the semantic formalism. So, for us, the nondeterminate choice *skip* $\|$ *abort* differs semantically both from *skip* (do nothing) and from *abort* (loop forever).

For the ease of computation with commands as mathematical objects, the abstract syntax is kept as small as possible. It only contains simple commands, sequential composition, unbounded nondeterminate choice and (mutually) recursive procedures. In examples and applications we use a concrete syntax which also contains conditional statements, while–loops and procedure parameters. The translation of these constructs into the abstract syntax turns out to be straightforward.

0.3 Program transformations

We describe several kinds of program transformations:

- modification of expressions in assignments, in 1.7
- unfolding: replacing a procedure name by its body, in 2.5
- distributivity, in 3.3
- insertion of guards, in 5.3
- commutation of commands, in 5.4 and 12.4
- stack implementation of recursive procedures in 9.1 and 9.2
- procedure abstraction, in 10.3 and 10.4
- computational induction, in 11.3 and 12.2
- storage of procedure parameters, in 11.5
- change of procedure declaration, in 11.6

In most of these cases, what we actually present is a rule to prove semantic equality. An important property is that semantic equality is compositional with respect to sequential composition and (unbounded) choice. So, if we use '$\cong$' to denote semantic equality, we have

$$c0 \cong c \quad \wedge \quad d0 \cong d \quad \Rightarrow \quad c0; d0 \cong c; d \quad \wedge \quad c0 \,\|\, d0 \cong c \,\|\, d .$$

Semantic equality, however, is not compositional with respect to declarations of recursive procedures. If the body of procedure h is semantically equal to a command expression q that may contain h, the semantics of h can change if we replace the declaration of h by $\mathbf{body}.h = q$. In fact, every procedure h satisfies $\mathbf{body}.h \cong h$, but, if the declaration is replaced by $\mathbf{body}.h = h$, then h becomes equivalent to *abort*. This situation suggests that we need to look for an equivalence relation on command expressions stronger than semantic equality and compositional with respect to recursive declarations. In Chapter 11, we introduce such a relation. It is called the *strong congruence*. It is responsible for the last three items of the above list.

In [Hesselink 1990], we constructed a related congruence, but the formalism was too restrictive for the application in [Hesselink 1989a]. In fact, our previous formalism did not provide unbounded choice as a constructor. Here, we allow unbounded choice and obtain the results needed.

0.4 Overview

The book can be divided into four parts. Part A consists of Chapters 1, 2, 3, 4 and 5; it contains the introduction, the formal foundation and some additional material. Part B consists of Chapters 6, 7, 8 and 9; it contains the relational semantics and a treatment of disjunctivity properties of commands. Part C consists of Chapters 10, 11, 12 and 13; it deals with program transformation. Part D consists of Chapters 14 and 15; in this part the semantic framework is extended to include some temporal properties of commands. The main dependencies of the chapters are indicated in the directed graph shown below.

$$
\begin{array}{ccccccccc}
& & & & 5 & & & 14 & \to & 15 \\
& & & & \uparrow & & & \nearrow & & \\
1 & \to & 2 & \to & 3 & \to & 4 & \to & 10 & \\
& \searrow & & \nearrow & & & & \downarrow & & \\
& & 6 & \to & 7 & \to & 8 & \to & 11 & \to & 12 & \to & 13 \\
& & & \searrow & & & & & & & \uparrow & & \\
& & 4 & \to & 9 & & & & & & 5 & &
\end{array}
$$

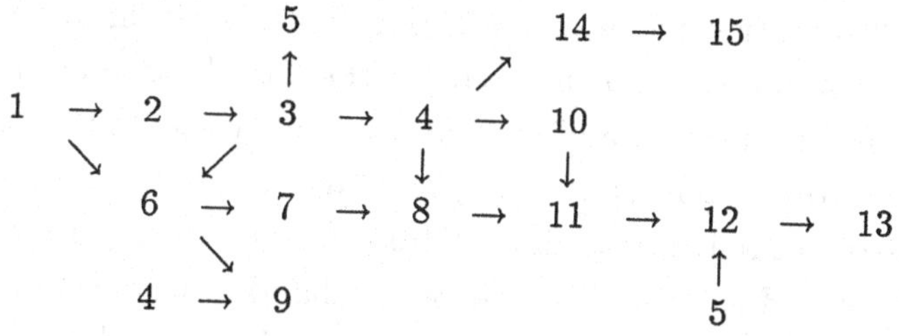

For clarity of the graph, the nodes 4 and 5 have been duplicated. The arrow between 3 and 6 can be reversed at will. The arrow between 8 and 11 is rather weak.

We regard part A as the most important one, for it contains the development of a very simple model that is yet effective and powerful. We hope that parts B, C and D can be appreciated independently from each other. Part B provides an operational background, which can be seen as a foundation for part A, and which is also useful for some details in parts C and D. Part C contains the results on program transformation and computational induction. In order to obtain sharp results, we were forced to develop a complicated theory. Part D consists of less heavy material. It sheds new light on concepts like termination, stability, progress and fairness, but we do not claim practical applicability.

It is our intention that each chapter adds a layer of understanding that is useful without support from later chapters. To this end we sometimes use the postulational method. For example, in Chapter 2, recursion is introduced by means of proof rules that are used in programming. The semantics of recursion are formally defined in Chapter 4, and the proofs of some proof rules are postponed until Section 4.9. The heaviest material of the book is concentrated in Chapter 9, which leads to an independent goal, and in Chapters 8 and 13, which are needed to prove the results postulated in Chapters 11 and 12.

0.5 The chapters in detail

We proceed with a brief description of the chapters. First Part A. Chapter 1 is an introduction to the predicate–transformation semantics of straight–line commands. In particular, we treat guards, assertions, assignments, sequential composition and unbounded choice. It is a survey of known material with some new points of view. The only result with a substantial proof is the substitution rule for the weakest precondition of the assignment.

In Chapter 2 we introduce Hoare triples as a specification method and a tool to prove program correctness. The next step is the introduction of procedures with correctness rules for declaration and invocation. The postulate that a procedure is semantically equal to its body is used to prove the soundness of the proof rule for total correctness of recursive procedures. Hoare's Induction Rule for conditional correctness is presented as well, followed by a related induction rule to prove necessity of preconditions. Finally the results on recursive procedures are specialized to the repetition.

In Chapter 3, we introduce Dijkstra's healthiness conditions, and we investigate their formal consequences. One of the consequences discussed is the distributivity of sequential composition over unbounded choice.

Chapter 4 is the heart of the book. It contains the formal definition of the semantics of recursive procedures and the proofs of the properties of commands that were postulated and used in the previous chapters. It begins with a brief excursion into lattice theory that culminates in a version of the theorem of Knaster–Tarski. We then come back to programming, fix the abstract syntax, define the semantics of recursive procedures and prove the fundamental properties of recursive procedures.

Chapter 5 is a kind of appendix to Part A. It has only weak ties with the rest of the book. It contains a number of different subjects: refinement of commands, refinement of procedures, some examples of semantic equality, strongest postconditions and proof rules with well–founded sets.

Part B begins with Chapter 6. Here we present the relational semantics. We give the relational interpretations of totality and nontermination, composition and nondeterminate choice. We show that, under assumption of the healthiness laws, the expressive power of relational semantics equals the expressive power of predicate transformation semantics.

In Chapter 7, we treat determinacy of commands and disjunctivity properties of the associated predicate transformers. The concept of determinacy of commands is split into liberal determinacy and termination determinacy. We prove that liberal determinacy of a command is equivalent to positive disjunctivity of the weakest liberal precondition and that finite nondeterminacy is equivalent to upper continuity of the weakest precondition.

In Chapter 8, we obtain syntactic results concerning total, disjunctive, determinate, and finitely nondeterminate commands. A command is said to be of finite nondeterminacy if every initial state in which the command is bound to terminate, allows only finitely many resulting states. This concept played a crucial rôle in some early treatments of the semantics of nondeterminacy, cf. [Dijkstra 1976] and [de Bakker 1980] p. 263. We do not need finite nondeterminacy for the basic properties of recursive procedures. The concept is necessary, however, in our treatment of the strong congruence.

In Chapter 9, we treat a stack implementation of recursive procedures. Actually, the problem of proving the validity of such a stack implementation in terms of the axiomatic semantics was the challenge that triggered our investigations. We then define the relational or operational semantics of recursive procedures, and prove the equivalence with the semantics of Chapter 4.

Chapter 10 is the opening chapter of Part C. It introduces substitution of procedure names and treats a kind of program transformation that can be characterized as the introduction of intermediate procedures.

In Chapter 11, we postulate the existence of the strong congruence and some of its properties. It is compositional with respect to sequential composition and unbounded choice, and it implies semantic equality. Moreover, it satisfies a so–called accumulation rule, which is our version of the induction rule of De Bakker and Scott (cf. [de Bakker 1980] Section 9.3 and [Hesselink 1990] Section 5). This rule is illustrated by some examples. It is used to prove that the strong congruence is compositional with respect to recursive declarations.

In many applications, refinement is more important than semantic equality. Therefore, in Chapter 12, we introduce a 'strong preorder', which plays the same rôle with respect to refinement as the strong congruence plays with respect to semantic equality. This preorder is also used to prove the postulates concerning the strong congruence. In Chapter 13, we construct the strong preorder and prove its properties.

In Part D that consists of Chapters 14 and 15, the semantics are extended to include predicates concerning states that are visited during execution of the commands. In Chapter 14, we introduce temporal predicate transformers related to those of [Morris 1990] and [Lukkien 1991]. They can be characterized by the key–words 'always' and 'eventually', to be interpreted here as 'at every induced procedure call' and as 'at some induced procedure call', respectively. Following Morris, we use these predicate transformers in Chapter 15 for a treatment of predicative fairness. The examples of this chapter are illuminating and show that our formalism interprets fairness in unexpected ways, especially in cases of more complicated recursion.

0.6 Notation

We use the operator '.' for function application. This operator has the highest binding power. It binds from left to right to allow currying. Thus, typically, the expression $D.w.h.p$ stands for $((D.w).h).p$. The set of functions from a set X to a set Y is denoted by Y^X or $X \to Y$ (the second notation is preferred if X is a complicated expression). Accordingly, $f \in X \to Y$ means that f is a function from X to Y. If W is a subset of X, we write $(f|W)$ to denote the restriction of f to W, which is a function in $W \to Y$. Multiplication of integers is denoted by '$\cdot$' which takes more white space than function application, compare $2 \cdot i$ with $f.x$. Functional composition is denoted by means of the infix operator $\circ$, so that typically $(f \circ g).x = f.(g.x)$.

We use Dijkstra's quantification format. For example, the quantification

$$(\forall i \in I : P.i : Q.i)$$

expresses that $Q.i$ holds for all values $i \in I$ such that $P.i$. We enclose the whole expression in parentheses, since that makes it easier to parse formulae where such an expression is an operand of a binary operator. Domain expression $P.i$ is omitted if it is identically true. The same format is used for other quantifiers like $\exists$, sup, $\bigcup$, $\|$, etc.

A quantification can be regarded as the application of a quantifier to a family, where the concept of family is defined as follows. If I and X are sets, P is a boolean function on I and $f.i \in X$ for every $i \in I$ with $P.i$, then the *family* $(i \in I : P.i : f.i)$ is the entity consisting of the terms $f.i$ with $i \in I$ and $P.i$. Formally speaking, a family of elements of X is a function with values in X, but conceptually the emphasis is on the elements of X and not on the function. The family is called a *sequence* if the set I consists of natural numbers.

We use the following boolean operators (logical connectives) in order of decreasing priority. The negation '$\neg$' has the highest priority, followed by conjunction '$\wedge$' and disjunction '$\vee$' of equal priority, followed by the implication symbols '$\Rightarrow$' and '$\Leftarrow$' of equal priority, followed '$\equiv$' for logical equivalence, i.e. equality of boolean values. Equality of functions (even of boolean valued functions) is denoted by '$=$'. We use the symbol '$\subset$' to denote (nonstrict) subset inclusion

$$A \subset B \quad \equiv \quad (\forall x \in A :: x \in B) .$$

Strict subset inclusion $A \subset B \wedge A \neq B$ does not occur very often, and will therefore be stressed accordingly.

Whenever convenient, we use Feijen's proof format for calculational proofs, with braces '{' and '}' to enclose comment, cf. [Dijkstra-Scholten 1990]. For example, in order to prove that X follows from Z we may write

$$\begin{array}{ll} & X \\ \equiv & \{\text{indication why } X \text{ and } Y \text{ are equivalent}\} \\ & Y \\ \Leftarrow & \{\text{indication why } Y \text{ follows from } Z\} \\ & Z . \end{array}$$

If Z is trivially true, this format will be used as a proof of X. A similar format is used for other transitive relational operators.

Braces are also used in Hoare triples (cf. Section 2.1), and for enumerated sets. For example, $\{p, q\}$ is the set with two elements p and q. We write $\emptyset$ to denote the empty set. We write $\mathbb{Z}$ for the set of the integers and $\mathbb{N}$ for the set of the integers ≥ 0.

If P is a boolean function on a set X, the set of the elements $x \in X$ with $P.x$ is conventionally defined by $Y = \{x \in X | P.x\}$. Instead of this braces notation, we prefer to define Y as the subset of X given by $x \in Y \equiv P.x$ for all $x \in X$. For calculational purposes, this way of introducing Y is more convenient. In fact, the equivalence is directly used in all references to the definition of Y. The wish to avoid overloading of the braces is a second reason.

0.7 Design decisions

In the composition of the theory we have made various choices and rejected several alternatives. Of course, a reader satisfied by the results need not be interested in the alternatives, but nevertheless a justification of the main choices should be given.

We use predicate–transformation semantics instead of relational semantics or denotational semantics, since it is more useful for programming and reduces the temptation to use operational arguments. Moreover, we do not know a construction of the strong congruence in terms of relational semantics.

Theoretically minded computer scientists often prefer to define the meanings of programs by means of denotational semantics. Denotational semantics are sometimes characterized by key properties like compositionality, usage of environments to bind the meanings of procedure names and usage of extreme fixpoints to define the semantics of recursion. Our semantics are denotational in that sense. On the other hand, denotational semantics are also sometimes thought to capture the essential results of completed computations in terms of the initial situation. In this sense, weakest precondition semantics are never denotational.

In [Apt-Plotkin 1986], denotational semantics is assigned to a class of while–programs over a countable state space. The authors also define operational semantics and *wp*–semantics, and prove the equivalence of the semantical paradigms. It seems that this work (without the results on completeness and complexity) can be extended to our language and an arbitrary state space. We have refrained from doing so, since it is not our aim to compare semantical paradigms.

Our treatment of predicate–transformation semantics does not require a separate logic. We present a mathematical theory with definitions, axioms, theorems and proofs, rather than a version of dynamic logic. To quote from [McCarthy 1980] p. 37: *In our opinion, it is better to avoid modifying the logic if at all possible, because there are many temptations to modify the logic, and it would be very difficult to keep them compatible.* For example, we use Dijkstra's pair of square brackets not as a primitive predicate symbol but as a convenient abbreviation: we have a fixed state space X, and for a boolean function p on X we write $[\,p\,] \equiv (\forall x \in X :: p.x)$, cf. Section 1.1.

A second fundamental decision is the choice to use the implication order of predicates and predicate transformers, and not the approximation order of [Nelson 1989] p. 518, which is a kind of translation of the so-called Egli–Milner order to pairs of predicate transformers. Our choice has the advantage that the functions *wp* and *wlp* for recursive procedures can be defined independent of each other. Since we do not use Nelson's order, we cannot admit Nelson's constructors '$\boxtimes$' and '**if–fi**' (see loc.cit. p. 534 and p. 557) in bodies of recursive procedures.

A third design decision is to impose two of Dijkstra's healthiness laws (the universal conjunctivity of *wlp* and the termination law, see Chapter 3 below) and to abolish Dijkstra's law of the excluded miracle. These decisions work together. The accepted laws imply that sequential composition of commands distributes over unbounded choice:

$$q;(\,[\!]\, r \in C :: r) \quad \cong \quad (\,[\!]\, r \in C :: q; r).$$

Freedom for miracles implies that the conditional combination can be expressed in terms of composition and choice, see Section 1.5. These two observations enable us to model all command expressions (in Section 4.3) as nonempty sets of sequences of elementary commands. This greatly simplifies the formal syntax. A second reason for postulating the universal conjunctivity and the termination law is that some of the crucial technical arguments (e.g. in Section 10.2) need positive conjunctivity of the predicate transformers involved.

For the sake of simplicity we do not use the terminology of command algebras of [Hesselink 1990]. Unbounded choice would have required a rather heavy construction of completions of command algebras, whereas in the present framework it suffices to work with sets of strings of commands.

It has been proposed that we might include an account of the history of the subject. This, however, is beyond the scope of the present monograph. To give a minimum of historical references, the function '*wp*' was introduced in [Dijkstra 1975]. Its relational interpretation was discussed in [de Roever 1976]. The distinction between '*wp*' and '*wlp*' was introduced in [Dijkstra 1976], but the idea of '*wlp*' goes back to [de Bakker-Meertens 1975]. For other aspects of axiomatic semantics, we refer to [Apt 1981]. Many concepts are quite old, but the importance is often recognized later, by researchers who are not aware of the earlier occurrences. For example, Hoare's inductive assertion method is usually attributed to Floyd, but, according to [de Bakker-Meertens 1975] p. 328, it was in essence proposed in [Turing 1949].

CHAPTER 1

WEAKEST PRECONDITIONS

1.0. In this chapter, we introduce straight–line commands and the semantic framework. It is a survey of known material with some new points of view. The stress is on the semantics, to prepare the ground for general recursion with unbounded nondeterminacy. The issues of formal syntax related to unbounded choice are postponed to Chapter 4.

If j is a program variable, command j := j + 1 specifies a change of the state of the computer. If j = 2 in the initial state, the resulting state satisfies j = 3. If we want the resulting state to satisfy j < 5, it is necessary and sufficient that the initial state satisfies j < 4. This is expressed in

$$wp.(\mathtt{j} := \mathtt{j}+1).(\mathtt{j} < 5) \quad = \quad (\mathtt{j} < 4)\ ,$$

in words, the weakest precondition for command j := j+1 and postcondition j < 5 is j < 4.

We regard expressions like j < 5 as boolean functions on the state space. If x is a state where j has value 9 then $(\mathtt{j} < 5).x$ = false. Boolean functions on the state space are called predicates. Thus, *wp*.(j := j + 1) is a function from predicates to predicates, a so–called predicate transformer, and *wp* is a function from commands to predicate transformers. Function *wp* and its twin *wlp* to be introduced below form the central concept of this book. In fact, for a command *c*, the pair (*wp.c*, *wlp.c*) is regarded as the meaning of *c*, i.e., its predicate–transformation semantics.

In Section 1.1, we formalize our view of predicates and predicate transformers. In Section 1.2, we introduce the functions *wp* and *wlp* and discuss their interpretation and some of their properties. In the remainder of the chapter, we define *wp.c* for straight–line commands *c*, i.e., commands that are constructed from simple commands by means of composition and choice, but without recursion or repetition.

1.1 Predicates and predicate transformers

Let X denote the state space of a computer. The elements of X are called *states*. We let $\mathbb{B}$ denote the set of the two boolean values false and true, so that we can define $\mathbb{P} = \mathbb{B}^X$ to be the set of the boolean functions on the state space. The elements of $\mathbb{P}$ are called *predicates*.

Warning: many authors use the term predicate syntactically, for boolean expression. For us, however, the predicates form a semantic concept: they are boolean functions.

We define *false*, *true* $\in \mathbb{P}$ as the constant functions with the values false and true, respectively. For predicates $p, q \in \mathbb{P}$, we define predicates $\neg p$, $p \wedge q$, $p \vee q$, $p \equiv q$, $p \Rightarrow q$ by pointwise application, so that for all $x \in X$:

(0)
$$\begin{aligned} \neg p.x &\equiv \neg(p.x) \ , \\ (p \wedge q).x &\equiv p.x \wedge q.x \ , \\ (p \vee q).x &\equiv p.x \vee q.x \ , \\ (p \equiv q).x &\equiv (p.x \equiv q.x) \ , \\ (p \Rightarrow q).x &\equiv p.x \Rightarrow q.x \ . \end{aligned}$$

Similarly, the conjunction and disjunction of a family of predicates $(i \in I :: p.i)$ are given by

(1)
$$\begin{aligned} (\forall i \in I :: p.i).x &\equiv (\forall i \in I :: p.i.x) \ , \\ (\exists i \in I :: p.i).x &\equiv (\exists i \in I :: p.i.x) \ . \end{aligned}$$

The universal quantification $[\,p\,]$ of a predicate p over the state space is defined by

(2) $$[\,p\,] \ \equiv \ (\forall x \in X :: p.x) \ .$$

By definition, the equality $p = q$ is an abbreviation of $[\,p \equiv q\,]$. It follows that $[\,p\,]$ is equivalent to $p =$ *true*.

Example. The truth of $[(\exists i \in I :: p.i)]$ means that in every state there is some index i such that $p.i$ holds in that state. This is weaker than the truth of $(\exists i \in I :: [p.i])$: there is some i such that $p.i$ holds everywhere.

More concretely, let $f \in \mathbb{Z}^X$ be an integer valued function on the state space. For integer i, let $f = i$ denote the predicate given by $(f = i).x \equiv (f.x = i)$. For every state x, there is a value i with $f.x = i$; this proves that $[\,(\exists i :: \ f = i)\,]$. If function f is not constant, there is no value i such that $f.x = i$ holds for all x; this shows that $\neg(\exists i :: [\,f = i\,])$. (End of example)

Calculations with predicates can be reduced to calculations with boolean values, and these can be performed by means of truth tables, i.e., by extensive case distinction. Experience shows that this method is very inefficient and error prone. The method of natural deduction may be more secure, but is not efficient either. Therefore, we use the equational style of reasoning developed by Dijkstra and others, which is called predicate calculus. This calculus can be presented in an axiomatic way, see [Dijkstra-Scholten 1990]. For our purposes, however, it is sufficient to know a number of basic equalities. A sample of useful rules is contained in the appendix at the end of this chapter and in the exercises.

Since elements of $\mathbb{P}$ are called predicates, a function $f \in \mathbb{P} \to \mathbb{P}$ is called a *predicate transformer*. Functions preserve equality. So, for all predicates p and q, the equality $p = q$ implies $f.p = f.q$, or equivalently

$$[p \equiv q] \quad \Rightarrow \quad [f.p \equiv f.q] \; .$$

An important application of definition (2) is the concept of strength of predicates: p is called ***stronger*** than predicate q if and only if $[p \Rightarrow q]$. This defines an order on $\mathbb{P}$. A predicate transformer $f \in \mathbb{P} \to \mathbb{P}$ is called *monotone* if and only if, for all p, $q \in \mathbb{P}$,

(3) $$[p \Rightarrow q] \quad \Rightarrow \quad [f.p \Rightarrow f.q] \; .$$

Remark. Following [Barr-Wells 1990], we use the terms order, ordered set and monotone where other authors often use partial order, poset and monotonic. (End of remark)

Example. Let there be precisely one program variable v, which is of type integer. A state x is characterized by the value of v. We may therefore regard state x as an integer. Let predicate transformer f be given by

$$(f.p).x \quad = \quad p.(x+1) \wedge x > 0 \qquad \text{for all } p \in \mathbb{P},\ x \in X \; .$$

Then f is monotone, as is proved in

$$\begin{array}{ll} & [f.p \Rightarrow f.q] \\ \equiv & \{(2),\text{ and definition of } f\} \\ & (\forall x :: \; p.(x+1) \wedge x > 0 \Rightarrow q.(x+1) \wedge x > 0) \\ \Leftarrow & \{(2),\text{ and some calculus}\} \\ & [p \Rightarrow q] \; . \end{array}$$

Since f is defined in terms of states, we need states in the proof. In general, however, it is our aim to avoid states whenever possible. (End of example)

1.2 Weakest preconditions

A *command* is a syntactic unit intended to be executed by a computer. It specifies a relation between precondition and postcondition. It need not be deterministic or implementable. The semantics of a command c are given by predicate transformers *wp.c* and *wlp.c*. If p is a predicate, the predicate *wp.c.p* is the *weakest precondition* such that every execution of command c terminates in a state where predicate p holds. Predicate *wlp.c.p* is the *weakest precondition* such that every execution of c does not terminate or terminates in a state where p holds. Since the operator '.' binds from left to right, we do not need the parentheses in $(wp.c).p$. The argument p is called the *postcondition*.

This description of the predicates *wp.c.p* and *wlp.c.p* is to be regarded as an informal interpretation upon which no formal conclusions can be based. In fact, we treat the functions *wp* and *wlp* as primitive concepts with properties given by axioms and definitions. The above description is only used as a justification of such axioms and definitions. Readers who want to take the above description literally, can try and read Chapter 6 first where the relational semantics is presented.

Example. Running ahead of the formal development, we illustrate these concepts by giving the weakest preconditions for some commands and predicates. Since we lack the foundation required, we cannot give meanings and proofs. The reader may skip the example or use previous experience for the interpretation. Let $\mathtt{j}$ be an integer program variable. As announced above, $\mathtt{j} := \mathtt{j}+1$ is a command with

$$wp.(\mathtt{j} := \mathtt{j}+1).(\mathtt{j} < 5) \quad = \quad (\mathtt{j} < 4) \; .$$

The same equality holds if *wp* is replaced by *wlp*. More interesting is a loop like

$$L \quad = \quad \mathbf{while}\ \mathtt{j} \neq 0\ \mathbf{do}\ \mathtt{j} := \mathtt{j} - 1\ \mathbf{od} \; .$$

This loop terminates if and only if $\mathtt{j}$ is initially at least 0. If it terminates, the postcondition $\mathtt{j} = 0$ is established. Therefore, we have

$$\begin{aligned} wp.L.(\mathtt{j} = 0) &\quad = \quad (\mathtt{j} \geq 0) \; , \\ wlp.L.(\mathtt{j} = 0) &\quad = \quad \mathit{true} \; , \\ wp.L.(\mathtt{j} \neq 0) &\quad = \quad \mathit{false} \; , \\ wlp.L.(\mathtt{j} \neq 0) &\quad = \quad (\mathtt{j} < 0) \; . \end{aligned}$$

Command $(\mathtt{j} := -\mathtt{j} \;[\!]\; \mathit{skip})$ is the nondeterminate choice between $\mathtt{j} := -\mathtt{j}$ and *skip* (do nothing). Since we do not prescribe the choice, we have

$$wp.(\mathtt{j} := -\mathtt{j} \;[\!]\; \mathit{skip}).(\mathtt{j} < 5) \quad = \quad (-\mathtt{j} < 5) \wedge (\mathtt{j} < 5) \; ,$$

and similarly for *wlp*. (End of example)

The above description of *wp* and *wlp* easily justifies the following three axioms:

(4) $[\, wp.c.p \Rightarrow wlp.c.p \,]$,

(5) $[\, p \Rightarrow q \,] \;\Rightarrow\; [\, wp.c.p \Rightarrow wp.c.q \,]$ {monotony of *wp.c*} ,

(6) $[\, p \Rightarrow q \,] \;\Rightarrow\; [\, wlp.c.p \Rightarrow wlp.c.q \,]$ {monotony of *wlp.c*} .

Rule (4) can be interpreted to say: if command c is guaranteed to terminate in a state where p holds then c can only terminate in a state where p holds. Rules (5) and (6) can be rephrased: if p implies q everywhere then termination in a state where p holds implies termination in a state where q holds.

The informal description can be used to justify some more stringent postulates. In program development, however, it is often useful to admit specifications as commands, even if they are not implementable. We therefore postpone the introduction of postulates that are not yet needed.

Example. The present formalism admits a command *serve* that establishes the postcondition if and only if there exists a state where the postcondition holds; otherwise *serve* does not terminate (see [Back–von Wright 1990]). The command is defined by stating that, for all states x and predicates p,

$$wp.serve.p.x \;\equiv\; (\exists\, y \in X :: p.y) \;,$$
$$wlp.serve.p.x \;\equiv\; \text{true} \;.$$

Command *serve* is not implementable. It seems that the executing mechanism needs to 'know' the postcondition that the user has in mind. The axioms that forbid such commands are introduced in Chapter 3. (End of example)

Since the semantics of our commands are defined by means of *wp* and *wlp*, we define *semantic equality* of commands c and d by

(7) $c \cong d \;\equiv\; (wp.c = wp.d) \wedge (wlp.c = wlp.d)$.

For commands c and d, the notation $c = d$ is reserved for definitions and syntactic equality.

Remark. Definition (7) may need some justification. Why not choose only one of the conjuncts at the righthand side? Theoretically, it is attractive to choose the *wlp*–conjunct, in which case we could speak of *wlp*–equivalence. As early as 1972, a good theory of *wlp*–equivalence was presented in [de Bakker-de Roever 1973]. Since equivalence with respect to termination is not included, however, *wlp*–equivalence is not sufficient for all purposes.

For practical purposes, *wp*–equivalence is often enough. There are useful programs, however, in which nondeterminate occurrence of error conditions cannot be precluded. The occurrence of error conditions being modelled as nontermination, such a program is *wp*–equivalent to an arbitrary nonterminating program. Therefore, its useful behaviour is completely characterized by *wlp*. For this reason, we have chosen to include both *wp* and *wlp* in definition (7). (End of remark)

1.3 Guards, assertions, termination and totality

The first commands we are going to introduce formally, are guards and assertions. Operationally speaking, these commands do not change the state but only test whether a given predicate holds. They have nice calculational properties and are important as building blocks of conditional commands.

For any predicate b, the *guard* $?b$ and the *assertion* $!\,b$ are commands characterized by

(8) $$wp.(?b).p \;=\; (b \Rightarrow p) \quad , \quad wlp.(?b).p \;=\; (b \Rightarrow p) \; ,$$
$$wp.(!\,b).p \;=\; (b \wedge p) \quad , \quad wlp.(!\,b).p \;=\; (b \Rightarrow p) \; .$$

In principle, we have to verify that definition (8) is in accordance with laws (4), (5) and (6). This verification is very simple. For example, command $!\,b$ satisfies rule (4) because of

$$[\, b \wedge p \;\Rightarrow\; (b \Rightarrow p)] \; .$$

Remark. The reader is advised not to think operationally about $!\,b$ and $?b$. Nevertheless, the following description can be offered. The assertion $!\,b$ tests whether b holds. If so, it skips. Otherwise it loops indefinitely. The guard $?b$ also tests whether b holds. If so, it skips. Otherwise it does not execute,— which means that every execution (there is none) establishes every postcondition. Guards are nontotal commands: not every initial state has a corresponding final state, the set of final states may be empty. We come back to this at the end of this section, and also in Chapter 6. (End of remark)

Three important special cases are *skip*, *abort* and *miracle*, given by

(9) $$skip \;=\; ?true \quad (\cong \,!\,true) \; ,$$
$$abort \;=\; !\,false \; ,$$
$$miracle \;=\; ?false \; .$$

It is easy to verify that for any predicate p:

(10) $$wp.skip.p = p \quad , \quad wlp.skip.p = p \; ,$$
$$wp.abort.p = false \quad , \quad wlp.abort.p = true \; ,$$
$$wp.miracle.p = true \quad , \quad wlp.miracle.p = true \; .$$

Thus, *skip* and *abort* have their conventional meanings, see [Dijkstra 1976]. Command *miracle* is introduced in [Morris 1987]. It is called *Fail* in [Nelson 1989] and **magic** in [Back-von Wright 1989a].

For an arbitrary command c we now consider the special predicates $wp.c.true$ and $wp.c.false$. For a state x, proposition $wp.c.true.x$ is interpreted to mean that every computation starting in x terminates in a state where *true* holds, i.e., in an arbitrary state. In other words, c necessarily terminates from x. By quantification over all states we get the following definition. Command c is defined to be *necessarily terminating* if and only if

(11) $[\, wp.c.true \,]$.

On the other hand, proposition $wp.c.false.x$ is interpreted to mean that every computation starting at x terminates in a state where *false* holds. Since there are no states where *false* holds, there are no computations starting in x: we might say that c is not defined at x. Command c could be called defined at x if $\neg wp.c.false.x$. We shall not use these local concepts,— we only use the following global definition. Command c is defined to be *total* (or feasible, cf. [Morgan 1990] Section 21.3.6) if and only if

(12) $[\, \neg wp.c.false \,]$.

Now we can prove that guard command $?b$ is total if and only if $b = true$:

$$\begin{array}{ll} & ?b \text{ is total} \\ \equiv & \{(12)\} \\ & [\, \neg wp.(?b).false \,] \\ \equiv & \{(8)\} \\ & [\, \neg(b \Rightarrow false) \,] \\ \equiv & \{\text{calculus}\} \\ & [\, b \,] \, . \end{array}$$

On the other hand, it is easy to verify that the assert command $!\,b$ is total for every predicate b.

Remark. The reader may object to nontotal commands. In [Dijkstra 1976] and [Dijkstra-Scholten 1990], it is postulated that all commands be total. We shall not do so, for —as argued in [Nelson 1989]— this postulate is an obstacle for the development of a simple calculus of commands. See also [Morris 1987] and [Morgan-Gardiner 1990]. Compare the discussion about the existence of the imaginary numbers.

To show that guards are very useful building blocks, we announce that, in section 1.5, we shall prove that

$$\textbf{if } b \textbf{ then } c \textbf{ else } d \textbf{ fi} \quad \cong \quad ?b; c \;[\!]\; ?\neg b; d \; .$$

In section 1.8, we shall use guards to model the call $q.f$ of a procedure q with an actual value parameter f. (End of remark)

1.4 Composition and nondeterminate choice

We only need two operators for composition of commands: the operator ';' for sequential composition and the operator '[]' for nondeterminate choice.

The *sequential composition* $(c; d)$ of commands c and d is the command to execute c first and then d. For any postcondition p, this suggests that $wp.(c; d).p = wp.c.q$, where $q = wp.d.p$. This implies $wp.(c; d).p = wp.c.(wp.d.p)$, and hence $wp.(c; d) = wp.c \circ wp.d$. In the notation of the last step, we use that function application by '.' has a higher binding power than function composition by '∘'. We use a similar argument for *wlp*. In this way, we arrive at the following formal definition.

With *wg* ranging over *wp* and *wlp*, we define

(13) $\qquad wg.(c; d) \quad = \quad wg.c \circ wg.d \; .$

Sequential composition of commands thus corresponds to the composition of the predicate transformers. If c and d satisfy the laws (4), (5) and (6), the composition $(c; d)$ satisfies the same laws. This is easily verified. For example, the case of law (4) is verified in

$$\begin{array}{ll} & wp.(c; d).p \\ = & \{(13)\} \\ & wp.c.(wp.d.p) \\ \Rightarrow & \{(5), \text{ and } (4) \text{ with } p := wp.d.p \, , \; q := wlp.d.p\} \\ & wp.c.(wlp.d.p) \\ \Rightarrow & \{(5)\} \\ & wlp.c.(wlp.d.p) \\ = & \{(13)\} \\ & wlp.(c; d).p \; . \end{array}$$

Without proof we mention the following rules:

(14) $\qquad c; (d; e) \;\cong\; (c; d); e \qquad \{\textit{associativity}\}\,,$

$\qquad c; skip \;\cong\; c \;\; , \;\; skip; c \;\cong\; c \qquad \{\textit{neutrality}\}\,,$

$\qquad abort; c \;\cong\; abort \;\; , \;\; miracle; c \;\cong\; miracle \qquad \{\textit{pre-emption}\}\,.$

In all these cases the proofs are easy.

We now introduce the operator '$[\!]$' for nondeterminate choice. Informally speaking, command $(c [\!] d)$ offers the executing mechanism a choice between all executions of c and d. Since command $(c [\!] d)$ does not specify the choice, $wp.(c [\!] d).p$ should guarantee that either choice leads to termination in a state where p holds. We use a similar argument for *wlp*. Therefore, we define '$[\!]$' as the infix operator given by

(15) $\quad wg.(c [\!] d).p \;=\; wg.c.p \wedge wg.d.p$,

where *wg* ranges over *wp* and *wlp*. We give operator '$[\!]$' a lower priority than the composition operator ';'.

We generalize the choice operator to a quantifier. For any nonempty set C of commands, the *choice* $(\,[\!]\, c \in C :: c)$ is defined as the command with the weakest (liberal) precondition equal to the conjunction of the weakest (liberal) preconditions of the members of C:

(16) $\quad wg.(\,[\!]\, c \in C :: c).p \;=\; (\forall c \in C :: wg.c.p)$,

where *wg* ranges over *wp* and *wlp*. The reason for not allowing the empty choice will be discussed later, in Sections 3.3 and 4.8. Henceforth, we assume that C is nonempty whenever $(\,[\!]\, c \in C :: c)$ is mentioned without qualification.

Since the semantics of composition and choice are defined in terms of the semantics of the constituents, these operators respect semantic equality. For example, we have

$$c0 \cong c1 \;\wedge\; d0 \cong d1 \;\Rightarrow\; c0; d0 \cong c1; d1 \;\wedge\; c0 [\!] d0 \cong c1 [\!] d1 \,.$$

In section 0.3, this property was called the compositionality of '$\cong$'.

1.5 Intermezzo on the conditional combination

In the abstract syntax, we do not provide a separate construct for the conditional combination. Theoretically, such a construct is superfluous. In fact, the usual conditional statement for a condition b and alternative commands c and d satisfies

(17) $\quad \textbf{if } b \textbf{ then } c \textbf{ else } d \textbf{ fi} \;\cong\; ?b; c [\!] ?\neg b; d$.

This is proved by observing that, for *wg* ranging over *wp* and *wlp* and p ranging over $\mathbb{P}$,

$$\begin{array}{ll} & wg.(\textbf{if } b \textbf{ then } c \textbf{ else } d \textbf{ fi}).p \\ = & \{\text{standard definition}\} \\ & (b \Rightarrow wg.c.p) \;\wedge\; (\neg b \Rightarrow wg.d.p) \\ = & \{(8)\} \\ & wg.(?b).(wg.c.p) \;\wedge\; wg.(?\neg b).(wg.d.p) \\ = & \{(13) \text{ and } (15)\} \end{array}$$

$$wg.(?b; c \,[\!]\, ?\neg b; d).p \; .$$

According to [de Bakker-de Roever 1973] p. 176, formula (17) goes back to [Karp 1959].

Dijkstra's more general nondeterministic conditional combination can also easily be expressed. In fact, for a nonempty family of predicates $(i \in I :: b.i)$ and a corresponding family of commands $(i \in I :: c.i)$, the conditional combination

$$IF \;=\; \mathbf{if} \,[\!]\, i \in I :: b.i \;\rightarrow\; c.i \;\mathbf{fi}$$

is defined by

$$\begin{aligned} wp.IF.p \;&=\; bb \wedge (\forall i \in I :: b.i \Rightarrow wp.(c.i).p) \;, \\ wlp.IF.p \;&=\; (\forall i \in I :: b.i \Rightarrow wlp.(c.i).p) \;, \end{aligned}$$

where $bb = (\exists i \in I :: b.i)$, the disjunction of the predicates $b.i$, see [Dijkstra 1976]. Informally speaking, *IF* offers the executing mechanism a choice between the executions of $c.i$ for which $b.i$ holds. If none of the guards $b.i$ holds, the mechanism does not terminate. Formally, the conditional combination *IF* can be expressed in our terms by

(18) $$IF \;\cong\; !\,bb\,;(\,[\!]\, i \in I :: \; ?b.i\,; c.i) \; .$$

The proof is a straightforward calculation.

Conversely, the choice operator and the assertions and guards can be expressed in terms of the conditional combination and the commands *skip* and *miracle*. In fact, one may verify that, for any predicate b,

$$\begin{aligned} ?b \;&\cong\; \mathbf{if}\; b \;\rightarrow\; skip \,[\!]\, true \;\rightarrow\; miracle \;\mathbf{fi} \;, \\ !\,b \;&\cong\; \mathbf{if}\; b \;\rightarrow\; skip \;\mathbf{fi} \; . \end{aligned}$$

The choice of a nonempty set C of commands can be constructed as

$$(\,[\!]\, c \in C :: c) \;\cong\; \mathbf{if} \,[\!]\, c \in C :: true \;\rightarrow\; c \;\mathbf{fi} \; .$$

These formulae show that the expressive power of the conditional combination together with *skip* and *miracle* is equal to the expressive power of the choice operator together with the assertions and guards. Since it has better algebraic properties, we use the latter combination.

1.6 Program variables, state functions and localized relations

In actual programming, the state space X has structure: there is a set V of names, which are called ***program variables***. The state is characterized by the values associated to these program variables; so it is a function from V to the set of values. We use typewriter fount to represent particular program variables, and italic for variables that range over program variables. Every program variable may have its own type, i.e., its own set of values. If we use T to denote the union of all occurring types, every program variable has values in T. Therefore, the state x is a function $x \in T^V$ and the state space X is a subset of T^V.

A function on the state space X with values in T is called a *state function*. So, T^X is the set of state functions. We assume that $\mathbb{B}$ is a subset of T, so that a predicate is a state function with values in $\mathbb{B}$.

State functions are usually constructed as expressions in the program variables. For example, if `j` is a program variable of type integer, we want to regard the expression $3 - \mathtt{j}$ as a state function with, in state x, the value $3 - x.\mathtt{j}$. To this end, we introduce the following definitions.

We construct state functions by means of constants, variables and operators. Every element $t \in T$ induces a constant state function, also denoted t, given by

(19) $\quad t.x = t \quad$ for all states x .

Every program variable $v \in V$ induces the function that delivers the value of the variable in the current state. We use the name of the variable to denote this function, so that

(20) $\quad v.x = x.v \quad$ for all states x .

Remark. We do not identify elements $t \in T$ and $v \in V$ with the state functions given by (19) and (20). Whenever necessary, we make the distinction by speaking of the value t (or the program variable v) or the state function t (or v). The reader who feels uncomfortable with the invisible coercions, may choose to decorate the state functions t and v, say as $t^\diamond$ and $v^\diamond$, so that $t^\diamond.x = t$ and $v^\diamond.x = x.v$. (End of remark)

The third way to construct state functions is to lift operators and quantifiers of the value domain T to the domain of the state functions T^X, just as we have done with the boolean operators and quantifiers in definitions (0) and (1). So, we introduce the convention that each binary operator $\oplus$ on T is lifted to state functions f and g by

(21) $\quad (f \oplus g).x = f.x \oplus g.x \quad$ for all states x .

Similarly, a quantifier $\oplus$ on T is lifted to T^X, so that

(22) $\quad (\oplus\, i \in I :: f.i).x \;=\; (\oplus\, i \in I :: f.i.x)$

for any family $(i \in I :: f.i)$ of state functions.

The interpretation of $\oplus$ in (21) and (22) is called the *localized* interpretation. It is the usual interpretation if $\oplus$ is an arithmetical operator like $+$ or $\times$. For relational operators like $=$ and $\leq$, however, it must often compete with the *globalized* interpretation, where for instance the expression $f = g$ stands for the boolean value that f and g are equal functions. In principle, if one uses the localized interpretation, the equality of functions f and g must be expressed by $[f = g]$, cf. definition (2) (see [Dijkstra-Scholten 1990] Chapter 1). For the relational operators $=$, $\leq$ and $\geq$, we shall use the localized interpretation only if the context requires a predicate (i.e. a boolean state function). For elements of V, the equality symbol has yet a third interpretation, namely *name identity*, that is, equality as element of V. We write $v =_V w$ to denote the name identity of v and w, and $v \neq_V w$ to express that the names denoted by v and w differ.

Example. A Pascal program may contain

‘**if** i = j **then** ... **else** ...’

Clearly, i and j are different program variables (i.e. different elements of V and different functions on the state space), so the boolean value would be false. The Pascal interpretation of i = j, however, is the localized one, so that by (20) and (21) the expression i = j is the state function with

$$(\mathtt{i} = \mathtt{j}).x \quad \equiv \quad (x.\mathtt{i} = x.\mathtt{j}) \quad \text{for any state } x \in X \ .$$

Similarly, if i and j are integer program variables, the Pascal interpretation of i < j is the localized relation with $(\mathtt{i} < \mathtt{j}).x \ \equiv \ (x.\mathtt{i} < x.\mathtt{j})$. (End of example)

1.7 The assignment

The main command for state modification is the assignment $v := f$, where v is a program variable and f is a state function of the type of v. The operational meaning is that state x is updated at location v with new value $f.x$. In other words, state x is replaced by state $(v \leftarrow f).x$ given by

(23) $$(v \leftarrow f).x.v = f.x \ ,$$
$$(v \leftarrow f).x.w = x.w \quad \text{if } w \neq_V v \ .$$

Therefore, letting *wg* stand for *wp* or *wlp*, the predicate–transformation semantics of command $v := f$ is defined by

(24) $$wg.(v := f).p.x \quad = \quad p.((v \leftarrow f).x)$$

for all predicates p and all states x, or equivalently

$$wg.(v := f).p \quad = \quad p \circ (v \leftarrow f) \ .$$

The standard way to determine $wg.(v := f).p$ is captured in the *substitution rule:*

(25) **Theorem.** Let p be a predicate expression, i.e., a predicate given as an expression in constants, program variables, operators and quantifiers by means of formulae (19), (20), (21) and (22). Then

$$wg.(v := f).p \quad = \quad p^v_f$$

where p^v_f is the expression obtained from p by substituting f for every occurrence of v in expression p.

Proof. We use induction on the structure of expression p. Since the constituents of p need not be predicates, we generalize the assertion. By definition (24), it suffices to prove

$$e.((v \leftarrow f).x) \quad = \quad (e^v_f).x$$

for every state x and every state function e that is given as an expression in constants, program variables, operators and quantifiers by means of (19), (20), (21) and (22). This is done by structural induction on expression e. If $e = t \in T$ then

$$\begin{array}{ll} & t.((v \leftarrow f).x) \\ = & \{(19), \text{ twice}\} \\ & t.x \\ = & \{v \text{ does not occur in the simple expression } t\} \\ & (t^v_f).x \ . \end{array}$$

If $e = w \in V$ and $w \neq_V v$, then

$$\begin{array}{ll} & w.((v \leftarrow f).x) \\ = & \{(20)\} \\ & (v \leftarrow f).x.w \\ = & \{(23)\} \\ & x.w \\ = & \{(20)\} \\ & w.x \\ = & \{v \text{ does not occur in the simple expression } w\} \\ & (w^v_f).x \ . \end{array}$$

If $e = v$ then

$$\begin{array}{ll} & v.((v \leftarrow f).x) \\ = & \{(20)\} \\ & (v \leftarrow f).x.v \\ = & \{(23)\} \\ & f.x \\ = & \{\text{substitution}\} \\ & (v^v_f).x \ . \end{array}$$

If $e = e0 \oplus e1$ then

$$\begin{array}{cl} & (e0 \oplus e1).((v \leftarrow f).x) \\ = & \{(21)\} \\ & e0.((v \leftarrow f).x) \ \oplus \ e1.((v \leftarrow f).x) \\ = & \{\text{induction hypothesis}\} \\ & (e0^v_f).x \ \oplus \ (e1^v_f).x \\ = & \{(21) \text{ and definition of substitution}\} \\ & (e0 \oplus e1)^v_f.x \ . \end{array}$$

The case of a quantifier is completely analogous to the case of an operator, provided that the dummy of the quantification is renamed when necessary. (End of proof)

Example. For an integer program variable j, the substitution rule gives

$$wp.(\mathsf{j} := \mathsf{j}+1).(\mathsf{j} < 5) \quad = \quad (\mathsf{j}+1 < 5)$$

Compare the example in 1.0. (End of example)

Example. It is not our aim to provide or discuss data structuring facilities, but the formalism presented is rich enough to model variable arrays. In fact, since V is the set of program variables, a variable array a with index set I can be regarded as a function $\mathsf{a} \in V^I$. Assume that a is an array of integers, i.e., that all variables $\mathsf{a}.i$ are of type integer. Let us consider the postcondition $(\forall i :: \mathsf{a}.i > 0)$ and the assignment $v := n$. Then we have

$$\begin{array}{cl} & wp.(v := n).(\forall i :: \mathsf{a}.i > 0) \\ = & \{(25)\} \\ & (\forall i :: (\mathsf{a}.i > 0)^v_n) \\ = & \{\text{case distinction}\} \\ & (\forall i : \mathsf{a}.i \neq_V v : \mathsf{a}.i > 0) \\ \wedge & (n > 0 \vee (\forall i :: \mathsf{a}.i \neq_V v)) \ . \end{array}$$

Notice that the formalism requires that name v be independent of the state (it may be a.5). In Section 1.8, we show how to model general array modification $a.f := g$ for state functions f and g. (End of example)

Example. One of the first rules of program transformation is that an assignment $v := f$ can be replaced by $v := g$ under the precondition $(f = g)$, in the sense of (21). This rule is of course well-known and often used. For example, in [Dijkstra 1990], Chapter 2, Gries uses the rule very effectively in the derivation of a program for the maximum–segment–sum problem.

Our formalization of the rule is

(26) $\qquad ?(f = g); v := f \ \cong \ ?(f = g); v := g \ .$

This formula can be proved as follows. By (8), (13) and (24), we have for any predicate p

$$wg.(?(f=g); v := f).p \quad = \quad (f=g) \Rightarrow (p \circ (v \leftarrow f)) \ ,$$

where wg is wp or wlp. Therefore, by definition (7), formula (26) follows from the observation that for any predicate p

$$\begin{array}{ll} & [(f=g) \Rightarrow (p \circ (v \leftarrow f)) \ \equiv \ (f=g) \Rightarrow (p \circ (v \leftarrow g))] \\ \equiv & \{(r \Rightarrow) \text{ distributes over } \equiv, \text{ see exercise 1.1.6}\} \\ & [(f=g) \ \Rightarrow \ (p \circ (v \leftarrow f) \ \equiv \ p \circ (v \leftarrow g))] \\ \Leftarrow & \{\text{composition and (2)}\} \\ & (\forall x \in X : f.x = g.x : (v \leftarrow f).x = (v \leftarrow g).x) \\ \equiv & \{(23)\} \\ & \text{true} \ . \end{array}$$

(End of example)

1.8 Deterministic choice

A deterministic choice is a choice between (possibly infinitely many) different commands that depends on the value of a given state function. The deterministic choice can be regarded as a procedure call with the state function as an actual parameter.

The formal treatment is as follows. Recall that T is the 'universal' set of values, as introduced in the first paragraph of section 1.6. Let $(t \in I :: q.t)$ be a family of commands with $I \subset T$. We want to be able to treat this family as a procedure with a formal input parameter t. Therefore, if $f \in I^X$ is an I–valued state function, we define the call $q.f$ as the command

(27) $\quad q.f \quad = \quad ([\!] \, t \in I :: ?(f=t); q.t) \ .$

This definition implies, with wg for wp and wlp,

(28) $\quad wg.(q.f).p = (\forall t \in I :: \ (f=t) \ \Rightarrow \ wg.(q.t).p) \ .$

This is proved by

$$\begin{array}{ll} & wg.(q.f).p \\ = & \{(27), (16)\} \\ & (\forall t \in I :: \ wg.(?(f=t); q.t).p) \\ = & \{(8), (13)\} \\ & (\forall t \in I :: \ (f=t) \ \Rightarrow \ wg.(q.t).p) \ . \end{array}$$

It follows from (28) that, if $wg.(q.t).p$ is an expression E in t, then $wg.(q.f).p = E^t_f$.

Example. If we regard the constant assignments $v := t$ with $t \in T$ as simple commands, the general assignment $v := f$ with $f \in T^X$ is a special case of the above construction. (End of example)

Example. If f is a predicate, so that $I = \mathbb{B}$, then $q.f$ is the construction

$$\textbf{if } f \textbf{ then } q.\text{true} \textbf{ else } q.\text{false} \textbf{ fi} \quad .$$

(End of example)

Example. Array modification. Let a be an array with index set I, regarded as a function $\mathrm{a} \in I \to V$. The array modification $\mathrm{a}.f := g$ for an I–valued state function f and a T–valued state function g can be modelled as

$$(\, [\!] \, t \in I :: ?(f = t);\ \mathrm{a}.t := g) \ .$$

(End of example)

Example. The bounded repetition. Let $(i \in \mathbb{N} :: q.i)$ be a family of commands. Let $(i \in \mathbb{N} :: p.i)$ be a family of predicates such that for all $i \in \mathbb{N}$

$$[\, p.i \quad \Rightarrow \quad wp.(q.i).(p.(i+1))\,] \ .$$

For an integer valued state function f, the bounded repetition

$$loop \quad = \quad \textbf{for } i := 0 \textbf{ to } f \textbf{ do } q.i \textbf{ od}$$

is supposed to satisfy the specifications

$$?(f < 0); loop \quad \cong \quad ?(f < 0)$$

and for all $j \in \mathbb{N}$

$$[\, p.0 \wedge (f = j) \quad \Rightarrow \quad wp.loop.(p.(j+1))\,] \ .$$

The deterministic choice allows us to express *loop* in terms of the basic formalism. In fact, we can define commands

$$r.0 \quad = \quad skip \ ,$$
$$r.(i+1) \quad = \quad r.i; q.i \quad \text{for all } i \in \mathbb{N} \ .$$

A straightforward verification shows that

$$loop \quad = \quad ?(f < 0) \, [\!] \, (\, [\!] \, i \in \mathbb{N} :: ?(f = i); r.(i+1))$$

satisfies the above specification. (End of example)

1.9 Appendix on predicate calculus

For programming practice and programming theory, we need the ability to calculate effectively with boolean values and boolean functions. We need not reconsider the foundations of classsical logic but only isolate a number of useful theorems (rules). These theorems make it easier to avoid the pitfalls of state based reasoning and enable a calculational style which leads to shorter proofs than with natural deduction. We do not provide a complete set of rules, but we give some important ones and show how such rules can be justified. Afterwards the readers can extend their repertoire by means of the exercises of Section 1.1.

The lowest level is propositional calculus without quantification. Here, we have well-known rules like the commutativity and the associativity of '$\wedge$' and '$\vee$', the double negation rule, and De Morgan's laws. The implication operator satisfies

$$a \Rightarrow b \quad \equiv \quad \neg a \vee b \ .$$

The equivalence operator satisfies

$$(a \equiv b) \quad \equiv \quad (a \Rightarrow b) \wedge (b \Rightarrow a) \ .$$

There are two distributivity laws

$$a \wedge (b \vee c) \quad \equiv \quad (a \wedge b) \vee (a \wedge c) \ ,$$
$$a \vee (b \wedge c) \quad \equiv \quad (a \vee b) \wedge (a \vee c) \ .$$

The next level contains the universal and existential quantification. The above distributivity laws generalize to distributivity laws of '$\wedge$' over '$\exists$' and of '$\vee$' over '$\forall$'. For a proposition a and a family of propositions $(i \in I :: b.i)$, the second one reads

$$a \vee (\forall i \in I :: b.i) \quad \equiv \quad (\forall i \in I :: a \vee b.i) \ .$$

If it is not an axiom, this rule can be proved by case distinction. Indeed, if proposition a holds, the lefthand side holds and the righthand side reduces to $(\forall i \in I :: \text{true})$ which is also true (regardless whether I is empty or not). If a is false, both sides reduce to $(\forall i \in I :: b.i)$. This concludes the proof.

The third level consists of the predicates introduced in Section 1.1. The distributivity law now gets the form

$$p \vee (\forall i \in I :: q.i) \quad = \quad (\forall i \in I :: p \vee q.i)$$

for every predicate p and every family of predicates $(i \in I :: q.i)$. This can be proved by observing that for every $x \in X$

$$\begin{array}{ll} & (p \vee (\forall i \in I :: q.i)).x \\ = & \{(0) \text{ and } (1)\} \\ & p.x \vee (\forall i \in I :: q.i.x) \\ = & \{\text{distributivity law for propositions}\} \\ & (\forall i \in I :: p.x \vee q.i.x) \\ = & \{(0) \text{ and } (1)\} \\ & (\forall i \in I :: p \vee q.i).x \ . \end{array}$$

The universal quantification over the state space, cf. formula (2), has its special rules like

$$[\, true \,] \quad \equiv \quad \text{true} \ ,$$

$$[p \wedge q] \ \equiv \ [p] \wedge [q] \ ,$$

and for a family of predicates

$$[(\forall i \in I :: q.i)] \ \equiv \ (\forall i \in I :: [q.i]) \ .$$

For example, the last rule is proved in

$$\begin{array}{ll} & [(\forall i \in I :: q.i)] \\ \equiv & \{(2) \text{ and } (1)\} \\ & (\forall x \in X :: (\forall i \in I :: q.i.x)) \\ \equiv & \{\text{interchange of quantifications}\} \\ & (\forall i \in I :: (\forall x \in X :: q.i.x)) \\ \equiv & \{(2)\} \\ & (\forall i \in I :: [q.i]) \ . \end{array}$$

For further extension we refer to the exercises of Section 1.1.

1.10 Exercises

Exercises of Section 1.1.

Whenever possible the reader should try and avoid to use states.

Exercise 0. Prove that for all predicates p, q, r

(a) $\quad (p \Rightarrow q) \ = \ (p \equiv p \wedge q)$,

(b) $\quad (p \Rightarrow q \vee r) \ = \ (p \wedge \neg q \Rightarrow r) \quad$ {shunting} ,

(c) $\quad (p \Rightarrow (q \Rightarrow r)) \ = \ (p \wedge q \Rightarrow r)$,

(d) $\quad (p \Rightarrow q \wedge r) \ = \ (p \Rightarrow q) \wedge (p \Rightarrow r)$,

(e) $\quad (p \vee q \Rightarrow r) \ = \ (p \Rightarrow r) \wedge (q \Rightarrow r)$,

Exercise 1. Prove that for every set U of predicates

$$[(\exists p \in U :: p)] \ \Leftarrow \ (\exists p \in U :: [p]) \ .$$

Exercise 2. Distributivity of '$\wedge$' over '$\forall$'. Prove that for every predicate p and every family of predicates $(i \in I :: q.i)$

$$I \neq \emptyset \ \Rightarrow \ (p \wedge (\forall i \in I :: q.i) \ = \ (\forall i \in I :: p \wedge q.i)) \ .$$

Why do we need the condition on I?

Exercise 3. The distributivity rules for $\exists$. Prove that for every predicate p and every family of predicates $(i \in I :: q.i)$

(a) $\quad p \wedge (\exists i \in I :: q.i) \ = \ (\exists i \in I :: p \wedge q.i)$,

(b) $\quad I \neq \emptyset \ \Rightarrow \ (p \vee (\exists i \in I :: q.i) \ = \ (\exists i \in I :: p \vee q.i))$.

Exercise 4. Prove that for every predicate q and every set U of predicates

(a) $\quad [q \Rightarrow (\forall p \in U :: p)] \ \equiv \ (\forall p \in U :: [q \Rightarrow p])$,

(b) $\quad [(\exists p \in U :: p) \Rightarrow q] \ \equiv \ (\forall p \in U :: [p \Rightarrow q])$.

Exercise 5. Prove that for all predicates p and q

$$p = q \quad \equiv \quad (\forall r \in \mathbb{P} : [p \Rightarrow r] \equiv [q \Rightarrow r]) .$$

Exercise 6. Prove that for all predicates p, q, r

$$(p \Rightarrow q) \equiv (p \Rightarrow r) \quad = \quad p \Rightarrow (q \equiv r) .$$

Exercise 7. Let p and q be predicates.
(a) Prove that $[p] \vee [q] \quad \Rightarrow \quad [p \vee q]$.
(b) Prove that $[p \Rightarrow q] \quad \Rightarrow \quad ([p] \Rightarrow [q])$.
(c) Give examples to show that the outer implications in (a) and (b) cannot be replaced by equivaleces.

Exercises of Section 1.3.

From now onward, the reader is urged to avoid the usage of states $x \in X$ whenever possible.

Exercise 0. Prove that $!\,b$ is total for every predicate b.

Exercises of Section 1.4.

Exercise 0. Prove that for any command c:
(a) ♡ $\quad c; miracle \cong miracle \quad \equiv \quad [\, wp.c.true \,]$,
(b) $\quad c; abort \cong abort \quad \equiv \quad [\neg wp.c.false] \wedge [\, wlp.c.true \,]$.

Exercise 1. Let c and d be total commands.
(a) Prove that $(c; d)$ and $(c \,[\!]\, d)$ are total.
(b) Prove that $(?b; c \,[\!]\, ?\neg b; d)$ is total for every predicate $b \in \mathbb{P}$.

Exercise 2. Prove that for predicates a and b

$$?a;\ ?b \quad \cong \quad ?(a \wedge b) .$$

Exercise 3. Prove that for every family $(i \in I :: b.i)$ of predicates

$$(\,[\!]\, i \in I :: ?b.i) \quad \cong \quad ?(\exists i \in I :: b.i) .$$

Exercise 4. Prove that for all commands c and d:

$$c \,[\!]\, ?false; d \quad \cong \quad c .$$

Exercise 5. Prove the postdistributivity rule

$$(\,[\!]\, c \in C :: c); q \quad \cong \quad (\,[\!]\, c \in C :: c; q)$$

for any command q and any nonempty set of commands C.

Exercise 5. Prove the rules (14).

Exercises of Section 1.5.

Exercise 0. Prove that IF as defined by formula (18) satisfies the equations given for $wp.IF$ and $wlp.IF$.

Exercises of Section 1.6.

Exercise 0. Let j and k be integer program variables. Prove that

$$skip \,[\!]\; !(j = k) \quad \cong \quad !(j \leq k) \,[\!]\; !(k \leq j) \; .$$

Exercises of Section 1.7.

Exercise 0. Let v be an integer program variable. Discuss all errors in the following calculation:

$$\begin{array}{ll} & wp.(v := 3 \; ; \; v := 5).(v > 4) \\ = & \{(13)\} \quad wp.(v := 3).(wp.(v := 5).(v > 4)) \\ = & \{(25)\} \quad wp.(3 := 5).(3 > 4) \\ = & \{\text{calculus}\} \quad wp.(3 := 5).false \\ = & \{(25)\} \quad false \; . \end{array}$$

Give a correct calculation of the initial expression.

Exercises of Section 1.8.

Exercise 0. Prove that command *loop*, as defined at the end of Section 1.8, satisfies its specification.

CHAPTER 2

ANNOTATION, RECURSION AND REPETITION

2.0. This chapter is devoted to the introduction of annotations, procedures, recursion and repetitions, all concepts highly relevant to programming practice and programming methodology. In 2.1 we introduce Hoare triples as a specification method. Hoare triples are used in 2.2 for correctness proofs by annotation. In 2.3 and 2.4 we treat procedures in a programming language like Pascal. The specification and invocation rules are discussed in Section 2.3. The correctness of recursive procedures is treated in Section 2.4. The methods presented here are not new but deserve to be promoted.

In Section 2.5 we present and prove an abstract version of the rule for total correctness of recursive procedures. In 2.6 we introduce homomorphisms, functions from commands to predicate transformers that satisfy the standard laws of *wp* and *wlp*. Homomorphisms are used in 2.7 to give Hoare's Induction Rule for conditional correctness of recursive procedures, and a related rule for the necessity of preconditions. Finally, in Section 2.8, the results on recursive procedures are specialized to the repetition.

With respect to recursive procedures, this chapter is not 'well–founded'. We only postulate some properties and proof rules, but the definition of the semantics of recursion (i.e., of the functions *wp* and *wlp*) and the proof of the postulates are postponed to Chapter 4.

2.1 Specification with Hoare triples

Weakest preconditions provide the easiest way to present predicate–transformation semantics. The formalism of Hoare triples, however, is completely equivalent and more convenient for program derivations and proofs of program correctness. Since we use *wp* as the foundation, Hoare triples are defined concepts. For predicates p and q and a command c, the Hoare triple $\{p\}\ c\ \{q\}$ is defined as the boolean value given by

(0) $\{p\}\ c\ \{q\} \quad \equiv \quad [p \Rightarrow wp.c.q]$.

Actually, Hoare introduced (cf. [Hoare 1969] and [Manna-Vuillemin 1972]) the notation

(1) $p\ \{c\}\ q \quad \equiv \quad [p \Rightarrow wlp.c.q]$.

In (0), we speak of *total* correctness: precondition p implies that execution of c terminates in a state that satisfies q. In (1), we speak of *partial* or *conditional* correctness: precondition p implies that if c terminates in some state that state satisfies q.

Example. If p is a predicate expression, cf. 1(25), the assignment $v := f$ is easily seen to satisfy

$$\{p^v_f\} \quad v := f \quad \{p\} \ .$$

For predicates p and b, the assertion $!\,b$ satisfies

$$\{p \wedge b\} \quad !\,b \quad \{p\} \ .$$

On the other hand, the guard $?b$ satisfies the Hoare triple

$$\{p\} \quad ?b \quad \{p \wedge b\}$$

$\equiv$ {definitions (0) and 1(8)}

$$[p \Rightarrow (b \Rightarrow p \wedge b)]$$

$\equiv$ {calculus}

true .

(End of example)

Remark. Formulae (0) and (1) are by no means the standard view of Hoare triples. For example, in [de Bakker 1980] definition 3.29, the triple $\{p\}\ c\ \{q\}$ is the predicate $(p \Rightarrow wlp.c.q)$. In other books (e.g. [Chandy-Misra 1988] Chapter 3), Hoare triples are part of a logical deduction system, so that the validity of a Hoare triple includes its derivability.

Hoare triples often contain free variables, over which an implicit universal quantification is intended. For example, the intention of

$$\{\mathrm{v} = t\}\ \mathrm{v} := \mathrm{v} - 1\ \{\mathrm{v} < t\}$$

is that whatever the initial value (t) of v may be, the final value is smaller. This is made explicit by writing

$$(\forall t :: \{\mathrm{v} = t\}\ \mathrm{v} := \mathrm{v} - 1\ \{\mathrm{v} < t\}\ ).$$

Notice that the rôle of variable t is totally different from the rôle of v. Variables like t will be called *specification constants*. Some authors use the term logical variables.
(End of remark)

Hoare triples satisfy the following two weakening rules

(2) $$[p \Rightarrow q] \ \land \ \{q\}\, c\, \{r\} \quad \Rightarrow \quad \{p\}\, c\, \{r\} \ ,$$
$$\{p\}\, c\, \{q\} \ \land \ [q \Rightarrow r] \quad \Rightarrow \quad \{p\}\, c\, \{r\} \ .$$

The first weakening rule follows from definition (0). In the proof of the second rule, axiom 1(5) is also needed.

The composition rule for Hoare triples is

(3) $$\{p\}\, c\, \{q\} \ \land \ \{q\}\, d\, \{r\} \quad \Rightarrow \quad \{p\}\, c; d\, \{r\} \ .$$

This rule is proved in

$$\begin{array}{ll} & \{p\}\, c\, \{q\} \ \land \ \{q\}\, d\, \{r\} \\ \equiv & \{(0)\} \\ & [p \Rightarrow wp.c.q] \ \land \ [q \Rightarrow wp.d.r] \\ \Rightarrow & \{1(5) \text{ with } p := q \text{ and } q := wp.d.r\} \\ & [p \Rightarrow wp.c.q] \ \land \ [wp.c.q \Rightarrow wp.c.(wp.d.r)] \\ \Rightarrow & \{\text{transitivity of `}\Rightarrow\text{' and } 1(13)\} \\ & [p \Rightarrow wp.(c;d).r)] \\ \equiv & \{(0)\} \\ & \{p\}\, c; d\, \{r\} \ . \end{array}$$

The rule for the choice operator is that, for every nonempty family of commands $(i \in I :: c.)$,

(4) $$\{p\}\, (\, [\!] \, i \in I :: c.i)\, \{q\} \quad \equiv \quad (\forall i \in I :: \ \{p\}\, c.i\, \{q\}\ ) \ .$$

This rule follows from definition 1(16) and exercise 1.1.4(a).

The above rules are often used and easily recognized in program annotations. The next result is less familiar, but well-known and very useful.

(5) **Covering rule.** Let p and q be predicates, c a command and $(i \in I :: r.i)$ a family of predicates with $[p \Rightarrow (\exists i :: r.i)]$. Then we have

$$\{p\}\, c\, \{q\} \quad \equiv \quad (\forall i :: \ \{p \land r.i\}\, c\, \{q\}\ ) \ .$$

Remark. The condition $[p \Rightarrow (\exists i :: r.i)]$ says that the set of states where p holds is contained in the union of the family of sets of states corresponding to the predicates $r.i$. This family of sets can be regarded as a covering of the set where p holds. Hence the name of the rule. (End of remark)

Proof. We begin with the righthand side.

$$\begin{array}{ll} & (\forall i :: \ \{p \land r.i\}\, c\, \{q\}\ ) \\ \equiv & \{(0)\} \\ & (\forall i :: [p \land r.i \Rightarrow wp.c.q]) \\ \equiv & \{\text{exercise } 1.1.4(b)\} \end{array}$$

$$[(\exists i :: p \wedge r.i) \Rightarrow wp.c.q]$$
$$\equiv \quad \{\text{exercise 1.1.3(a)}\}$$
$$[p \wedge (\exists i :: r.i) \Rightarrow wp.c.q]$$
$$\equiv \quad \{\text{use given implication}\}$$
$$[p \Rightarrow wp.c.q]$$
$$\equiv \quad \{(0)\}$$
$$\{p\}\ c\ \{q\}\ .$$

(End of proof)

2.2 Proofs by annotation

It is of practical importance that in cases where the correctness proof of a program is not very involved, this proof can be integrated in the program text. For this purpose we use the Floyd–Hoare method of inductive assertions, which is a direct application of the Hoare triple rules of the previous section.

In this method the correctness of a Hoare triple $\{p\}\ c\ \{q\}$ is proved in a top–down fashion by induction on the structure of command c. The result is called an *annotation*. This is an extension of the syntactic structure of c in which every constituent of c is replaced by a Hoare triple. The following annotation rules are available.

0. Simple commands. In view of the example in the previous section, the following Hoare triples are accepted without further proof:

$$\{p^v_f\} \quad v := f \quad \{p\}\ ,$$
$$\{p\} \quad ?b \quad \{p \wedge b\}\ .$$

1. Weakening Rule. If A is an argument that proves $[p \Rightarrow q]$, then it is allowed to use the annotation

$$\{p\} \quad (* \ A \ *) \quad \{q\}\ .$$

2. Sequencing Rule. In order to prove $\{p\}\ c; d\ \{q\}$, it suffices to provide a predicate r and to prove $\{p\}\ c\ \{r\}$ and $\{r\}\ d\ \{q\}$. This reduction is recorded in the annotation

$$\{p\}\ c\ \{r\}\ d\ \{q\}\ .$$

3. Choice Rule. In order to prove $\{p\}\ (\,[\!]\ i \in I :: c.i)\ \{q\}$ for a family of commands $(i \in I :: c.i)$, it suffices to prove $\{p\}\ c.i\ \{q\}$ for all $i \in I$. This reduction is recorded in the annotation

$$\{p\}\ (\,[\!]\ i \in I :: \{p\}\ c.i\ \{q\}\ )\ \{q\}\ .$$

4. Covering Rule. In order to prove $\{p\}\ c\ \{q\}$, it suffices to provide a family of predicates $(i \in I :: r.i)$, to prove that $[p \Rightarrow (\exists i :: r.i)]$ and to prove all Hoare triples $\{p \wedge r.i\}\ c\ \{q\}$. If A is an argument that proves the implication, this reduction can be recorded in the annotation

$\{p\}$ (* A introduces i *)
$\{p \wedge r.i\}\ c\ \{q\}$.

The soundness of rule 1 follows from the weakening rules (2), together with the transitivity of the implication if rule 1 is applied repeatedly. The soundness of the rules 2, 3 and 4 follows from (3), (4) and (5).

For other programming languages, the repertoire of annotation rules can be extended to cover the conditional statement and the repetition as well. An annotation rule for the repetition is given in section 2.8 below. The annotation rule for the conditional statement is:

5. Conditional Rule. If $\{p \wedge b\}\ c\ \{q\}$ and $\{p \wedge \neg b\}\ d\ \{q\}$ then

$\{p\}$ **if** b **then** c **else** d **fi** $\{q\}$.

This reduction is recorded in the annotation:

$\{p\}$
if b **then** $\{p \wedge b\}$ c $\{q\}$
else $\{p \wedge \neg b\}$ d $\{q\}$ **fi**
$\{q\}$.

Example. Let `i`, `j`, `k` be integer program variables. Command c assigns to `k` the maximum of `i` and `j`. This is specified by means of a specification constant t in the following way:

$\{p:\ \mathtt{i}\ \mathbf{max}\ \mathtt{j} = t\}$ c $\{q:\ \mathtt{k} = t\}$.

We take $c = (?(\mathtt{j} \le \mathtt{i})\ ;\ \mathtt{k} := \mathtt{i}\ [\!]\ ?(\mathtt{i} \le \mathtt{j})\ ;\ \mathtt{k} := \mathtt{j})$. The correctness is proved in the annotation

$\{p:\ \mathtt{i}\ \mathbf{max}\ \mathtt{j} = t\}$
($\{p\}$ $?(\mathtt{j} \le \mathtt{i})$ $\{p\ \wedge\ \mathtt{j} \le \mathtt{i}\}$
(* calculus *) $\{\mathtt{i} = t\}$ $\mathtt{k} := \mathtt{i}$ $\{q:\ \mathtt{k} = t\}$
[] $\{p\}$ $?(\mathtt{i} \le \mathtt{j})$ $\{p\ \wedge\ \mathtt{i} \le \mathtt{j}\}$
(* calculus *) $\{\mathtt{j} = t\}$ $\mathtt{k} := \mathtt{j}$ $\{q:\ \mathtt{k} = t\}$
) $\{q\}$.

Notice that we have used each of the rules 0, 1, 2, and 3. (End of example)

The covering rule allows us to introduce a new specification constant for the value of an expression at a point in the program text, provided that the new constant is eliminated in the remainder of the program. This point is illustrated in the next example.

Example. Let k be an integer program variable. Let c be the squaring command specified by

$$(\forall i \in \mathbb{Z} :: \ \{\mathrm{k} = i\} \ c \ \{\mathrm{k} = i^2\} \ ) \ .$$

It may be clear that $\{\mathrm{k} \geq 3\} \ c \ \{\mathrm{k} \geq 9\}$. This is formally proved in the following annotation, based on the covering rule

$\{\mathrm{k} \geq 3\}$ (∗ there is $i \geq 3$ with $\mathrm{k} = i$: introduction of i ∗)
$\{\mathrm{k} \geq 3 \wedge \mathrm{k} = i\}$ (∗ weakening ∗)
$\{\mathrm{k} = i\}$
c (∗ specification ∗)
$\{\mathrm{k} = i^2\}$ (∗ range $i \geq 3$, weakening ∗)
$\{\mathrm{k} \geq 9\}$.

(End of example)

2.3 Specification and invocation of procedures

Procedures are introduced to allow a separation between the application of a command and its implementation. This is especially useful if the command is to be applied several times. Parametrization is helpful to allow application under different circumstances. Recursion may be regarded as the accident that the procedure can be applied in its own implementation.

Ideally, the specification of a procedure is the only bridge between implementation and application. In principle, it is possible to specify procedures by means of weakest preconditions. In practice, this is not convenient: prescribing the weakest precondition of a procedure is often overspecific. We therefore assume that a procedure is specified by means of Hoare triples and the list of all external variables involved.

For a programming language like Pascal we prefer the following declaration format, which is inspired by [Gries 1981] and [Martin 1983]. For simplicity, we assume that the procedure has precisely one variable for each of the variable modalities.

(6) **proc** $h(x : \mathit{item};$ **var** $y : \mathit{item})$
{**ext** $u, v! : \mathit{item};$
all $i \in \mathit{item} : C :$ **pre** P, **post** $Q\}$.

The meaning of the specification is defined by

(7) **Correctness Rule.** An implementation of procedure h is correct if it satisfies the conditions:
(a) all external variables used in the body of h are listed after the key word **ext**; external variables that are threatened to be modified (in the sense of [Jensen–Wirth 1985]) are marked with '!',
(b) the value parameters (x) do not occur in postcondition Q,
(c) for all values of the specification constants (i) that satisfy condition C the body of h satisfies $\{P\}$ **body**.h $\{Q\}$. If C is omitted, the default value *true* is meant.

Of course, variable modalities that do not occur can be omitted from the specification. The list after key word **ext** is needed to exclude aliasing upon invocation of h. Condition (b) may seem unnecessarily restrictive. There are three reasons for imposing it. Firstly, it encourages specifications with simple postconditions (J.E. Jonker). Secondly, if value parameters would be allowed in the postcondition, the invocation rule (to be treated below) would be complicated by the fact that the value of the expression for the actual parameter can be modified by the call. Finally, condition (b) is necessary if one wants to combine condition (c) with the exploitation of value parameters as local variables. Compare [Gries 1981] chapter 12. For recursive implementations rule (7) is correct but inadequate, for requirement (c) is too strong; we come back to this in Section 2.4.

Example. Let i be a program variable. Procedure *copy0* copies the value of i into the parameter, procedure *copy1* copies the parameter into i:

proc *copy0* (**var** p : *item*)
{ **ext** i ; **all** $v \in$ *item* :: **pre** i $= v$, **post** $p = v$} ;
    begin $p :=$ i **end** ;
proc *copy1* (p : *item*)
{ **ext** i! ; **all** $v \in$ *item* :: **pre** $p = v$, **post** i $= v$} ;
    begin i $:= p$ **end** .

(End of example)

As this example may indicate, it is not our aim to discuss the methods for disciplined and effective usage of procedures in every day programming. We only want to indicate that full specifications of procedures are feasible. In the next paragraph we show that these specifications can be used to prove the correctness of invocations of procedures. From the semantic point of view the most interesting cases are the recursive invocations to be treated in the next section. We first treat the easier case of an invocation of a procedure outside of its own body.

An *invocation* or *call* of procedure h declared in (6) is of the form $h(E,t)$ where E is an expression and t is a program variable, both of which are well-defined at the position of the call. To avoid aliasing we require that the actual **var**–parameter is not used as an external variable:

(8) $t \notin Ext$,

where Ext is the list headed by **ext**. We let $Ext!$ be the sublist of Ext that consists of the variables that are threatened to modified. Precondition P and postcondition Q of specification (6) need not mention that external variables outside of $Ext!$ are unchanged. In the specification of the call an additional predicate R is used to express this fact. Predicate R is supposed to satisfy

(9) $Var.R \cap (\{t\} \cup Ext!) = \emptyset$

where $Var.R$ is the list of program variables that occur in R. If $Ext! = Ext$, conditions (8) and (9) are more symmetrically expressed by stating that the three lists Ext, $Var.R$ and the list of actual **var**–parameters are pairwise disjoint.

The call $h(E,t)$ is specified by

(10) **Invocation Rule.** If (8) and (9), then for all i such that C:

$$\{P^{x,y}_{E,t} \wedge R\} \quad h(E,t) \quad \{Q^{y}_{t} \wedge R\} \ .$$

In words: in the expressions for P and Q the formal parameters are replaced by the actual parameters.

Remark. If there are more **var**–parameters, the avoidance of aliasing also requires that all actual **var**–parameters differ. For simplicity we do not allow calls of the form $h(E,a[F])$ where the actual **var**–parameter is an array field. (End of remark)

Example. A procedure to compute natural powers of integers can be specified by

$$\textbf{proc}\ pow\,(x : integer\ ;\ \textbf{var}\ y : integer)$$
$$\{\ \textbf{all}\ Z \in integer\ ::\ \textbf{pre}\ y \geq 0 \wedge Z = x^y\ ,\ \textbf{post}\ y = Z\}\ .$$

Let $\mathtt{i}$ and $\mathtt{t}$ be external variables. We use an annotation to prove

$$\{\mathtt{i} \geq 1 \wedge \mathtt{t} \geq 3\} \quad pow\,(\mathtt{i}+1, \mathtt{t}) \quad \{\mathtt{i} \geq 1 \wedge \mathtt{t} \geq 8\}\ .$$

We first use the covering rule, then weakening, then the invocation rule, and finally weakening again.

$\{\mathtt{i} \geq 1 \wedge \mathtt{t} \geq 3\}$
  (∗ $(\mathtt{i}+1)^{\mathtt{t}}$ has some value Z ∗)
$\{\mathtt{i} \geq 1 \wedge \mathtt{t} \geq 3 \wedge Z = (\mathtt{i}+1)^{\mathtt{t}}\}$
  (∗ calculus ∗)
$\{\mathtt{t} \geq 0 \wedge Z = (\mathtt{i}+1)^{\mathtt{t}} \wedge (R:\ \mathtt{i} \geq 1 \wedge Z \geq 8)\}$
$pow\,(\mathtt{i}+1, \mathtt{t})$ (∗ invocation ∗)

$$\begin{array}{l}
\quad (*\ Var.R = \{\mathtt{i}\} \text{ and hence } Var.R \cap \{\mathtt{t}\} = \emptyset\ *) \\
\{\mathtt{t} = Z \land (R\colon\ \mathtt{i} \geq 1 \land Z \geq 8)\} \\
\quad (*\ \text{calculus}\ *) \\
\{\mathtt{i} \geq 1 \land \mathtt{t} \geq 8\}\ .
\end{array}$$

(End of example)

2.4 Correctness of recursive declarations

If the body of procedure h in declaration (6) is recursive, it is difficult to guarantee condition (7)(c). Therefore, Correctness Rule (7) had better be adapted in such a way that Invocation Rule (10) can be applied to the recursive calls in the proof of condition (7)(c).

(11) **Correctness Rule.** A recursive implementation of procedure h specified as in (6) is correct if conditions (7)(a) and (7)(b) are satisfied, together with condition (d) given by

(d) There is an integer valued function *vf* (to be called the *variant function*) in the specification constant (i), the parameters x, y and the variables in *Ext*, such that for every $m \in \mathbb{Z}$ and every i with C the induction hypothesis given below implies

(12) $\{P \land vf \leq m\}$ **body**.h $\{Q\}$.

The induction hypothesis is that every recursive call $h(E,t)$ satisfies for all j with C^i_j and for all predicates R with (9) the Hoare triple

(13) $$\begin{array}{l}\{(P \land vf < m)^{i,x,y}_{j,E,t} \quad \land \quad m \geq 0 \quad \land \quad R\} \\ h(E,t) \\ \{Q^{i,y}_{j,t} \quad \land \quad R\}\ .\end{array}$$

The soundness of this rule can be proved by induction on the value of *vf* in the state where procedure h is called. If *vf* is negative in the precondition of (12), we can use $m = -1$. In that case the precondition of the induction hypothesis is false and, hence, the induction hypothesis is true. This case serves as the base case of the induction. For states with $vf \leq m$ and $m \geq 0$, the execution uses recursive calls with $vf < m$. Below in Section 2.5 we give a formal proof of an abstract version of rule (11).

The conjunct $m \geq 0$ in the precondition of induction hypothesis (13) must not be forgotten: it provides the base case of the induction. See also exercise 2.7.4.

Notice that condition $m \geq 0$ enters only in the precondition of (13), that is in the precondition of the recursive call(s). This observation may guide the design of an implementation. Other correctness rules for recursive procedures often require more case distinctions or additional proof obligations. Rule (11) allows a correctness proof (or rather a verification of condition (11)(d)) that consists of an annotation of the body. This is illustrated in the next examples.

Example. We first provide a very simple example with a complete annotation. Procedure *pow3* computes the natural powers of 3, as specified in

proc *pow3* (x : *integer*; **var** y : *integer*)
{**all** $i \in$ *integer* :: **pre** $P: \ x \geq 0 \wedge i = 3^x$, **post** $Q: \ y = i$} .

We take variant function $vf = x$. The instantiation of the induction hypothesis (13) is that for every expression E, every variable t, every specification constant j and every predicate R with $Var.R \cap \{t\} = \emptyset$:

$\{E \geq 0 \wedge j = 3^E \wedge E < m \wedge m \geq 0 \wedge R\}$
pow3 (E, t)
$\{t = j \wedge R\}$.

We give a body of *pow3* with an annotation to show that condition (12) is satisfied.

$\{P \wedge vf \leq m\}$ (* definitions of P and vf *)
$\{x \geq 0 \wedge i = 3^x \wedge x \leq m\}$
if $x = 0$ **then** $\{x \geq 0 \wedge i = 3^x \wedge x \leq m \wedge x = 0\}$
(* $3^0 = 1$ *) $\{1 = i\}$
$y := 1$ $\{Q: \ y = i\}$
else $\{x \geq 0 \wedge i = 3^x \wedge x \leq m \wedge x \neq 0\}$
(* $3^{x-1} = j$ for some j; calculus *)
$\{x - 1 \geq 0 \wedge j = 3^{x-1} \wedge x - 1 < m \wedge m \geq 0 \wedge (R : 3 \cdot j = i)\}$
pow3 $(x - 1, y)$ (* induction hypothesis; $Var.R \cap \{y\} = \emptyset$ *)
$\{y = j \wedge 3 \cdot j = i\}$
(* calculus *) $\{3 \cdot y = i\}$
$y := 3 \cdot y$ $\{Q: \ y = i\}$
fi $\{Q\}$.

This proves that the induction hypothesis implies the properly instantiated version of (12). Therefore, procedure *pow3* is correctly implemented. (End of example)

Example. Consider a procedure for integer division as specified in

proc *divi* (y : *integer*)
{**ext** $\mathtt{x}!, \mathtt{q}!$: *integer* ; **all** $X, Y \in$ *integer* : $X \geq 0 \ \wedge \ Y > 0$:
pre $P: \mathtt{x} = X \ \wedge \ y = Y$,
post $Q: X = \mathtt{q} \cdot Y + \mathtt{x} \ \wedge \ 0 \leq \mathtt{x} < Y$} .

Specification constant X captures the initial value of the external variable x. We use a specification constant Y to denote the value of y. Postcondition Q is easily established if $\mathtt{x} < y$. Therefore, we use the variant function $vf = \mathtt{x} - y$. The induction hypothesis is that, if $Var.R \cap \{\mathtt{x}, \mathtt{q}\} = \emptyset$ and $W \geq 0$ and $T > 0$, then

$$\{\mathtt{x} = W \ \wedge \ E = T \ \wedge \ \mathtt{x} - E < m \ \wedge \ m \geq 0 \ \wedge \ R\}$$
$$divi\ (E)$$
$$\{W = \mathtt{q} \cdot T + \mathtt{x} \quad \wedge \quad 0 \leq \mathtt{x} < T \quad \wedge \quad R\} \ .$$

The annotated body is

$\{\mathtt{x} = X \ \wedge \ y = Y \ \wedge \ \mathtt{x} - y \leq m\}$
if $\mathtt{x} < y$ **then** $\{\mathtt{x} = X \geq 0 \ \wedge \ \mathtt{x} < y = Y\}$
$\{X = 0 \cdot Y + \mathtt{x} \ \wedge \ 0 \leq \mathtt{x} < Y\}$
$\mathtt{q} := 0 \quad \{Q\}$
else $\{\mathtt{x} = X \ \wedge \ y = Y > 0 \ \wedge \ 0 \leq \mathtt{x} - y \leq m\}$
$\{\mathtt{x} = X \wedge 2 \cdot y = 2 \cdot Y \wedge \mathtt{x} - 2 \cdot y < m \wedge m \geq 0 \wedge y = Y\}$
divi $(2 \cdot y)$;
$\{X = \mathtt{q} \cdot 2 \cdot Y + \mathtt{x} \ \wedge \ 0 \leq \mathtt{x} < 2 \cdot Y \ \wedge \ y = Y\}$
$\mathtt{q} := \mathtt{q} \cdot 2$;
$\{X = \mathtt{q} \cdot Y + \mathtt{x} \ \wedge \ 0 \leq \mathtt{x} < 2 \cdot Y \ \wedge \ y = Y\}$
if $\mathtt{x} < y$ **then** *skip* $\{Q\}$
else $\{X = \mathtt{q} \cdot Y + \mathtt{x} \ \wedge \ y \leq \mathtt{x} < 2 \cdot Y \ \wedge \ y = Y\}$
$\mathtt{x} := \mathtt{x} - y \quad \{X = (\mathtt{q}+1) \cdot Y + \mathtt{x} \ \wedge \ 0 \leq \mathtt{x} < Y\}$;
$\mathtt{q} := \mathtt{q} + 1 \quad \{Q\}$
fi $\{Q\}$
fi $\{Q\}$.

(End of example)

2.5 An abstract version of recursive procedures

We now leave the realm of Pascal procedures in order to prepare the treatment of procedures in a more abstract setting.

A direct proof of correctness rule (11) would have to use induction hypothesis (13) with its mess of renamings. Therefore, we apply abstraction. A procedure with parameters can be regarded as a family of procedures. If the procedure is recursive, it is a family of mutually recursive procedures. Each of these procedures, say $h.\alpha$, may be specified by a family of Hoare triples

$$\{p.\alpha.\beta\} \quad h.\alpha \quad \{q.\alpha.\beta\} \ .$$

In this way, specification constants and additional predicates R as used above, can be accommodated. If we now encode the pair $\langle \alpha, \beta \rangle$ in a single symbol i and write $h.i = h.\alpha$, we get a family of procedures $h.i$ with preconditions $p.i$ and postconditions $q.i$, where i ranges over some set I.

The declaration of a procedure is a recipe that associates the name of the procedure to its body. This body is a command expression that may contain one or more recursive calls, i.e. occurrences of procedure names. We allow parameters but, for simplicity, no local variables. We treat the parameters as part of the procedure name. Therefore, we use an arbitrary set H of procedure names and we assume that every name $h \in H$ is equipped with a procedure body **body**.h, which is a command expression that may contain occurrences of elements of H. A syntactic formalism for these expressions is given later.

Example. In this abstract setting, the last example of Section 2.4 can be represented by a family of procedure names $(y : y > 0 : divi.y)$ with the declaration

$$\begin{array}{l} \mathbf{body}.(divi.y) = \\ \quad (\ ?(\mathtt{x} < y);\ \mathtt{q} := 0 \\ \quad [\!]\ ?(y \leq \mathtt{x});\ divi.(2 \cdot y);\ \mathtt{q} := \mathtt{q} \cdot 2\ ; \\ \qquad (\ ?(\mathtt{x} < y)\ [\!]\ ?(y \leq \mathtt{x});\ \mathtt{x} := \mathtt{x} - y;\ \mathtt{q} := \mathtt{q} + 1) \\ \quad) . \end{array}$$

(End of example)

The function **body**, which maps procedure names to command expressions, is regarded as the declaration of the procedures. We postpone the definition of $wp.h$ and $wlp.h$ for procedure names h. For the moment we only postulate $h \cong \mathbf{body}.h$, or equivalently

(14) $\quad wp.h = wp.(\mathbf{body}.h)$,

(15) $\quad wlp.h = wlp.(\mathbf{body}.h)$.

If the declaration of h does not contain recursion, these postulates are clearly consistent and strong enough to define the semantics of h. In the case of a recursive declaration it is not clear that they are consistent or applicable. The proof of consistency is postponed to chapter 4. The applicability is shown presently.

The next theorem is the abstract version of rule (11).

(16) **Recursion Theorem.** Let $(i \in I :: h.i)$ be a family of procedure names. Let $(i \in I :: p.i)$ and $(i \in I :: q.i)$ be families of predicates. Let $vf \in I \to \mathbb{Z}^X$ be a function such that for every $m \in \mathbb{Z}$

$$(\forall i \in I :: \{p.i \wedge vf.i < m \wedge m \geq 0\} \quad h.i \quad \{q.i\}\,) \qquad \{\text{ind.hyp.}\}$$
$$\Rightarrow \quad (\forall i \in I :: \{p.i \wedge vf.i \leq m\} \quad \mathbf{body}.(h.i) \quad \{q.i\}\,)\,.$$

Then $\{p.i\}\ h.i\ \{q.i\}$) for all indices $i \in I$.

Remark. The antecedent of the implication is called the induction hypothesis. The theorem implicitly allows mutual recursion. In fact, the body of $h.i$ may call $h.j$. (End of remark)

Proof. In view of postulate (14) and definition (0), we have

(17) $$(\forall i \in I :: \{p.i \wedge vf.i \leq m-1 \wedge m \geq 0\} \quad h.i \quad \{q.i\}\,)$$
$$\Rightarrow \quad (\forall i \in I :: \{p.i \wedge vf.i \leq m\} \quad h.i \quad \{q.i\}\,)\,.$$

If $m = -1$, the precondition of the antecedent is *false*. Therefore, all Hoare triples of the antecedent are true, so that formula (17) implies

(18) $$(\forall i \in I :: \{p.i \wedge vf.i \leq -1\} \quad h.i \quad \{q.i\}\,)\,.$$

By natural induction with (18) for the base case and (17) for the step, we obtain that for all integers $m \geq -1$

$$(\forall i \in I :: \{p.i \wedge vf.i \leq m\} \quad h.i \quad \{q.i\}\,)\,.$$

Interchanging quantifications we see that for all $i \in I$

$$(\forall m \in \mathbb{N} :: \{p.i \wedge vf.i \leq m\} \quad h.i \quad \{q.i\}\,)\,.$$

On the other hand, for every $i \in I$, we have $[\,(\exists m \in \mathbb{N} :: vf.i \leq m)]$; in fact, for every state x there is m with $vf.i.x \leq m$. Therefore, covering rule (5) implies that, for all $i \in I$,

$$\{p.i\} \quad h.i \quad \{q.i\}\,.$$

(End of proof)

2.6 Homomorphisms and simple commands

In this section we prepare the ground for two additional proof rules for recursive procedures. They do not follow from the postulates (14) and (15), but from the formal definitions of *wp* and *wlp* to be given in Chapter 4. We present these rules in this chapter, since they are useful for proofs of correctness and incorrectness of concrete programs. At the same time they form motivation for the theory of Chapter 4.

The above Theorem (16) is a form of induction over the state space. The induction rules to be presented below are based on induction over the possible interpretation functions. We therefore generalize the functions *wp* and *wlp* in the following definition.

A function w is called a ***homomorphism*** if and only if it is a function from commands to monotone predicate transformers that satisfies

(19) $$w.(c; d) = w.c \circ w.d \qquad \text{for all commands } c,\ d,$$
$$w.(\,[\!]\, j \in J :: c.j).p = (\forall j \in J :: w.(c.j).p)$$

for all predicates p and all nonempty families $(j \in J :: c.j)$ of commands $c.j$. Notice that the axioms 1(5), 1(6), 1(13) and 1(16) are summarized in the statement that *wp* and *wlp* are homomorphisms.

When we use arbitrary homomorphisms instead of *wp* and *wlp* we allow more freedom of interpretation of commands. We do not want to allow too much freedom, however. There are usually some commands the interpretation of which is supposed to be known. We therefore introduce a set S of commands the interpretation of which will be fixed. The elements of S are called ***simple commands***.

In the examples we always assume that all guards and all assignments are simple commands. In actual programming, for instance with abstract data types, there is usually a layer of procedures with fixed interpretation, upon which a layer of application oriented procedures can be build. In that case the lower level procedures can also be regarded as simple commands. In other words, in applications of the theory, one can choose a convenient set of simple commands. The introduction of the set S was needed for the following two definitions.

The set *WP* is defined as the set of homomorphisms w with

(20) $$w.s = wp.s \qquad \text{for all } s \in S.$$

The set *WLP* is defined as the set of homomorphisms w with

(21) $$w.s = wlp.s \qquad \text{for all } s \in S.$$

With respect to the syntax, we asssume that every simple command is atomic in the sense that it is not a sequential composition or a nondeterminate choice of other commands (it may be a procedure name). We write $S^{\odot}$ to denote the set of commands that can be obtained from S by repeated application of composition and choice. Since *wp* and *wlp* are homomorphisms, it follows from (19) that the equalities of (20) and (21) can be extended to the elements of $S^{\odot}$: if $c \in S^{\odot}$ then

(22) $$(\forall w \in WP :: w.c = wp.c)\ ,$$
$$(\forall w \in WLP :: w.c = wlp.c)\ .$$

We come back to these syntactic issues in Chapter 4.

2.7 Induction rules

The first induction rule is Hoare's proof rule for the conditional correctness of recursive procedures, cf. [Hoare 1971] and [Manna-Vuillemin 1972]. In Hoare's logic, it looks like

$$\frac{p\,\{h\}\,q \quad \vdash \quad p\,\{\mathbf{body}.h\}\,q}{p\,\{h\}\,q} \;,$$

where $\vdash$ is the derivability symbol: '$A \vdash B$' is pronounced as 'B can be derived from A'. Therefore, by definition (1), Hoare's Rule means that, if $[\,p \Rightarrow wlp.(\mathbf{body}.h).q\,]$ can be derived from $[\,p \Rightarrow wlp.h.q\,]$ then $[\,p \Rightarrow wlp.h.q\,]$.

Since we do not construct a separate logic, but only develop a mathematical theory, the derivability symbol $\vdash$ is to be eliminated. This is done by quantification over all interpretation functions $w \in WLP$. In this way the above rule leads to

Induction Rule. Assume that for every $w \in WLP$

$$[\,p \Rightarrow w.h.q\,] \quad \Rightarrow \quad [\,p \Rightarrow w.(\mathbf{body}.h).q\,] \;.$$

Then $[\,p \Rightarrow wlp.h.q\,]$.

Actually, Hoare's rule is stronger than this one, for it allows implicit quantification over free variables (parameters to the procedure as well as specification constants in the pre– and postconditions). These free variables can be incorporated in the same way as in Theorem (16). Thus we arrive at the following theorem.

(23) **Hoare's Induction Rule.** Assume that for every $w \in WLP$

(24) $$(\forall i :: [\,p.i \Rightarrow w.(h.i).(q.i)\,]) \quad \Rightarrow \quad (\forall i :: [\,p.i \Rightarrow w.(\mathbf{body}.(h.i)).(q.i)\,]) \;.$$

Then $[\,p.i \Rightarrow wlp.(h.i).(q.i)\,]$ for all i.

Remark. This rule is proved in Section 4.9 below. It is based on the definition of *wlp* as the weakest solution of equation (15). Just as in Theorem (16), the antecedent of (24) is called the induction hypothesis. (End of remark)

Example. We give an example where Hoare's Induction Rule is used to prove conditional correctness. In this example, total correctness fails, so that Theorem (16) cannot be used.

Let v be an integer program variable. Let procedure h be declared by

(25) $$\mathbf{body}.h \quad = \quad (skip \,[\!]\, \mathrm{v} := \mathrm{v}+2; h; \mathrm{v} := \mathrm{v}-1) \;.$$

Operationally, it is clear that h need not terminate, but that if h terminates then v is not smaller than it was before. We therefore guess that

$$[\,\mathrm{v} \geq i \quad \Rightarrow \quad wlp.h.(\mathrm{v} \geq i)\,] \qquad \text{for all } i \in \mathbb{Z}.$$

This is proved by means of Hoare's rule in the following way. We let i range over $\mathbb{Z}$, choose all $h.i = h$, and the predicates $p.i$ and $q.i$ equal to $\mathrm{v} \geq i$. We have to prove the proper instantiation of (24). So, we let $w \in \mathit{WLP}$ be a function that satisfies the induction hypothesis

$$[\,\mathrm{v} \geq i \;\; \Rightarrow \;\; w.h.(\mathrm{v} \geq i)\,] \qquad \text{for all } i \in \mathbb{Z}.$$

Now it suffices to observe

$$
\begin{array}{ll}
 & w.(\mathbf{body}.h).(\mathrm{v} \geq i) \\
= & \{\text{declaration (25) of } h\} \\
 & w.(\mathit{skip} \;[\!]\; \mathrm{v} := \mathrm{v}+2; h; \mathrm{v} := \mathrm{v}-1).(\mathrm{v} \geq i) \\
= & \{w \text{ is a homomorphism}\} \\
 & w.\mathit{skip}.(\mathrm{v} \geq i) \;\; \wedge \;\; w.(\mathrm{v} := \mathrm{v}+2).(w.h.(w.(\mathrm{v} := \mathrm{v}-1).(\mathrm{v} \geq i))) \\
= & \{(21),\ 1(10) \text{ and } 1(25)\} \\
 & \mathrm{v} \geq i \;\; \wedge \;\; w.(\mathrm{v} := \mathrm{v}+2).(w.h.(\mathrm{v} \geq i+1)) \\
\Leftarrow & \{\text{induction hypothesis with } i := i+1 \\
 & \quad \text{and monotony of } w.(\mathrm{v} := \mathrm{v}+2)\} \\
 & \mathrm{v} \geq i \;\; \wedge \;\; w.(\mathrm{v} := \mathrm{v}+2).(\mathrm{v} \geq i+1) \\
= & \{(21) \text{ and } 1(25)\} \\
 & \mathrm{v} \geq i \;\; \wedge \;\; \mathrm{v}+2 \geq i+1 \\
= & \{\text{calculus}\} \\
 & \mathrm{v} \geq i\ .
\end{array}
$$

(End of example)

As far as I know, the second induction rule is new. It deals with necessity of preconditions instead of sufficiency. In fact, when dealing with correctness, we are only interested in the question whether a given predicate implies the weakest (liberal) precondition. In program transformation or in proofs of incorrectness, we can also be interested in the necessity of certain preconditions. Necessity of preconditions is usually shown by means of scenarios. Since scenarios require careful operational reasoning, we prefer a formal instrument like the following Necessity Rule for *wp*.

(26) **Necessity Rule.** Assume that for every $w \in \mathit{WP}$

$$(\forall i :: [\,w.(h.i).(q.i) \Rightarrow p.i\,])$$
$$\Rightarrow \quad (\forall i :: [\,w.(\mathbf{body}.(h.i)).(q.i) \Rightarrow p.i\,])\ .$$

Then $[\,wp.(h.i).(q.i) \Rightarrow p.i\,]$ for all i.

The rule is proved in Section 4.9. It is based on the postulate that *wp* is the strongest solution of (14). The rule is not useful for proofs of program correctness. It can be used, however, for proofs of totality, proofs of incorrectness, and proofs of (in–)equivalence of commands.

It is not useful to imagine an operational interpretation of the rule. The specialization of the rule to the repetition is given below in Theorem (30)(b). An operational interpretation in that special case is offered after the proof of Theorem (30).

Example. We use rule (26) to prove that, for every initial state, procedure h of declaration (25) need not terminate. This is formalized in $wp.h.true = false$, or equivalently $[\, wp.h.true \Rightarrow false \,]$. By Rule (26), it suffices to prove that for every $w \in WP$

$$[\, w.h.true \Rightarrow false \,] \quad \Rightarrow \quad [\, w.(\mathbf{body}.h).true \Rightarrow false \,] \ ,$$

or equivalently

$$[\, \neg w.h.true \,] \quad \Rightarrow \quad [\, \neg w.(\mathbf{body}.h).true \,] \ .$$

Therefore, it suffices to use the induction hypothesis $[\, \neg w.h.true \,]$ and to observe

$$
\begin{array}{ll}
 & \neg w.(\mathbf{body}.h).true \\
= & \{\text{declaration (25) of } h\} \\
 & \neg w.(skip \;[\!]\; \mathrm{v} := \mathrm{v}+2; h; \mathrm{v} := \mathrm{v}-1).true \\
= & \{w \text{ is a homomorphism}\} \\
 & \neg w.skip.true \quad \vee \quad \neg w.(\mathrm{v} := \mathrm{v}+2).(w.h.(w.(\mathrm{v} := \mathrm{v}-1).true)) \\
= & \{(21),\ 1(10) \text{ and } 1(25)\} \\
 & \neg w.(\mathrm{v} := \mathrm{v}+2).(w.h.true) \\
= & \{\text{induction hypothesis}\} \\
 & \neg w.(\mathrm{v} := \mathrm{v}+2).false \\
= & \{(21) \text{ and } 1(25)\} \\
 & true \ .
\end{array}
$$

This proves that $wp.h.true = false$. Notice that, since $false$ implies $true$ and $wp.h$ is monotone, it also follows that $wp.h.false = false$, so that h is total. (End of example)

2.8 The repetition

We can now treat the repetition in terms of recursion. Let c be a command and let b be a predicate. The repetition $L = (\mathbf{while}\ b\ \mathbf{do}\ c\ \mathbf{od})$ is defined as the recursive procedure L with

(27) $\quad$ $\textbf{body}.L \quad = \quad (?\neg b \, [\!] \, ?b; c; L)$.

The main proof rule for the repetition is

(28) **Theorem.** Let p be a predicate and $vf \in \mathbb{Z}^X$ a state function such that

(29) $\quad$ $(\forall m \in \mathbb{Z} :: \{p \wedge b \wedge vf \leq m\}\ c\ \{p \wedge vf < m \wedge m \geq 0\})$.

Then it holds $\{p\}\ L\ \{p \wedge \neg b\}$.

Remark. Here m is a specification constant. For negative m, the postcondition of (29) is *false*. So, if condition (29) holds and $m \leq -1$, the precondition of (29) is *false* or command c is not total. In programming methodology one may prefer to require the conjunction

$$[p \wedge b \;\Rightarrow\; vf \geq 0] \;\wedge$$
$$(\forall m \in \mathbb{N} :: \{p \wedge b \wedge vf \leq m\}\ c\ \{p \wedge vf < m\})\ .$$

For nontotal commands our version is stronger. The main advantage, however, is that Theorem (28) leads to the simplest possible annotation rule, see below. In Section 3.5 below, a third version is discussed. (End of remark)

Proof. The theorem is proved by application of Theorem (16) with a singleton set I and the instantiations $p.i := p$, $q.i := p \wedge \neg b$ and $h.i := L$. It suffices to observe that, for every integer m,

$$\{p \wedge vf \leq m\}\ \textbf{body}.L\ \{p \wedge \neg b\}$$
$$\equiv \quad \{(27) \text{ and } (4)\}$$
$$\{p \wedge vf \leq m\}\ ?\neg b\ \{p \wedge \neg b\} \quad \wedge \quad \{p \wedge vf \leq m\}\ ?b; c; L\ \{p \wedge \neg b\}$$
$$\equiv \quad \{\text{eliminating guards}\}$$
$$\{p \wedge vf \leq m \wedge b\}\ c; L\ \{p \wedge \neg b\}$$
$$\Leftarrow \quad \{(3) \text{ and } (29)\}$$
$$\{p \wedge vf < m \wedge m \geq 0\}\ L\ \{p \wedge \neg b\}\ .$$

(End of proof)

Theorem (29) leads to the following annotation rule:

6. Repetition Rule. The correctness of $\{p\}\ L\ \{p \wedge \neg b\}$ can be proved in the annotation

```
{p}
while b do    {vf = ···}
    {p ∧ b ∧ vf ≤ m}
    c  {p ∧ vf < m ∧ m ≥ 0}
od  {p ∧ ¬b} .
```

Theorem (29) is used for proving total correctness of repetitions. There are easier rules for proving conditional correctness and necessity.

When arguing about command L, we may assume that the meaning of command c, the body of L, is given. In other words, we may assume that $c \in S^{\odot}$, the set of commands obtained from simple commands by composition and choice. Recall that the set S of simple commands may also contain lower level procedures, see Section 2.6.

(30) **Theorem.** Let repetition L be given by declaration (27) with $c \in S^{\odot}$. Let p be a predicate.
(a) Let $[\, p \wedge b \Rightarrow wlp.c.p]$. Then $[\, p \Rightarrow wlp.L.(p \wedge \neg b)]$.
(b) Let $[\, b \wedge wp.c.p \Rightarrow p]$. Then $[\, wp.L.(b \vee p) \Rightarrow p]$.

Proof. (a) We apply Hoare's Induction Rule (23) with the same instantiations as in the proof of Theorem (28). In fact, by (23), it suffices to consider an element $w \in WLP$ with

$$[\, p \Rightarrow w.L.(p \wedge \neg b)] \ ,$$

and to prove

$$[\, p \Rightarrow w.(\mathbf{body}.L).(p \wedge \neg b)] \ .$$

This is done in the following calculation

$$\begin{array}{ll} & [\, p \Rightarrow w.(\mathbf{body}.L).(p \wedge \neg b)] \\ \equiv & \{(27)\} \\ & [\, p \Rightarrow w.(?\neg b \,[\!]\, ?b; c; L).(p \wedge \neg b)] \\ \equiv & \{w \text{ is a homomorphism, (21), 1(8)}\} \\ & [\, p \;\Rightarrow\; (\neg b \Rightarrow p \wedge \neg b) \wedge (b \Rightarrow w.c.(w.L.(p \wedge \neg b)))] \\ \equiv & \{\text{predicate calculus}\} \\ & [\, p \wedge b \Rightarrow w.c.(w.L.(p \wedge \neg b))] \\ \Leftarrow & \{w.c \text{ is monotone}\} \\ & [\, p \wedge b \Rightarrow w.c.p] \;\wedge\; [\, p \Rightarrow w.L.(p \wedge \neg b)] \\ \equiv & \{[\, p \wedge b \Rightarrow wlp.c.p],\ c \in S^{\odot} \text{ and (22)}\} \\ & [\, p \Rightarrow w.L.(p \wedge \neg b)] \ . \end{array}$$

(b) Now we use Necessity Rule (26). It suffices to observe that, for every $w \in WP$,

$$\begin{array}{ll} & [\, w.(\mathbf{body}.L).(b \vee p) \Rightarrow p] \\ \equiv & \{(27)\} \\ & [\, w.(?\neg b \,[\!]\, ?b; c; L).(b \vee p) \;\Rightarrow\; p] \\ \equiv & \{w \text{ is a homomorphism, (20), 1(8)}\} \end{array}$$

$$[(\neg b \Rightarrow b \vee p) \wedge (b \Rightarrow w.c.(w.L.(b \vee p))) \quad \Rightarrow \quad p]$$
$$\equiv \quad \{\text{predicate calculus, a number of steps}\}$$
$$[b \wedge w.c.(w.L.(b \vee p)) \quad \Rightarrow \quad p]$$
$$\Leftarrow \quad \{w.c \text{ is monotone}\}$$
$$[w.L.(b \vee p) \Rightarrow p] \quad \wedge \quad [b \wedge w.c.p \Rightarrow p]$$
$$\equiv \quad \{[b \wedge wp.c.p \Rightarrow p],\ c \in S^{\odot} \text{ and } (22)\}$$
$$[w.L.(b \vee p) \Rightarrow p]\ .$$

(End of proof)

Remark. Rule (30)(a) is the well–known rule that if predicate p is an invariant, i.e., $[p \wedge b \Rightarrow wlp.c.p]$, and if p holds initially, and if the repetition terminates, then it terminates in a state that satisfies $p \wedge \neg b$.

Rule (30)(b) seems to be new. Operationally, it can be understood as follows. Assume that $[b \wedge wp.c.p \Rightarrow p]$. Let initially $\neg p$ hold. We claim that there is an execution sequence that keeps $\neg p$ valid. In fact, we have $[b \wedge \neg p \Rightarrow \neg wp.c.p]$. Therefore, whenever $b \wedge \neg p$ holds, there is an execution of c that does not establish p. Repeating this argument, we arrive at an execution sequence of L that either does not terminate or terminates in a state where $\neg p$ holds and also $\neg b$, that is $\neg(b \vee p)$. This shows that

$$[b \wedge wp.c.p \Rightarrow p] \quad \Rightarrow \quad [\neg p \Rightarrow \neg wp.L.(p \vee b)]\ .$$

This suffices. (End of remark)

Remark. In [Nelson 1989], a more general repetition $N = (\textbf{do}\ c\ \textbf{od})$ is defined by

$$\textbf{body}.N \quad = \quad (c\ ;\ N \boxtimes skip)\ ,$$

where operator '$\boxtimes$' is defined by

$$q \boxtimes r \quad = \quad q \mathbin{[\!]} ?(wp.q.false); r.$$

In repetition N, command c is repeatedly executed. The repetition terminates when c 'fails'. Our framework does not allow operator '$\boxtimes$' in such recursive declarations. The operator is unnecessary and has complicated monotony properties. For similar reasons, we do not admit Nelson's **if–fi** constructor, which could be defined by

$$\textbf{if}\ q\ \textbf{fi} \quad = \quad q \boxtimes abort\ .$$

(End of remark)

The next result is a nice characterization of totality of repetitions.

Theorem. Repetition L is a total command if and only if $(\,!\,b; c)$ is total.

Proof. By definition 1(12), command s is total if and only if $wp.s.false = false$. Therefore, one implication is proved in

$$\begin{array}{ll}
& wp.L.false \;=\; false \\
\equiv & \{(27)\} \\
& wp.(?\neg b \,[\!]\, ?b; c; L).false \;=\; false \\
\equiv & \{1(8),\ 1(13),\ 1(16)\} \\
& (\neg b \Rightarrow false) \wedge (b \Rightarrow wp.(c; L).false) \;=\; false \\
\equiv & \{\text{calculus and } 1(13)\} \\
& b \wedge wp.c.(wp.L.false) \;=\; false \\
\Rightarrow & \{[\, false \Rightarrow wp.L.false\,];\ wp.c \text{ monotone; contrapositive}\} \\
& b \wedge wp.c.false \;=\; false \\
\equiv & \{1(8),\ 1(13)\} \\
& wp.(!b; c).false \;=\; false\ .
\end{array}$$

By the last step, the other implication follows from

$$\begin{array}{ll}
& b \wedge wp.c.false \;=\; false \\
\Rightarrow & \{(30)(\text{b}) \text{ with } p := false\} \\
& [\, wp.L.b \Rightarrow false\,] \\
\Rightarrow & \{wp.L \text{ is monotone}\} \\
& wp.L.false \;=\; false\ .
\end{array}$$

(End of proof)

2.9 Exercises

Exercises of Section 2.1.

Exercise 0. Prove the weakening rules (2) and the choice rule (4).

Exercises of Section 2.2.

Exercise 0. Prove the annotation rule for the conditional statement.

Exercise 1. Let k be an integer program variable. For all $i \in \mathbb{Z}$, let $p.i$ be the predicate

$$p.i \;=\; \mathtt{k} > 0 \wedge (\mathtt{k} = 2 \cdot i + 1 \vee \mathtt{k} = -2 \cdot i)\ .$$

Determine commands c and d that satisfy

$$\{\mathtt{k} = i\}\quad c \quad \{p.i\}\ ,$$
$$\{p.i\}\quad d \quad \{\mathtt{k} = i\}\ ,$$

for all $i \in \mathbb{Z}$. Give proofs by annotation. Notice that commands c and d must not depend on i.

Exercises of Section 2.3.

Exercise 0. ♡ Given are integer program variables t and w. Procedure h is declared by

$$\begin{array}{l} \textbf{proc } h\ (x : integer\ ; \textbf{var } y : integer)\ ; \\ \quad (\ x := x + \mathtt{t} \\ \quad ;\ \mathtt{t} := y \\ \quad ;\ y := x\ ) . \end{array}$$

(a) Give a correct and sharp specification of procedure h and prove the correctness.
(b) Give an invocation of h that satisfies for all values of specification constant X the Hoare triple

$$\{\mathtt{w} = X\} \quad h(?,?) \quad \{\mathtt{w} = 0 \quad \wedge \quad \mathtt{t} = X\} \ ,$$

and prove the correctness by means of the specification given in part (a) and invocation rule (10).

Exercise 1. Let j and k be program variables of type *item*. Procedure h is specified by

$$\begin{array}{l} \textbf{proc } h\ (x : item;\ \ \textbf{var } y : item) \\ \{\textbf{ext } \mathtt{j}!\ ;\ \textbf{all } U, V \in item :: \\ \quad \textbf{pre } x = U \wedge \mathtt{j} = V,\ \textbf{post } \mathtt{j} = U \wedge y = V\} \ . \end{array}$$

(a) Give an invocation of h that satisfies, for all values of S and T,

$$\{\mathtt{j} = S \wedge \mathtt{k} = T\} \quad h(?,?) \quad \{\mathtt{j} = T \wedge \mathtt{k} = S\} \ ,$$

and prove its correctness.
(b) Give an implementation of h and prove its correctness.

Exercise 2. Given are integer program variables u and z. Procedure p is specified by

$$\begin{array}{l} \textbf{proc } p\ (x : integer\ ; \textbf{var } y : integer\ ) \\ \{\textbf{ext } \mathtt{u}!\ ;\ \textbf{all } U, Y \in integer\ :: \\ \quad \textbf{pre } x + y = U \wedge \mathtt{u} = Y\ ,\ \textbf{post } \mathtt{u} = U \wedge y = Y\} \ . \end{array}$$

(a) Give an invocation of p that satisfies, for every value of specification constant X,

$$\{\mathtt{u} = X\} \quad p(?,?) \quad \{\mathtt{z} = X \wedge \mathtt{u} = X\} \ ,$$

and prove the correctness.
(b) Give an implementation of p and prove that it satisfies the specification.

Exercises of Section 2.4.

Exercise 0. Given are an integer program variable x and a variable array

$$\mathtt{a} : \textbf{array } [0\,..\,9] \textbf{ of } 0\,..\,9 \ .$$

Function f is defined for natural numbers n by

$$f(0) = 0 \ ,$$
$$f(n) = 10 \cdot f(n \textbf{ div } 10) + \mathtt{a}[n \textbf{ mod } 10] \quad \text{for } n > 0 \ .$$

The question is to implement procedure cd specified by

proc cd
{**ext** x!, a;
all $X \in integer$ :: **pre** $\mathtt{x} \geq 0 \wedge f(\mathtt{x}) = X$, **post** $\mathtt{x} = X$} ,

and to prove the correctness.

Exercise 1. The function $g(n)$ of natural numbers n satisfies

$$g(0) = 0 \ ,$$
$$g(n) = n - g(g(n-1)) \quad \text{for all } n > 0 \ .$$

Give an implementation of procedure $makeg$ specified by

proc $makeg$ (x : $integer$)
{ **ext** w! : $integer$; **all** $X \in integer$ ::
pre P : $x = X \geq 0$, **post** Q : $\mathtt{w} = g(X) \wedge 0 \leq \mathtt{w} \leq X$} ,

and prove its correctness.

Exercises of Section 2.5.

Exercise 0. Let v be an integer program variable. Let procedure h be given by

$$\textbf{body}.h \ = \ (?(\mathtt{v} = 0); \mathtt{v} := 1 \ [\!] \ ?(\mathtt{v} \neq 0); \mathtt{v} := \mathtt{v} - 1; h; \mathtt{v} := 2 \cdot \mathtt{v}).$$

Prove that $(\forall i : i \geq 0 : \ \{\mathtt{v} = i\} \ h \ \{\mathtt{v} = 2^i\} \ )$.

Exercise 1. The simple euclidean algorithm determines the greatest common divisor (gcd) of integer program variables x and y in the following way. It is a procedure h specified by

$\{\mathtt{x} > 0 \wedge \mathtt{y} > 0 \wedge Z = gcd.\mathtt{x}.\mathtt{y}\}$
$h \ \ \{\mathtt{x} = Z \wedge \mathtt{y} = Z\}$

for all specification constants Z. Prove that h can be implemented by means of

body.h =
(?(x = y)
[] ?(x > y) ; x := x − y ; h
[] ?(y > x) ; y := y − x ; h) .

Exercise 2. The extended euclidean algorithm. Modify the algorithm of the previous exercise in such a way that the greatest common divisor of x and y is expressed as an integral linear combination of the initial values of x and y. There are four integer program variables x, y, s, t. Procedure h is specified by

$$\{\mathtt{x} = X \wedge \mathtt{y} = Y\}$$
$$h \quad \{\mathtt{s} \cdot X - \mathtt{t} \cdot Y = gcd.X.Y \wedge 0 < \mathtt{s} \leq Y \wedge 0 \leq \mathtt{t} < X\}$$

for all positive specification constants X and Y. Give an implementation of h and prove its correctness.

Exercise 3. Let k be an integer program variable. Let procedure h be declared by

$$\mathbf{body}.h \quad = \quad \mathtt{k} := \mathtt{k} + 1 \,;\, (\, ?(\mathtt{k} > 0) \,[\!]\, ?(\mathtt{k} \leq 0) \,;\, h \,;\, h) \,.$$

Find a function $f \in \mathbb{Z} \to \mathbb{Z}$ such that for all specification values t

$$\{f.\mathtt{k} = t\} \quad h \quad \{\mathtt{k} = t\} \;.$$

Exercise 4. Every rational number X with $0 \leq X \leq 1$ can be written as an alternating sum of inverses of positive integers. This result, a variation of a theorem of Leonardo di Pisa, can be proved as follows. The alternating sum of inverses $asi.s$ of sequence s is defined recursively by

$$asi.\varepsilon = 0 \;,$$
$$asi.(j;s) = \tfrac{1}{j} - asi.s \quad \text{for integer } j \neq 0.$$

Here, ε is the empty sequence, the operator ';' stands for concatenation and the integer j is identified with the singleton sequence. Let q be a rational program variable and let s be a program variable for sequences of integers. The algorithm is specified by

$$\{\mathtt{q} = X\} \quad g \quad \{X = asi.\mathtt{s}\}$$

for every rational number X with $0 \leq X \leq 1$. Prove that g is implemented by

$$\mathbf{body}.g \quad =$$
$$(\, ?(\mathtt{q} = 0) \,;\, \mathtt{s} := \varepsilon$$
$$[\!]\, ?(\mathtt{q} \neq 0) \,;\, (\,[\!]\, j :: ?(\tfrac{1}{j+1} < \mathtt{q} \leq \tfrac{1}{j}) \,;\, \mathtt{q} := \tfrac{1}{j} - \mathtt{q} \,;\, g \,;\, \mathtt{s} := (j;\mathtt{s}))) \,,$$

where j ranges over the positive integers.
Hint: use the numerator of q as a variant function.

Exercise 5. Prove that the sequence s generated by procedure g in the previous exercise is increasing.

Exercises of Section 2.7.

Exercise 0. Use Hoare's rule to prove that procedure h given by

$$\mathbf{body}.h \quad = \quad (\mathtt{v} := \mathtt{v} + 1 \,[\!]\, h \,;\, h)$$

satisfies $[\,\mathtt{v} = i \;\Rightarrow\; wlp.h.(\mathtt{v} > i)]$. Hint: weaken the precondition.

Exercise 1. Let **body**.h = $(h; h)$. Prove that h does not terminate and is total. Do not use operational arguments.

Exercise 2. Let i be an integer program variable. Let procedure h be declared by

$$\mathbf{body}.h \quad = \quad (\mathtt{i} := 0 \; ; \; h \, [\!] \, ?(\mathtt{i} \neq 0) \; ; \; c)$$

for some command c. Prove that for every predicate p

$$wp.h.p \quad = \quad \mathit{false} \; ,$$
$$wlp.h.p \quad = \quad (\mathtt{i} = 0 \vee wlp.c.p) \; .$$

Exercise 3. Let procedure h be declared by

$$\mathbf{body}.h \quad = \quad (\mathit{skip} \, [\!] \, \mathtt{v} := \mathtt{v} + 1 \; ; \; h \; ; \; \mathtt{v} := \mathtt{v} - 2 \; ; \; h) \; .$$

Prove that $[\, \mathtt{v} < i \;\; \Rightarrow \;\; wlp.h.(\mathtt{v} < i)]$ for all integer values i.

Exercise 4. Let procedure h be declared by

$$\mathbf{body}.h \quad = \quad (?(\mathtt{v} = 7) \, [\!] \, ?(\mathtt{v} \neq 7) \; ; \; \mathtt{v} := \mathtt{v} - 1 \; ; \; h) \; .$$

(a) Show that $[\, wp.h.(\mathtt{v} = 7) \;\; \Rightarrow \;\; \mathtt{v} \geq 7]$.

(b) Show that the conjunct $m \geq 0$ in the precondition of the induction hypothesis of Theorem (16) cannot be omitted. For this purpose, show that, when $m \geq 0$ is omitted, the rule can be used to prove $[\, \mathit{true} \Rightarrow wp.h.(\mathtt{v} = 7)]$, thus contradicting the result of part (a).

Exercises of Section 2.8.

Exercise 0. Prove that repetition L of (27) satisfies

(a) $\quad [\, wlp.L.(\neg b)] \; ,$

(b) $\quad [\, wp.L.b \Rightarrow b] \; .$

Exercise 1. Prove that every repetition $L \; = \; \mathbf{while} \; b \; \mathbf{do} \; c \; \mathbf{od}$ with command c total satisfies $[\neg wp.L.b]$.

Exercise 2. Let i be an integer program variable. Consider the repetition

$$L: \quad \mathbf{while} \; \mathtt{i} \neq 0 \; \mathbf{do} \; (\mathtt{i} := \mathtt{i} - 1 \, [\!] \, \mathtt{i} := \mathtt{i} - 2) \; \mathbf{od} \; .$$

(a) Prove that

$$[\, wlp.L.(\mathtt{i} \neq 0) \quad \equiv \quad (\mathtt{i} < 0)] \; .$$

Use Theorem (30) and the previous exercise.

(b) Determine the predicates $wp.L.(\mathtt{i} \neq 0)$, $wlp.L.(\mathtt{i} = 0)$, $wp.L.(\mathtt{i} = 0)$. Guess the results first, and then give formal proofs.

Exercise 3. Prove that the repetition

$$L: \quad \mathbf{while} \; \mathtt{i} > 1 \; \mathbf{do} \; (\mathtt{i} := \mathtt{i} - 2 \, [\!] \, \mathtt{i} := \mathtt{i} - 3) \; \mathbf{od}$$

satisfies $wp.L.(\mathtt{i} \leq 0) \; = \; \mathtt{i} \leq 2 \wedge \mathtt{i} \neq 1$.

Exercise 4. Prove that the repetition

$L:$ **while** $\mathrm{v} \neq 0$ **do**

$?(\mathrm{v} < 0) \, [\!] \, ?(\mathrm{v} \leq 0); \mathrm{v} := 0 \, [\!] \, ?(\mathrm{v} > 0); \mathrm{v} := \mathrm{v} - 1$ **od**

satisfies $wp.L.true = (\mathrm{v} \geq 0)$.

Exercise 5. ♡ Let L be given by formula (27). Let p be a predicate. Let $vf \in \mathbb{Z}^X$ be a state function such that

$$[\, b \;\Rightarrow\; p \vee vf \geq 0] \,,$$
$$(\forall n \in \mathbb{Z} :: [\, b \wedge wlp.c.(p \vee vf \geq n) \;\Rightarrow\; p \vee vf > n]) \,.$$

Prove that $[\, wlp.L.(p \vee b) \Rightarrow p]$. Hint: use postulate (15).

Exercise 6. In this exercise we compare repetition L as given by formula (27) with what can be called the angelic repetition $L0$ given by

$$L0: \quad ([\!] \, n : n \geq 0 : (?b; c)^n; ?\neg b) \,.$$

We show that $L0$ is wlp–equivalent to L, but not wp–equivalent.

Let p be a predicate.

(a) Prove that for all $n \geq 0$

$$[\, wlp.L.p \Rightarrow wlp.(?b; c)^n.(b \vee p)] \,,$$

and similarly for wp.

(b) Prove that $[\, wlp.L.p \Rightarrow wlp.L0.p]$, and similarly for wp.

(c) Give an example with $c = skip$ to show that for wp the implication need not be an equivalence.

(d) Use Theorem 2(30)(a) with $p := wlp.L0.p$ to prove that $[\, wlp.L0.p \Rightarrow wlp.L.p]$.

CHAPTER 3

HEALTHINESS LAWS

3.0. We come back to the informal description of *wp* and *wlp* given in Section 1.2. This description is used to justify two more postulates concerning *wp* and *wlp*, the so-called healthiness laws. These postulates are due to [Dijkstra 1976]). They are theorems of the standard relational semantics, but in predicate-transformation semantics they need not be imposed. In fact, recently, some investigators (cf. [Back-von Wright 1989b], [Morgan-Gardiner 1990]) have proposed specification constructs that lead to violations of the laws (so these constructs cannot be expressed in relational semantics). Command *serve* from the second example in 1.2 belongs to this category.

In the remainder of this book the healthiness laws are imposed since they form the natural boundary of the theory of Chapter 4. Another reason for imposing them is that they hold for all practical imperative languages and for the relational model of computation (see Chapter 6).

In this chapter, we introduce the laws with an informal justification and we treat the main formal implications.

3.1 Conjunctivity properties of predicate transformers

Since the healthiness laws prescribe certain properties of the predicate transformers *wp.c* and *wlp.c* for commands *c*, it is useful to introduce these properties for arbitrary predicate transformers.

A predicate transformer $f \in \mathbb{P} \to \mathbb{P}$ is called *finitely conjunctive* if and only if for all predicates $p, q \in \mathbb{P}$

(0) $\quad f.(p \wedge q) \quad = \quad f.p \wedge f.q.$

It is called *universally conjunctive* if and only if, for every set of predicates $U \subset \mathbb{P}$,

(1) $\quad f.(\forall p \in U :: p) \quad = \quad (\forall p \in U :: f.p).$

Notice that formula (1) with $U = \emptyset$ implies

(2) $\quad f.true = true.$

Predicate transformer f is called ***positively conjunctive*** if and only if formula (1) holds for every nonempty subset U of $\mathbb{P}$.

It is well–known that every finitely conjunctive predicate transformer is monotone, cf. [Dijkstra-Scholten 1990]. In fact, by definition 1(3), it suffices to verify that for a finitely conjunctive f and predicates p and q:

$$
\begin{array}{ll}
 & [\,f.p \;\Rightarrow\; f.q] \\
\equiv & \{\text{a rule of predicate calculus, see exercise 1.1.0(a)}\} \\
 & [\,f.p \;\equiv\; f.p \wedge f.q] \\
\equiv & \{f \text{ is finitely conjunctive}\} \\
 & [\,f.p \;\equiv\; f.(p \wedge q)] \\
\Leftarrow & \{f \text{ is a function}\} \\
 & [p \;\equiv\; p \wedge q] \\
\equiv & \{\text{the rule of exercise 1.1.0(a)}\} \\
 & [p \;\Rightarrow\; q]\,.
\end{array}
$$

It is clear that every universally conjunctive predicate transformer is positively conjunctive and that every positively conjunctive one is finitely conjunctive. We refer to [Dijkstra-Scholten 1990] Chapter 6 for a more detailed investigation of properties of predicate transformers.

3.2 Two laws

Let c be a command and p a predicate. According to the informal description, predicate $wp.c.p$ holds in a state x if and only if every execution of c starting in x terminates in a state where p holds. Consequently, $wp.c.true$ holds in x if and only if every execution starting in x terminates. On the other hand, $wlp.c.p$ holds in x if and only if every execution starting in x does not terminate or terminates in a state where p holds. This argument yields the first healthiness law (see [Dijkstra-Scholten 1990] Chapter 7, formula (2)):

(3) $\quad wp.c.p \;=\; wp.c.true \wedge wlp.c.p \quad \{\textit{termination law}\}\,.$

Formula (3) can be interpreted as saying that correctness is the conjunction of termination and conditional correctness.

Now let U be a set of predicates. Predicate $(\forall p \in U :: wlp.c.p)$ holds in a state x if and only if, for every predicate $p \in U$, every execution of c starting in x does not terminate or terminates in a state where p holds. This is equivalent to the condition that every execution of c starting in x does not terminate or terminates in a state where all predicates $p \in U$ hold, that is to condition $wlp.c.(\forall p \in U :: p)$. By definition (1), this justifies the other healthiness law (see [Dijkstra-Scholten 1990] Chapter 7, formula (0)):

(4) $\quad wlp.c$ is universally conjunctive.

These laws are precisely the conditions needed for a good correspondence between predicate–transformation semantics as considered here and relational semantics. This is proved in Section 6.4 below.

Let us now consider, for a command c, the predicates $wlp.c.true$ and $wlp.c.false$. By formula (2), law (4) implies

(5) $\quad wlp.c.true \quad = \quad true.$

For a state x, proposition $wlp.c.false.x$ is interpreted to mean that every computation starting at x does not terminate. Therefore, $\neg wlp.c.false.x$ says that the initial state x has a terminating computation. After quantification over all states, we arrive at the following definition. Command c is said to be *potentially terminating* if and only if $[\neg wlp.c.false]$.

One might expect that whenever a command necessarily terminates (see 1(11)), it also potentially terminates. It turns out that this is only true under assumption of totality. More precisely, we have

$$\text{command } c \text{ is total} \quad \equiv \quad [\, wp.c.true \Rightarrow \neg wlp.c.false \,] \ .$$

This is proved in

$$
\begin{array}{ll}
 & [\, wp.c.true \Rightarrow \neg wlp.c.false \,] \\
\equiv & \{\text{predicate calculus}\} \\
 & [\, \neg(wp.c.true \wedge wlp.c.false) \,] \\
\equiv & \{(3)\} \\
 & [\, \neg wp.c.false \,] \\
\equiv & \{1(12)\} \\
 & c \text{ is total} \ .
\end{array}
$$

3.3 Some important implications

In this section, we use the healthiness laws (3) and (4) to derive some important results. The first observation is that for any nonempty set U of predicates and any command c

$$
\begin{array}{ll}
 & wp.c.(\forall u \in U :: u) \\
= & \{(3), (4)\} \\
 & wp.c.true \wedge (\forall u \in U :: wlp.c.u)
\end{array}
$$

$$= \quad \{U \text{ nonempty}\}$$
$$(\forall u \in U :: wp.c.true \wedge wlp.c.u)$$
$$= \quad \{(3)\}$$
$$(\forall u \in U :: wp.c.u).$$

This proves

(6) $wp.c$ is positively conjunctive.

The postulates 1(4), 1(5) and 1(6) of Section 1.2 follow from the healthiness laws (3) and (4). In fact, it is clear that law 1(4) follows from termination law (3). On the other hand, by the results of Section 3.1, the facts (4) and (6) imply monotony of $wp.c$ and $wlp.c$ as postulated in 1(5) and 1(6).

The healthiness laws imply that the choice operator '$[\!]$' distributes over composition in the following strong sense. For any pair of nonempty sets C, D of commands, we have

(7) $$(\,[\!]\, c \in C :: c); (\,[\!]\, d \in D :: d) \quad \cong \quad (\,[\!]\, c \in C,\, d \in D :: \; c; d)\;.$$

This distributivity law is proved as follows. We let c and d range over the sets C and D, respectively. For any predicate p, we have, with wg ranging over wp and wlp,

$$wg.((\,[\!]\, c :: c); (\,[\!]\, d :: d)).p$$
$$= \quad \{1(13)\}$$
$$wg.(\,[\!]\, c :: c).(wg.(\,[\!]\, d :: d).p)$$
$$= \quad \{1(16) \text{ twice}\}$$
$$(\forall c :: wg.c.(\forall d :: wg.d.p))$$
$$= \quad \{(4) \text{ for } wlp\text{; for } wp\text{: } (6) \text{ and } D \text{ is nonempty}\}$$
$$(\forall c, d :: wg.c.(wg.d.p))$$
$$= \quad \{1(13),\ 1(16)\}$$
$$wg.(\,[\!]\, c, d :: \; c; d).p.$$

By 1(7), this concludes the proof of (7).

Remark. Formula (7) is one of the reasons for not allowing a choice of the empty set. It is tempting to define the choice of the empty set by $(\,[\!]\, c \in \emptyset :: c) = miracle$. Then distributivity (cf. (7)) would fail for empty D, since

$$abort; (\,[\!]\, d \in \emptyset :: d) \quad \cong \quad abort\;, \quad \text{whereas}$$
$$(\,[\!]\, d \in \emptyset :: abort; d) \quad \cong \quad miracle\;.$$

This anomaly does not completely justify our decision to forbid the empty choice. The main reason for the decision is that to admit the empty choice here would introduce awkward anomalies in Chapter 4, especially in Sections 4.3, 4.7 and 4.8. (End of remark)

3.4 Guards, assertions, assignments

Guards and assertions satisfy the healthiness laws. We provide some of the proofs. For a predicate b, the assertion $!\,b$ satisfies (3) because of

$$\begin{aligned}
& wp.(!\,b).p \;=\; wp.(!\,b).true \wedge wlp.(!\,b).p\\
\equiv\;& \{1(8)\}\\
& b \wedge p \;=\; (b \wedge true) \wedge (b \Rightarrow p)\\
\equiv\;& \{\text{calculus}\}\\
& true.
\end{aligned}$$

The proof of (3) for $?b$ is even simpler, and therefore omitted.

In order to verify law (4) with $?b$ and $!\,b$ substituted for c, it suffices to note that the predicate transformer $(b \Rightarrow)$ given by $(b \Rightarrow).p = (b \Rightarrow p)$ is universally conjunctive because of the distributive law

$$(b \Rightarrow (\forall p \in U :: p)) \;=\; (\forall p \in U :: b \Rightarrow p).$$

Every assignment $v := f$ also satisfies the healthiness laws. In fact, the termination law (3) is proved by observing that for any predicate p

$$\begin{aligned}
& wp.(v := f).p \;=\; wp.(v := f).true \wedge wlp.(v := f).p\\
\equiv\;& \{1(24)\}\\
& p \circ (v \leftarrow f) \;=\; (true \circ (v \leftarrow f)) \wedge (p \circ (v \leftarrow f))\\
\equiv\;& \{true \circ (v \leftarrow f) = true \text{ by } 1(23);\; true \wedge q = q \text{ for } q \in \mathbb{P}\}\\
& true\;.
\end{aligned}$$

The universal conjunctivity of $wlp.(v := f)$ is proved by observing that for any set U of predicates and any state x

$$\begin{aligned}
& wlp.(v := f).(\forall p \in U :: p).x\\
\equiv\;& \{1(24)\}\\
& (\forall p \in U :: p).((v \leftarrow f).x)\\
\equiv\;& \{1(1) \text{ with } x := (v \leftarrow f).x\}\\
& (\forall p \in U :: p.((v \leftarrow f).x))\\
\equiv\;& \{1(24)\}\\
& (\forall p \in U :: wlp.(v := f).p.x)\\
\equiv\;& \{1(1)\}\\
& (\forall p \in U :: wlp.(v := f).p).x\;.
\end{aligned}$$

3.5 The termination law and repetitions

In our main proof rule for the repetition, Theorem 2(28), invariance and termination are closely coupled in one Hoare triple. Usually these aspects are distinguished into three separate proof obligations. We combined these aspects, since this combination allows the integration of a complete correctness proof of a repetition into the annotated program text. An unexpected asset is that rule 2(28) is independent of the healthiness laws, as opposed to the usual proof rule. We now present a proof rule in which three proof obligations are separated.

Let c be a command and let b be a predicate. Let $L =$ (**while** b **do** c **od**), cf. Section 2.8.

(8) **Theorem.** Let p be a predicate and $vf \in \mathbb{Z}^X$ a state function such that
(a) $[p \wedge b \;\Rightarrow\; vf \geq 0]$,
(b) $\{p \wedge b\}\; c\; \{p\}$,
(c) $(\forall m \in \mathbb{N} :: \{p \wedge b \wedge vf \leq m\}\; c\; \{vf < m\})$.
Then it holds $\{p\}\; L\; \{p \wedge \neg b\}$.

Proof. By Theorem 2(28), it suffices to observe that for all integers $m < 0$:

$$\begin{array}{ll} & wp.c.(p \wedge vf < m \wedge m \geq 0) \\ \Leftarrow & \{\text{trivially}\} \\ & \mathit{false} \\ \equiv & \{m < 0 \text{ and condition (a)}\} \\ & p \wedge b \wedge vf \leq m \,, \end{array}$$

and that for all integers $m \geq 0$:

$$\begin{array}{ll} & wp.c.(p \wedge vf < m \wedge m \geq 0) \\ = & \{m \geq 0;\ (6)\} \\ & wp.c.p \;\;\wedge\;\; wp.c.(vf < m) \\ \Leftarrow & \{m \geq 0 \text{ and conditions (b) and (c)}\} \\ & (p \wedge b) \;\;\wedge\;\; (p \wedge b \wedge vf \leq m) \\ = & \{\text{calculus}\} \\ & p \wedge b \wedge vf \leq m \,. \end{array}$$

(End of proof)

Remark. In Theorem (8), condition (c) can be replaced by
(c') $(\forall m \in \mathbb{N} :: \{p \wedge b \wedge vf = m\}\; c\; \{vf < m\})$.
Formally, this is a weaker proof obligation, but we prefer condition (c) since it seems to be a better guide of the intuition than (c'). (End of remark)

3.6 Exercises

Exercises of Section 3.2.

Exercise 0. Let f be a positively conjunctive predicate transformer. Prove that command c specified by $wp.c = f$ and $wlp.c.p = (f.true \Rightarrow f.p)$ for all $p \in \mathbb{P}$ satisfies the healthiness laws.

Exercises of Section 3.3.

Exercise 0. Prove that a command c is necessarily terminating if and only if

$$wp.c = wlp.c.$$

Exercise 1. Prove that for any command c and predicates $p, q \in \mathbb{P}$

$$wp.c.(p \wedge q) = wp.c.p \wedge wlp.c.q.$$

Exercise 2. Use the previous exercise to prove that, for every predicate p, a command c is total if and only if

$$[\, wp.c.p \quad \Rightarrow \quad \neg wlp.c.(\neg p)\,] \; .$$

Exercise 3. Let c be a command. Let $(i \in I :: p.i)$ and $(i \in I :: q.i)$ be families of predicates with $\{p.i\}\; c\; \{q.i\}$ for all $i \in I$. Prove that, if I is nonempty,

$$\{(\forall i \in I :: p.i)\} \quad c \quad \{(\forall i \in I :: q.i)\} \; .$$

Exercises of Section 3.5.

Exercise 0. ♡ Let L be given by formula 2(27).

(a) Show that $[\, wp.(!b; c).false \Rightarrow wp.L.false]$.

(b) Let $\mathtt{i}$ be an integer program variable. Prove that repetition L given by

$$L: \quad \textbf{while } true \textbf{ do } ?(\mathtt{i} \neq 0); \mathtt{i} := \mathtt{i} - 1 \textbf{ od}$$

satisfies $\{\mathtt{i} \geq 0\}\; L\; \{false\}$.

(c) Use the repetition of (b) to prove that the implication in (a) need not be an equivalence.

Exercise 1. Let there be an integer program variable $\mathtt{i}$. Let L be given by

$$L: \quad \textbf{while } \mathtt{i} > 0 \textbf{ do } (\, [\!]\, n \in \mathbb{N} :: ?(n < \mathtt{i}); \mathtt{i} := n) \textbf{ od} \; .$$

Prove that L is total and satisfies $[\, wp.L.(\mathtt{i} \leq 0)]$.

Exercise 2. In this exercise we explore some consequences of *not* postulating law (4). Let $\mathtt{j}$ be an integer program variable. Let command c be specified by $wlp.c = wp.c$ and

$$wp.c.p \quad = \quad p \vee wp.(\mathtt{j} := \mathtt{j} - 1).p \quad \text{for all } p \in \mathbb{P}.$$

(a) Prove that c satisfies the laws (3), (5), 1(4), 1(5) and 1(6). Use the conjunction of $\mathtt{j} = 0$ and $\mathtt{j} = 1$ to show that c violates law (4).

(b) Consider repetition

$$L: \textbf{while } \mathrm{j} > 0 \textbf{ do } c \textbf{ od} \ .$$

Use Theorem 2(30) to prove $[\, wp.L.(\mathrm{j} > 0) \Rightarrow \mathit{false}\,]$.

(c) Prove $wp.L.\mathit{false} = \mathit{false}$.

(d) Show that Theorem (8) is not applicable to repetition L, in the sense that application of Theorem (8) with $\mathit{vf} = \mathrm{j}$ and $p = (\mathrm{j} > 0)$ leads to a contradiction with part (c).

CHAPTER 4

SEMANTICS OF RECURSION

4.0. This chapter is devoted to the formal definition of the semantics of sequential composition, unbounded choice and recursion and to the proofs of the properties of commands that were introduced and used in the previous chapters. The semantics of the simple commands is taken for granted, but otherwise the reader should not rely on old knowledge but only use facts that have already been justified in the new setting. At the end of the chapter, the foundations of the previous chapters will be complete.

Some examples of the theory are given in the exercises at the end of the chapter. The text of the chapter has almost no examples. One reason is that the chapters 1, 2 and 3 may be regarded as examples of the theory. On the other hand, every nontrivial example tends to constitute additional theory.

In Section 4.1, we introduce complete lattices and investigate the lattice of the predicate transformers and some important subsets. Section 4.2 contains our version of the theorem of Knaster–Tarski. A syntactic formalism for commands with unbounded choice is introduced in Section 4.3.

Section 4.4 contains the main definition. From the definition on simple commands, the functions *wp* and *wlp* are extended to procedure names and command expressions. In Sections 4.5 and 4.6, the healthiness laws, which are postulated for simple commands, are extended to procedure names and command expressions.

The operators for command expressions ('$;$' and '$[\!]$') are introduced in Section 4.7. In Section 4.8, we prove that the functions *wp* and *wlp* treat these operators in the way postulated in Chapter 1. Section 4.9 contains the formal treatment of the induction rules for recursive procedures postulated in Section 2.7.

4.1 Complete lattices and predicate transformers

Recall that an ordered set is a pair $\langle W, \leq \rangle$, such that W is a set and '$\leq$' is an order (i.e. a reflexive, transitive, antisymmetric relation) on set W. An element $x \in W$

is called a *supremum* (least upper bound) of a subset U of W if and only if for all $w \in W$

(0) $\qquad x \leq w \;\equiv\; (\forall u \in U :: u \leq w)$,

i.e. $x \leq w$ if and only if w is an upper bound of U. If it exists, the supremum of U in W is unique. We use the quantifier notation

$$x = (\sup u \in U :: u)$$

or the shorter notation $x = (\sup U)$ to indicate that x is the supremum of U (so that, in particular, it exists).

Remark. Usually, the supremum x of U is defined by the condition

$$(\forall u \in U :: u \leq x) \;\;\wedge$$
$$(\forall w \in W : (\forall u \in U :: u \leq w) : x \leq w) \; .$$

It is easy to verify that our definition is equivalent to the usual one. We prefer our definition, since it is shorter, and more convenient in many proofs. (End of remark)

An element x is called an *infimum* (greatest lower bound, notation $x = (\inf u \in U :: u)$ or $x = (\inf U)$) of U if and only if for all $w \in W$

(1) $\qquad w \leq x \;\equiv\; (\forall u \in U :: w \leq u)$.

The ordered set $\langle W, \leq \rangle$ is called a *complete lattice* if and only if every subset has a supremum and an infimum.

A subset V of a complete lattice W is called *sup–closed* if and only if $(\sup U) \in V$ for every subset U of V. Similarly, V is called *inf–closed* if and only if $(\inf U) \in V$ for every subset U of V.

An important way to construct complete lattices out of smaller ones is as follows. For any set Y, the set of functions W^Y is equipped with the *induced order* '$\leq$' given by

(2) $\qquad f \leq g \;\equiv\; (\forall y \in Y :: f.y \leq g.y)$.

It is well–known and easy to verify that this defines an order on W^Y. It is also well–known and easy to prove (e.g. see [Hesselink 1990] Theorem 3(1)), that, if W is complete, W^Y is complete and infima and suprema in W^Y can be calculated pointwise:

(3) **Theorem.** Let $\langle W, \leq \rangle$ be a complete lattice. Then W^Y is a complete lattice and for any subset U of W^Y,

$$(\inf U).y = (\inf f \in U :: f.y) \quad , \quad (\sup U).y = (\sup f \in U :: f.y) \; .$$

We now specialize to lattices of boolean valued functions. The set $\mathbb{B}$ of the booleans is ordered by *false* < *true*. One can easily show that $\langle \mathbb{B}, \leq \rangle$ is a complete lattice. By Theorem (3), it follows that the set $\mathbb{P}$ of the predicates on the state space X with the induced order $\leq$ is a complete lattice. By (2) and 1(2), we have

(4) $\quad p \leq q \;\equiv\; [p \Rightarrow q]$,

so that the induced order on $\mathbb{P}$ is the strength order of Section 1.1. Notice that we now use the globalized interpretation of '$\leq$' in the sense of Section 1.6.

For any set U of predicates we have

(5) $\quad (\sup U) = (\exists p \in U :: p)$,
$\quad\quad (\inf U) = (\forall p \in U :: p)$.

In order to show the power of definition (0), we provide the straightforward proof of the first formula of (5):

$$
\begin{array}{ll}
& (\sup U) = (\exists p \in U :: p) \\
\equiv & \{(0)\} \\
& (\forall r \in \mathbb{P} :: \; (\exists p \in U :: p) \leq r \equiv (\forall p \in U :: p \leq r)) \\
\equiv & \{(4)\} \\
& (\forall r \in \mathbb{P} :: \; [(\exists p \in U :: p) \Rightarrow r] \equiv (\forall p \in U :: [p \Rightarrow r])) \\
\equiv & \{\text{exercise 1.1.4(b)}\} \\
& \text{true} .
\end{array}
$$

The proof of the second formula is analogous.

By a second application of Theorem (3), we see that the set $\mathbb{P} \to \mathbb{P}$ of the predicate transformers with the induced order is a complete lattice. This set is used so often that we introduce the notation $PT = (\mathbb{P} \to \mathbb{P})$. It follows from (3) and (5) that for any subset U of PT and any predicate $p \in \mathbb{P}$

(6) $\quad (\sup U).p = (\exists f \in U :: f.p)$,
$\quad\quad (\inf U).p = (\forall f \in U :: f.p)$.

We define MT to be the subset of PT that consists of the monotone predicate transformers. We write MC, MP, MU to denote the sets of finitely conjunctive predicate transformers, of positively conjunctive ones, of universally conjunctive ones, respectively. By Section 3.1, we have the inclusions

$$MU \subset MP \subset MC \subset MT \subset PT .$$

(7) **Theorem.** (a) The set MT is sup–closed and inf–closed in PT.
(b) MT is a complete lattice in its own right and every subset of MT has the same supremum and infimum in MT as in PT.
(c) The sets MU, MP, MC are inf–closed in PT.
(d) For f, g, $h \in MT$ with $f \leq g$, we have $f \circ h \leq g \circ h$ and $h \circ f \leq h \circ g$.

Proof. (a) We prove that MT is sup–closed in PT by showing for every subset U of MT that the supremum of U in PT satisfies $(\sup U) \in MT$, i.e. that $(\sup U)$ is monotone (cf. 1(3)): for every p, $q \in \mathbb{P}$, we have

$$
\begin{array}{ll}
 & [\,(\sup U).p \Rightarrow (\sup U).q\,] \\
\equiv & \{(6)\} \\
 & [\,(\exists f \in U :: f.p) \;\Rightarrow\; (\exists f \in U :: f.q)\,] \\
\Leftarrow & \{\text{predicate calculus}\} \\
 & (\forall f \in U :: [\, f.p \Rightarrow f.q\,]) \\
\Leftarrow & \{U \subset MT\} \\
 & [\, p \Rightarrow q\,] \,.
\end{array}
$$

A completely analogous argument shows that MT is inf–closed in PT.

(b) This follows from (a).

(c) We prove that MU is inf–closed by showing that for any subset U of MU function $(\inf U)$ is universally conjunctive. In fact, for any subset P of $\mathbb{P}$ we have

$$
\begin{array}{ll}
 & (\inf U).(\forall p \in P :: p) \;=\; (\forall p \in P :: (\inf U).p) \\
\equiv & \{(6)\} \\
 & (\forall f \in U :: f.(\forall p \in P :: p)) \;=\; (\forall p \in P :: (\forall f \in U :: f.p)) \\
\equiv & \{U \subset MU,\ 1(5),\ \text{interchange of quantifications}\} \\
 & \text{true.}
\end{array}
$$

To show that MP and MC are inf–closed, one uses the same calculation with certain conditions on P.

(d) It suffices to observe that for any $p \in \mathbb{P}$:

$$
\begin{array}{ll}
 & (f \circ h).p \le (g \circ h).p \;\wedge\; (h \circ f).p \le (h \circ g).p \\
\equiv & \{(4)\} \\
 & [\, f.(h.p) \Rightarrow g.(h.p)\,] \;\wedge\; [\, h.(f.p) \Rightarrow h.(g.p)\,] \\
\Leftarrow & \{\text{generalization (using } q := h.p \text{ and } q := p\text{), and } 1(3)\} \\
 & (\forall q \in \mathbb{P} :: [\, f.q \Rightarrow g.q\,]) \;\wedge\; h \in MT \\
\equiv & \{\text{assumptions}\} \\
 & \text{true}\,.
\end{array}
$$

(End of proof)

Remark. If the state space X has more than one element the sets MU, MP, MC are not sup–closed in PT, see exercise 4.1.3. This is the reason for using MT in the theory, even though it is our purpose to construct *wp* and *wlp* in such a way that *wp.c* is positively conjunctive and *wlp.c* is uniformly conjunctive. We do not use the set PT itself, since the composition in PT is not monotone (if X has at least one element). In fact, if $h \in PT$ is given by $h.p = \neg p$, then composition with h as first argument reverses the order:

$$f \leq g \quad \Rightarrow \quad h \circ f \geq h \circ g \, .$$

(End of remark)

4.2 Fixpoints in complete lattices

Let W be a complete lattice. A *fixpoint* of a function $D \in W \to W$ is defined to be an element $v \in W$ with $D.v = v$. If v is a fixpoint of D and $v \leq w$ for every fixpoint w of D, then v is a *least fixpoint* of D; clearly, there is at most one least fixpoint. Similarly, if v is a fixpoint of D and $v \geq w$ for every fixpoint w of D, then v is the *greatest fixpoint* of D; it is also unique. The existence of least and greatest fixpoints is contained in the theorem of Knaster–Tarski, cf. [Tarski 1955]. We shall mainly use the following variation of this theorem:

(8) **Theorem.** Let W be a complete lattice and let $D \in W \to W$ be a monotone function. Then D has a least fixpoint wa and a greatest fixpoint wb. Let V be a subset of W that is D–invariant, i.e. $(\forall v \in V :: D.v \in V)$.
(a) If V is sup–closed then $\mathrm{wa} \in V$.
(b) If V is inf–closed then $wb \in V$.

Remark. Notice that if V is sup–closed or inf–closed, it contains the supremum or infimum of the empty set, and is therefore nonempty. (End of remark)

Proof. By symmetry, it suffices to prove that D has a least fixpoint wa and that $\mathrm{wa} \in V$ for every D–invariant sup–closed subset V of W. Let a D–invariant sup–closed subset V be given. We construct wa as

(9) $\quad \mathrm{wa} = (\sup U)$

where U is the subset of W given by

(10) $\quad u \in U \quad \equiv \quad u \in V \quad \wedge \quad (\forall w : D.w \leq w : u \leq w) \, .$

Since $U \subset V$ and V is sup–closed in W, we have

(11) $\quad \mathrm{wa} \in V \, .$

The next step is to verify

(12) $\quad \mathrm{wa} \in U$

$\equiv \quad \{(10), (11)\}$

$(\forall w : D.w \leq w : \mathrm{wa} \leq w)$

$\equiv \quad \{(9) \text{ and } (0)\}$

$(\forall w : D.w \leq w : (\forall u \in U :: u \leq w))$

$$\begin{array}{ll} & \equiv \quad \{(10)\} \\ & \quad \text{true} \ . \end{array}$$

We then observe that

$$\begin{array}{lll}(13) & & D.\mathrm{wa} \le \mathrm{wa} \\ & \Leftarrow & \{(9)\} \\ & & D.\mathrm{wa} \in U \\ & \equiv & \{(10)\} \\ & & D.\mathrm{wa} \in V \quad \wedge \quad (\forall w : D.w \le w : D.\mathrm{wa} \le w) \\ & \Leftarrow & \{V \text{ is } D\text{–invariant, transitivity of } \le\} \\ & & \mathrm{wa} \in V \quad \wedge \quad (\forall w : D.w \le w : D.\mathrm{wa} \le D.w) \\ & \Leftarrow & \{D \text{ is monotone}\} \\ & & \mathrm{wa} \in V \quad \wedge \quad (\forall w : D.w \le w : \mathrm{wa} \le w) \\ & \equiv & \{(10) \text{ and } (12)\} \\ & & \text{true} \ . \end{array}$$

On the other hand, we have

$$\begin{array}{lll}(14) & & \mathrm{wa} \le D.\mathrm{wa} \\ & \Leftarrow & \{(10) \text{ with } u := \mathrm{wa} \text{ and } w := D.\mathrm{wa}\} \\ & & \mathrm{wa} \in U \quad \wedge \quad D.(D.\mathrm{wa}) \le D.\mathrm{wa} \\ & \equiv & \{(12);\ \text{monotony of } D \text{ and } (13)\} \\ & & \text{true} \ . \end{array}$$

It follows from (13) and (14) that wa is a fixpoint of D. From (10) and (12), it follows that $\mathrm{wa} \le w$ for every fixpoint w of D. Therefore, wa is the least fixpoint of D in W. (End of proof)

Remark. In Section 13.1, we give a stronger version of this theorem with a short proof based on Zorn's Lemma. (End of remark)

4.3 A syntax for commands with unbounded choice

In Chapter 2, we described the body of a procedure as a command expression that may contain some procedure names. Now we must be more formal. We shall define a command as a nonempty set of strings of elementary commands, i.e. a nonempty language over some possibly infinite alphabet.

Let A be a set of symbols that does not contain the symbols ε and ';'. We write A^* to denote the set of strings over A. The empty string is denoted by ε. Catenation of strings is denoted by means of the infix operator ';'. We write $A^{\odot}$

to denote the set of nonempty subsets of A^* (nonempty languages over A). The elements of $A^{\odot}$ are called *commands*.

The set A is regarded as a subset of A^* by identifying a symbol a with the corresponding singleton string. The set A^* is regarded as a subset of $A^{\odot}$ by identifying a string s with the singleton set $\{s\}$. An element $a \in A$ is called an *elementary* command. A string $s \in A^*$ is interpreted as a sequential composition of its terms. An element $r \in A^{\odot}$ is interpreted as the choice of its element strings.

Example. Assume that A contains the elementary commands $?b$ and $\mathtt{j} := 0$ and h. Then $(\mathtt{j} := 0; h) \in A^*$ and $\{?b, (\mathtt{j} := 0; h)\} \in A^{\odot}$. Elsewhere the latter command is written $(?b \,[\!]\, \mathtt{j} := 0; h)$. This notation is introduced formally below in Section 4.7. (End of example)

Recall that $PT = (\mathbb{P} \to \mathbb{P})$. For a function $v \in A \to PT$ from A to the set of the predicate transformers, the string extension $v^* \in A^* \to PT$ and the language extension $v^{\odot} \in A^{\odot} \to PT$ are defined by

(15) $\quad v^*.\varepsilon = identity \;\in \mathbb{P} \to \mathbb{P}$,

$\quad v^*.(a; s) = v.a \circ v^*.s \;$ for $a \in A$ and $s \in A^*$,

$\quad v^{\odot}.r = (\inf s \in r :: v^*.s) \;$ for $r \in A^{\odot}$.

By formula (6), it follows that for any predicate $p \in \mathbb{P}$

(16) $\quad v^{\odot}.r.p = (\forall s \in r :: v^*.s.p)$.

It is clear that function v is the restriction of v^* to the subset A, and that v^* is the restriction of $v^{\odot}$ to the subset A^*.

For later reference, we state the following result.

(17) **Lemma.** (a) Let V be an inf–closed subset of PT which contains the identity function and is closed under composition. Then $v^{\odot} \in A^{\odot} \to V$ for every function $v \in A \to V$.

(b) The subsets MT, MC, MP, MU of PT satisfy the conditions of part (a) on V.

Proof. (a) Let $v \in A \to V$. Since V contains the identity function and is closed under composition, we have by induction $v^*.s \in V$ for all $s \in A^*$. Since V is inf–closed, it follows that $v^{\odot}.r \in V$ for all $r \in A^{\odot}$.

(b) The sets listed are inf–closed by Theorem (7). It is easy to verify that they contain the identity function and are closed under composition. (End of proof)

4.4 The interpretation of recursion

This section contains the main definition of the book. We assume that *wp* and *wlp* are given on simple commands and we construct *wp* and *wlp* for all commands in such a way that the postulates 2(14) and 2(15) are satisfied. The homomorphism properties of *wp* and *wlp* are proved later, in Section 4.8. Since we want to treat *wp* and *wlp* in a unified way, whenever possible, we introduce a parameter $e \in \{0,1\}$ with $e = 0$ for *wp* and $e = 1$ for *wlp*.

We assume that the set A is the disjoint union of sets S and H. Here, S is the set of simple commands introduced in Section 2.6. The functions *wp* and *wlp* on simple commands, as given in Chapter 1, are renamed to $ws_0 \in S \to MT$ and $ws_1 \in S \to MT$, respectively. We assume that S contains at least all guards (see 1(8)) and all assignments (see 1(24)) that we might need.

The elements of H are called *procedure names*. As suggested in 2.5, we assume that the procedures are declared by means of a given function

$$\mathbf{body} \in H \to A^{\odot} .$$

In view of 2(14) and 2(15) the aim is now to construct functions wp, $wlp \in A^{\odot} \to MT$ such that

(18) $\quad wp|S = ws_0 \quad , \quad wlp|S = ws_1 \ ,$

and that for all $h \in H$ and $wg \in \{wp, wlp\}$

(19) $\quad wg.h = wg.(\mathbf{body}.h) \ .$

Remark. It is possible to introduce the simplification $ws_0 = ws_1$, or equivalently: all simple commands are everywhere terminating (see exercise 3.3.0). This simplification would eliminate many case distinctions, but the functions *wp* and *wlp* remain different since nonterminating recursive procedures do occur. The simplification would make the book easier to read, but would preclude applications with simple commands that are not everywhere terminating. For example, the applicability of Theorem 2(30) would be drastically reduced. (End of remark)

The functions *wp* and $wlp \in A^{\odot} \to MT$ are constructed in two steps. For $e \in \{0,1\}$, we first extend ws_e to a function in $A \to MT$. Since A is the disjoint union $S \cup H$, the extension of ws_e to A is of the form $ws_e \cup v$ where v is some function $v \in H \to MT$. Before choosing v, we describe the second step. For any $v \in H \to MT$, the extension $ws_e \cup v \in A \to MT$ has a language extension $(ws_e \cup v)^{\odot}$, cf. definition (15). By Lemma (17), this language extension satisfies

$$(ws_e \cup v)^{\odot} \in A^{\odot} \to MT \ .$$

We construct the extensions wp and wlp in the form $(ws_e \cup v)^{\odot}$.

In view of formula (19), we observe that

$$(20) \qquad \begin{array}{ll} & (\forall h \in H :: (ws_e \cup v)^{\odot}.h = (ws_e \cup v)^{\odot}.(\mathbf{body}.h)) \\ \equiv & \{(ws_e \cup v)^{\odot}.h = v.h \text{ for all } h, \text{ from (15)}\} \\ & (\forall h \in H :: v.h = (ws_e \cup v)^{\odot}.(\mathbf{body}.h)) \\ \equiv & \{\text{equality of functions, definition (21) below}\} \\ & v = D_e.v \end{array}$$

where function $D_e \in MT^H \to MT^H$ is defined by

$$(21) \qquad D_e.v = (ws_e \cup v)^{\odot} \circ \mathbf{body} .$$

By calculation (20), formula (19) can be established by extending ws_e by means of fixpoints of function D_e.

Since MT is a complete lattice, it follows from Theorem (3) that MT^H with the induced order is a complete lattice.

(22) **Theorem.** Function $D_e \in MT^H \to MT^H$ is monotone and has a least fixpoint wa_e and a greatest fixpoint wb_e in MT^H.

Proof. By completeness of MT^H and the Theorem of Knaster–Tarski (8), it suffices to prove that D_e is monotone. This is proved by verifying that for v, $w \in MT^H$

$$\begin{array}{ll} & D_e.v \le D_e.w \\ \equiv & \{\text{induced order, definition (21)}\} \\ & (\forall h \in H :: (ws_e \cup v)^{\odot}.(\mathbf{body}.h) \le (ws_e \cup w)^{\odot}.(\mathbf{body}.h)) \\ \Leftarrow & \{\text{generalization } r \text{ for } \mathbf{body}.h\text{; definition (15)}\} \\ & (\forall r \in A^{\odot} :: (\inf s \in r :: (ws_e \cup v)^*.s) \le (\inf s \in r :: (ws_e \cup w)^*.s)) \\ \Leftarrow & \{\text{if } s \in r \text{ and } r \in A^{\odot} \text{ then } s \in A^*\text{; monotony of inf}\} \\ & (\forall s \in A^* :: (ws_e \cup v)^*.s \le (ws_e \cup w)^*.s) \\ \Leftarrow & \{\text{remaining proof obligation (23)}\} \\ & v \le w . \end{array}$$

It remains to justify the last step by proving

$$(23) \qquad v \le w \quad \Rightarrow \quad (\forall s \in A^* :: (ws_e \cup v)^*.s \le (ws_e \cup w)^*.s) .$$

This is done by induction on the lengths of the strings s. In the base case, the string is empty and we have

$$(ws_e \cup v)^*.\varepsilon = identity = (ws_e \cup w)^*.\varepsilon .$$

The induction step is taken by observing that for any $a \in A$ and $s \in A^*$

$$\begin{array}{ll} & (ws_e \cup v)^*.(a;s) \le (ws_e \cup w)^*.(a;s) \\ \equiv & \{\text{definition (15)}\} \\ & (ws_e \cup v).a \circ (ws_e \cup v)^*.s \le (ws_e \cup w).a \circ (ws_e \cup w)^*.s \end{array}$$

$\Leftarrow$ {from (7)(d): composition is monotone in MT}
$(ws_e \cup v).a \le (ws_e \cup w).a \quad \wedge \quad (ws_e \cup v)^*.s \le (ws_e \cup w)^*.s$
$\Leftarrow$ {induction hypothesis}
$(ws_e \cup v).a \le (ws_e \cup w).a \quad \wedge \quad v \le w$
$\equiv$ {A is the disjoint union of S and H}
$((a \in S \wedge ws_e.a \le ws_e.a) \vee (a \in H \wedge v.a \le w.a)) \quad \wedge \quad v \le w$
$\Leftarrow$ {definition of order in MT^H}
$v \le w$.

(End of proof)

Using wa_e and wb_e as introduced in Theorem (22), we define the functions wp and wlp by

(24) $\qquad wp = (ws_0 \cup wa_0)^{\odot} \quad , \quad wlp \;=\; (ws_1 \cup wb_1)^{\odot}$.

So, wp is the extension of ws_0 by the least fixpoint of D_0 and wlp is the extension of ws_1 by the greatest fixpoint of D_1.

By calculation (20), the extended functions wp and wlp satisfy requirement (19), i.e., the postulates 2(14) and 2(15). In Section 7.5 below, we show that these definitions are in agreement with the operational semantics.

For reference below, we introduce for any $v \in MT^H$ and $e \in \{0,1\}$

(25) $\qquad v^e \;=\; (ws_e \cup v)^{\odot} \in A^{\odot} \to MT$.

It then follows that

(26) $\qquad D_e.v = v^e \circ \mathbf{body} \quad , \quad wp = (wa_0)^0 \quad , \quad wlp = (wb_1)^1$.

4.5 Healthiness laws: the universal conjunctivity of *wlp*

To be consistent with Chapter 3, we have to prove that the functions $wp, wlp \in A^{\odot} \to MT$ satisfy the healthiness laws 3(3) and 3(4). We treat rule 3(4) in this section and rule 3(3) in the next one. Some intermediate results are isolated and stressed because of their rôles in later chapters.

We begin with law 3(4): the universal conjunctivity of wlp. Since the semantics of simple commands is given, we postulate universal conjunctivity for these commands, i.e.

(27) $\qquad ws_1 \in S \to MU$.

By formula (18) this condition represents rule 3(4) for $s \in S$.

We shall use Theorem (8)(b) to prove that function wlp has values in MU as well. Now $wlp = (wb_1)^1$ where wb_1 is the greatest fixpoint of D_1 in MT^H.

Theorem (8)(b) is applied to this action of D_1. Since MU is inf–closed in MT by Theorem (7)(c), an easy argument with Theorem (3) shows that

(28) $\quad MU^H$ is inf–closed in MT^H .

In order to prove that MU^H is D_1–invariant, we observe, for any $v \in MT^H$,

$$\begin{array}{ll} & D_1.v \in MU^H \\ \equiv & \{(21)\} \\ & (ws_1 \cup v)^{\odot} \circ \mathbf{body} \in MU^H \\ \Leftarrow & \{\text{calculus}\} \\ & (ws_1 \cup v)^{\odot} \in A^{\odot} \to MU \\ \Leftarrow & \{\text{Lemma (17)}\} \\ & (ws_1 \cup v) \in A \to MU \\ \Leftarrow & \{A = S \cup H;\ (27)\} \\ & v \in MU^H \ . \end{array}$$

This proves that

(29) $\quad (\forall v \in MU^H :: D_1.v \in MU^H)$.

Notice that, by (25), the last part of this calculation also proves

(30) $\quad (\forall v \in MU^H :: v^1 \in A^{\odot} \to MU)$.

By Theorem (8)(b), it follows from (28) and (29), that the greatest fixpoint wb_1 of D_1 in MT^H is element of MU^H. Since $wlp = (wb_1)^1$ by formula (26), it now follows from (30) that condition (27) extends to the healthiness law

(31) **Theorem.** $wlp \in A^{\odot} \to MU$.

4.6 The termination law

The next aim is to prove that all elements of $A^{\odot}$ satisfy termination law 3(3). This can only be proved if we postulate that the simple commands satisfy this law. We therefore postulate

(32) $\quad (\forall s \in S, p \in \mathbb{P} :: ws_0.s.p = ws_0.s.true \wedge ws_1.s.p)$.

The termination law gives a relation between the functions wp and wlp. The functions wp and wlp are defined as extensions of the extreme fixpoints of D_e. Extreme fixpoints are characterized by their approximations. In order to prove relation 3(3), there are therefore three roads of attack. One can try to approximate the pair (wp, wlp), or to approximate wp while keeping wlp fixed, or to approximate wlp while keeping wp fixed. We use the second road, since the first road is more complicated and the third road leads astray.

More specifically, we fix function *wlp* and define a set WT of functions that satisfy a relation analogous to rule 3(3). We then use Theorem (8)(a) to show that the least fixpoint wa_0 of D_0 is element of this set WT. This leads to a proof of rule 3(3).

The set WT is defined as the subset of MT^H given by

(33) $\quad v \in WT \;\equiv\; (\forall h \in H, p \in \mathbb{P} :: v.h.p = v.h.true \wedge wlp.h.p)$.

Using abbreviation (25), we claim that

(34) $\quad (\forall v \in WT, r \in A^{\odot}, p \in \mathbb{P} :: v^0.r.p = v^0.r.true \wedge wlp.r.p)$.

To prove (34), let $v \in WT$ be given. Let K be the subset of $A^{\odot}$ given by

$$r \in K \;\equiv\; (\forall p \in \mathbb{P} :: v^0.r.p = v^0.r.true \wedge wlp.r.p) .$$

It suffices to prove that $K = A^{\odot}$, or equivalently $A^{\odot} \subset K$. This is done by induction over the structure of $A^{\odot}$.

It follows from the definitions (25) and (24) that the restriction of v^0 to S is ws_0 and that the restriction of wlp to S is ws_1. By postulate (32), this implies that $S \subset K$. It follows from (33) that $H \subset K$. Therefore, we have $A \subset K$.

The inclusion $A^* \subset K$ is proved by induction on the lengths of the strings $s \in A^*$. The base case is

$$\begin{array}{ll} & \varepsilon \in K \\ \equiv & \{\text{definition } K\} \\ & (\forall p :: v^0.\varepsilon.p = v^0.\varepsilon.true \wedge wlp.\varepsilon.p) \\ \equiv & \{(25),\ (24),\ (15)\} \\ & (\forall p :: p = true \wedge p) \\ \equiv & \{\text{calculus}\} \\ & \text{true} . \end{array}$$

The induction step is taken by observing that for every $a \in A$, every $s \in A^* \cap K$ and every $p \in \mathbb{P}$

$$\begin{array}{ll} & v^0.(a;s).true \wedge wlp.(a;s).p \\ = & \{(25),\ (24),\ (15)\} \\ & v^0.a.(v^0.s.true) \wedge wlp.a.(wlp.s.p) \\ = & \{a \in A \subset K\} \\ & v^0.a.true \wedge wlp.a.(v^0.s.true) \wedge wlp.a.(wlp.s.p) \\ = & \{wlp.a \in MU \text{ from } (31)\} \\ & v^0.a.true \wedge wlp.a.(v^0.s.true \wedge wlp.s.p) \\ = & \{s \in K\} \\ & v^0.a.true \wedge wlp.a.(v^0.s.p) \\ = & \{a \in A \subset K\} \end{array}$$

$$\begin{array}{ll} & v^0.a.(v^0.s.p) \\ = & \{(25), (15)\} \\ & v^0.(a;s).p\ , \end{array}$$

so that $(a;s) \in K$. By induction this proves that $A^* \subset K$. In order to show that $A^{\odot} \subset K$ we observe that for every $r \in A^{\odot}$ and every $p \in \mathbb{P}$

$$\begin{array}{ll} & v^0.r.true \wedge wlp.r.p \\ = & \{(25), (24), (15)\} \\ & (\forall s \in r :: v^0.s.true) \wedge (\forall s \in r :: wlp.s.p) \\ = & \{\text{calculus}\} \\ & (\forall s \in r :: v^0.s.true \wedge wlp.s.p) \\ = & \{s \in A^* \subset K\} \\ & (\forall s \in r :: v^0.s.p) \\ = & \{(25), (15)\} \\ & v^0.r.p\ , \end{array}$$

so that $r \in K$. This concludes the proof of formula (34).

The next aim is to prove that WT is D_0–invariant:

(35) $\quad (\forall v \in WT :: D_0.v \in WT)\ .$

This is proved by observing that for any $v \in MT^H$

$$\begin{array}{ll} & D_0.v \in WT \\ \equiv & \{(33)\} \\ & (\forall h \in H, p \in \mathbb{P} :: D_0.v.h.p = D_0.v.h.true \wedge wlp.h.p) \\ \equiv & \{(26)\} \\ & (\forall h \in H, p \in \mathbb{P} :: v^0.(\mathbf{body}.h).p = v^0.(\mathbf{body}.h).true \wedge wlp.h.p) \\ \Leftarrow & \{(19) \text{ for } wlp\} \\ & (\forall h \in H, p \in \mathbb{P} :: v^0.(\mathbf{body}.h).p = v^0.(\mathbf{body}.h).true \wedge wlp.(\mathbf{body}.h).p) \\ \Leftarrow & \{(34) \text{ with } r := \mathbf{body}.h\} \\ & v \in WT\ . \end{array}$$

In order to show that WT is sup–closed, we first observe that for any subset U of MT^H, any $h \in H$ and any $p \in \mathbb{P}$

(36)
$$\begin{array}{ll} & (\sup U).h.p \\ = & \{\text{Theorem (3)}\} \\ & (\sup v \in U :: v.h).p \\ = & \{\text{Theorem (7)(b) and formula (6)}\} \\ & (\exists v \in U :: v.h.p)\ , \end{array}$$

and therefore

$$(\sup U).h.p = (\sup U).h.true \wedge wlp.h.p$$

$$
\begin{aligned}
&\equiv \quad \{(36)\}\\
&\quad (\exists v \in U :: v.h.p) = (\exists v \in U :: v.h.true) \wedge wlp.h.p\\
&\equiv \quad \{\text{distributivity}\}\\
&\quad (\exists v \in U :: v.h.p) = (\exists v \in U :: v.h.true \wedge wlp.h.p)\\
&\Leftarrow \quad \{\text{equals for equals}\}\\
&\quad (\forall v \in U :: v.h.p = v.h.true \wedge wlp.h.p)\\
&\Leftarrow \quad \{(33)\}\\
&\quad U \subset WT\ .
\end{aligned}
$$

This proves

(37) WT is sup–closed in MT^H .

By Theorem (8)(a), it follows from (35) and (37) that the least fixpoint wa_0 of D_0 in MT^H is element of WT. Since $wp = (wa_0)^0$, it follows with (34) that

(38) **Theorem** (termination law 3(3)). For all $r \in A^{\odot}$ and $p \in \mathbb{P}$, we have

$$wp.r.p = wp.r.true \wedge wlp.r.p\ .$$

4.7 The syntactic algebra

Up to this point, $A^{\odot}$ is not more than the set of nonempty languages over $A = S \cup H$. In order to use expressions in $A^{\odot}$, we need operators for composition and (unbounded) choice.

We use the infix operator '$[\!]$' and the quantifier '$[\!]$' to denote nonempty unions of elements of $A^{\odot}$. In other words, $q \,[\!]\, r = q \cup r$ for commands q, $r \in A^{\odot}$. For a family of commands $(i \in I :: q.i)$ we have

(39) $([\!]\, i :: q.i) = (\bigcup i :: q.i)$.

We define the infix operator ';' for composition in $A^{\odot}$ by

(40) $s \in q; r \;\equiv\; (\exists t \in q, u \in r :: s = t; u)$.

Here, the lefthand semicolon is the new operator in $A^{\odot}$ and the righthand semicolon is the catenation operator in A^*. If q and r are singleton sets, so that they can be identified with elements of A^*, then $(q; r)$ is the singleton set consisting of the catenation of these elements. This proves that the operator ';' on $A^{\odot}$ is a genuine extension of the operator ';' on the subset A^* of $A^{\odot}$.

We use $S^{\odot}$ to denote the subset of $A^{\odot}$ that consists of the nonempty sets of strings over S. In view of (39) and (40), this definition is in accordance with the provisional definition in Section 2.6.

For every pair of nonempty subsets C, D of $A^{\odot}$ we have

(41) $$(\,[\!]\, q \in C :: q);(\,[\!]\, r \in D :: r) = (\,[\!]\, q \in C, r \in D :: q;r) \qquad \{\text{distributivity}\}\,.$$

This is proved by observing that for any string s

$$\begin{array}{ll} & s \in (\,[\!]\, q \in C :: q);(\,[\!]\, r \in D :: r) \\ \equiv & \{(40)\} \\ & (\exists t \in (\,[\!]\, q \in C :: q),\ u \in (\,[\!]\, r \in D :: r) ::\ s = t;u) \\ \equiv & \{(39) \text{ and calculus}\} \\ & (\exists q \in C, r \in D :: (\exists t \in q, u \in r ::\ s = t;u)) \\ \equiv & \{(39), (40) \text{ and calculus}\} \\ & s \in (\,[\!]\, q \in C, r \in D ::\ q;r)\,. \end{array}$$

4.8 The semantic homomorphisms

Now that we have operators ';' and '$[\!]$' on $A^{\odot}$, we must verify the postulates 1(13) and 1(16) of Section 1.4. Actually, it is useful to prove a more general result.

Recall from Section 2.6 that a function $w \in A^{\odot} \to MT$ is called a homomorphism if and only if it satisfies 2(19). By formula (6) this amounts to the conditions

$$(\forall q, r \in A^{\odot} :: w.(q;r) = w.q \circ w.r)\,,$$
$$(\forall C : \emptyset \neq C \subset A^{\odot} :: w.(\,[\!]\, c \in C :: c) = (\inf c \in C :: w.c))\,.$$

The main result of this section is

(42) **Theorem.** If $v \in A \to MP$ then $v^{\odot} \in A^{\odot} \to MP$ is a homomorphism.

Proof. It follows from Lemma (17) that $v^{\odot} \in A^{\odot} \to MP$. The first condition of 2(19) is verified by observing that for commands q, $r \in A^{\odot}$ and a predicate $p \in \mathbb{P}$, we have

$$\begin{array}{ll} & v^{\odot}.(q;r).p \\ = & \{(16)\} \\ & (\forall s \in (q;r) :: v^{*}.s.p) \\ = & \{(40)\} \\ & (\forall t \in q, u \in r :: v^{*}.(t;u).p) \\ = & \{\text{exercise } 4.3.2(\text{a})\} \\ & (\forall t \in q, u \in r :: v^{*}.t.(v^{*}.u.p)) \\ = & \{v^{*}.t \text{ is positively conjunctive by Lemma (17)};\ r \neq \emptyset;\ 3(1)\} \\ & (\forall t \in q :: v^{*}.t.(\forall u \in r :: v^{*}.u.p)) \\ = & \{(16) \text{ twice}\} \\ & v^{\odot}.q.(v^{\odot}.r.p)\,. \end{array}$$

The second condition of 2(19) is verified by observing that, for any nonempty subset C of $A^{\odot}$, we have

$$
\begin{aligned}
& v^{\odot}.(\,\|\, c \in C :: c) \\
= \quad & \{(39), (15), \text{calculus}\} \\
& (\inf s \in A^* : (\exists c \in C :: s \in c) : v^*.s) \\
= \quad & \{\text{calculus, see exercise 4.1.4}\} \\
& (\inf c \in C :: (\inf s \in c :: v^*.s)) \\
= \quad & \{(15)\} \\
& (\inf c \in C :: v^{\odot}.c)\ .
\end{aligned}
$$

(End of proof)

(43) **Corollary.** (a) For every $v \in MU^H$, function v^1 is a homomorphism in $A^{\odot} \to MU$. In particular, *wlp* is a homomorphism in $A^{\odot} \to MU$.
(b) For every $v \in WT$, function v^0 is a homomorphism in $A^{\odot} \to MP$. In particular, *wp* is a homomorphism in $A^{\odot} \to MP$.

Proof. (a) Since $ws_1 \in S \to MU$, we have $ws_1 \cup v \in A \to MU$. Lemma (17) then yields $v^1 = (ws_1 \cup v)^{\odot} \in A^{\odot} \to MU$. Since $MU \subset MP$, Theorem (42) implies that v^1 is a homomorphism. The assertion concerning *wlp* follows from $wlp = (wb_1)^1$.

(b) It follows from (31), (34) and the calculation used in the proof of 3(6) that $v^0.r$ is positively conjunctive for every $r \in A^{\odot}$. This proves that $v^0 \in A^{\odot} \to MP$. Since $v^0 = (ws_0 \cup v)^{\odot}$, it follows that $ws_0 \cup v \in A \to MP$. Now Theorem (42) implies that v^0 is a homomorphism. As for *wp*, it remains to observe that $wp = (wa_0)^0$ and that $wa_0 \in WT$. (End of proof)

Remark. This corollary shows that the formalism of this chapter satisfies the fundamental axioms 1(13) and 1(16). The validity of (43) relies on the healthiness laws, represented here by the postulates (27) and (32). The validity of $wp.(q;r) = wp.q \circ wp.r$ in combination with the simple definition (40) of ';' is the real reason that we did not admit the empty choice in Section 1.4 and the empty element in $A^{\odot}$, cf. Section 4.3.

Notice that the homomorphism property is proved in the end, whereas, in [Hesselink 1990], *wp* and *wlp* are defined as fixpoints in the set of homomorphisms. This important shift was forced upon us by the fact that the set *MP* is not sup–closed in *MT* (see exercise 4.1.3) and therefore not suited for direct application in Theorem (8)(a). Actually, even in the situation of loc.cit., where only finite choice is considered, the present order of presentation would be more convenient. (End of remark)

4.9 The induction rules

We can now prove the two induction rules of Section 2.7. Hoare's rule is very important for programming methodology. The necessity rule is occasionally useful for proving totality of a procedure or for proving that a procedure does not satisfy a specification.

Recall that the sets *WLP* and *WP* have been defined in Section 2.6. Hoare's Induction Rule 2(23) reads

(44) **Theorem.** Let $(i \in I :: h.i)$ be a family of procedure names. Let $(i \in I :: p.i)$ and $(i \in I :: q.i)$ be families of predicates such that for all $w \in WLP$

$$(\forall i :: [\, p.i \Rightarrow w.(h.i).(q.i)\,])$$
$$\Rightarrow \quad (\forall i :: [\, p.i \Rightarrow w.(\mathbf{body}.(h.i)).(q.i)\,]) \; .$$

Then $[\, p.i \Rightarrow wlp.(h.i).(q.i)\,]$ for all indices i.

Proof. We begin with massaging our goal

$$
\begin{array}{ll}
& (\forall i :: [\, p.i \Rightarrow wlp.(h.i).(q.i)\,]) \\
\equiv & \{h.i \in H \text{ and } wlp|H = wb_1\} \\
& (\forall i :: [\, p.i \Rightarrow wb_1.(h.i).(q.i)\,]) \\
\equiv & \{\text{definition } V1 \text{ below}\} \\
& wb_1 \in V1 \\
\Leftarrow & \{wb_1 \text{ is greatest fixpoint of } D_1\text{; Theorem (8)(b)}\} \\
& V1 \text{ is } D_1\text{–invariant and inf–closed in } MT^H \; ,
\end{array}
$$

where $V1$ is defined as the subset of MU^H of the functions v such that

$$(\forall i :: [\, p.i \Rightarrow v.(h.i).(q.i)\,]) \; .$$

Recall from (29) and (28) that MU^H is D_1–invariant and inf–closed in MT^H. The set $V1$ is D_1–invariant since for any $v \in MU^H$

$$
\begin{array}{ll}
& D_1.v \in V1 \\
\equiv & \{\text{definition of } V1 \text{ and (26); (29)}\} \\
& (\forall i :: [\, p.i \Rightarrow v^1.(\mathbf{body}.(h.i)).(q.i)\,]) \\
\Leftarrow & \{\text{assumption of theorem; } v^1 \in WLP \text{ by (43)(a)}\} \\
& (\forall i :: [\, p.i \Rightarrow v^1.(h.i).(q.i)\,]) \\
\equiv & \{\text{definition } V1 \text{ and } v^1|H = v\} \\
& v \in V1 \; .
\end{array}
$$

The set $V1$ is inf–closed in MT^H, since MU^H is inf–closed and for any subset U of $V1$ and any index i

$$[\, p.i \Rightarrow (\inf U).(h.i).(q.i)\,]$$

$\equiv$ {(3) and (6)}
$[\,p.i \Rightarrow (\forall v \in U :: v.(h.i).(q.i))\,]$
$\equiv$ {predicate calculus}
$(\forall v \in U :: [\,p.i \Rightarrow v.(h.i).(q.i)\,])$
$\equiv$ {definition $V1$ and $U \subset V1$}
true .

(End of proof)

Recall that the Necessity Rule 2(26) amounts to the following.

(45) **Theorem.** Assume that for every $w \in WP$

$$(\forall i :: [\,w.(h.i).(q.i) \;\Rightarrow\; p.i\,]) \;\Rightarrow\; (\forall i :: [\,w.(\mathbf{body}.(h.i)).(q.i) \;\Rightarrow\; p.i\,]) \;.$$

Then $[\,wp.(h.i).(q.i) \;\Rightarrow\; p.i\,]$ for all i.

Proof. The proof is analogous to the proof of (44). The main difference is that $wp = (wa_0)^0$ where wa_0 is the *least* fixpoint of function D_0. Therefore, we use Theorem (8)(a) and a sup–closed subset of WT. (End of proof)

Remark. A closer look at the proof reveals that Theorem (44) can be strengthened by weakening the assumption as follows. The set WLP can be replaced by the smaller set of the homomorphisms $w \in A^{\odot} \to MU$ with $w.\varepsilon = identity$ and $(w|S) = ws_1$. Similarly, in Theorem (45), the set WP can be replaced by the set of homomorphisms $w \in A^{\odot} \to MP$ with $w.\varepsilon = identity$ and $(w|S) = ws_0$ and

$$(\forall r \in A^{\odot}, p \in \mathbb{P} :: w.r.p = w.r.true \wedge wlp.r.p) \;.$$

(End of remark)

4.10 Conclusion

We have now justified all postulates of Chapters 1, 2 and 3, including the induction rules of Section 2.7 and the results in 2.8 based upon them. The theory is parametrized by the state space X, which induces the set of monotone predicate transformers, the set S of simple commands, the set H of procedure names, the functions ws_0 and ws_1 subject to the postulates (27) and (32), and the declaration function **body**. The fundamental definitions are (15), (24), (39) and (40).

The formalism is somewhat more specific than necessary. For example, in the distributivity law (41), we have syntactic equality whereas 3(8) only gives semantic equality.

4.11 Exercises

Exercises of Section 4.1.

Exercise 0. Let $\langle W, \leq \rangle$ be an ordered set. Let x and y both be suprema of the subset U of W. Prove that $x = y$.

Exercise 1. Prove that definition (0) is equivalent to the alternative suggested in the first remark of 4.1.

Exercise 2. Prove that $x \in W$ is the supremum of the empty set in W if and only if it is the smallest element of W. What about the infimum of the empty set?

Exercise 3. Let v be an integer program variable. Use the set containing $wp.(\mathtt{v} := 0)$ and $wp.(\mathtt{v} := 1)$ to show that MU, MP and MC are not sup–closed in PT. Construct a similar example for a boolean variable.

Exercise 4. ♡ Let Q be a set of subsets of a complete lattice W. Prove that

$$(\inf w \in W : (\exists U \in Q :: w \in U) : w) = (\inf U \in Q :: (\inf U)) \; .$$

Exercise 5. Assume that every subset of W has a infimum. Prove that $\langle W, \leq \rangle$ is a complete lattice, i.e. prove that every subset has an supremum. Hint: construct $(\sup U)$ as the infimum of the upper bounds of U.

Exercises of Section 4.2.

Exercise 0. The simplest version of the theorem of Knaster–Tarski. Let W be a complete lattice. Let $D \in W \to W$ be a monotone function. Give a direct proof of the following result:

Theorem. (a) The element $(\inf w \in W : D.w \leq w : w)$ is a fixpoint of D and, hence, the least fixpoint.
(b) The element $(\sup w \in W : w \leq D.w : w)$ is a fixpoint of D and, hence, the greatest fixpoint.

Exercise 1. Let W be a complete lattice. Let D, $D' \in W \to W$ be monotone functions with $D \leq D'$, cf. formula (2). Let a and a' be the least fixpoints of D and D', respectively.
(a) Prove that $a \leq a'$.
(b) Let V be a subset of W, which is D'–invariant and closed under suprema of **nonempty** subsets. Assume that $a \in V$. Prove that $a' \in V$. (Hint: adapt the proof of Theorem (8).)

Exercises of Section 4.3.

Exercise 0. Let $w \in A^{\odot} \to MT$ be a homomorphism (see Section 2.6). Assume $w.\varepsilon = identity$. Prove that $w = v^{\odot}$ for $v = (w|A)$.

Exercise 1. Let B be a subset of A. Identify $B^{\odot}$ as a subset of $A^{\odot}$. Let v and $w \in A \to PT$ be such that $v|B = w|B$. Prove that $v^{\odot}, w^{\odot} \in A^{\odot} \to PT$ satisfy $v^{\odot}|B^{\odot} = w^{\odot}|B^{\odot}$.

Exercise 2. Let $v \in A \to PT$.

(a) Prove that $v^*.(t;u) = v^*.t \circ v^*.u$ for all t, $u \in A^*$.

(b) Prove that $v^{\odot}.(r \cup s).p = v^{\odot}.r.p \wedge v^{\odot}.s.p$ for all r, $s \in A^{\odot}$ and all $p \in \mathbb{P}$.

Exercises of Section 4.4.

Exercise 0. Let the state space be spanned by one integer program variable i. Let $H = \{h\}$ with declaration

$$\mathbf{body}.h = (\mathtt{i} := \mathtt{i}+1 \,[\!]\, h) \ .$$

Let $w0$, $w1$, $w2 \in MT^H$ be defined by

$$w0.h.p = wp.(\mathtt{i} := \mathtt{i}+1).p \ ,$$
$$w1.h.p = (\forall j : j > \mathtt{i} : wp.(\mathtt{i} := j).p) \ ,$$
$$w2.h.p = false \ .$$

Prove that $w0$, $w1$, $w2$ are fixpoints of D_0, that $w0$ is the greatest fixpoint, and that $w2$ is the least fixpoint.

Exercise 1. Let $H = \{h\}$ with declaration $\mathbf{body}.h = (h \,[\!]\, \varepsilon)$. Determine $wp.h$ and $wlp.h$.

Exercise 2. For $n \in \mathbb{N}$ let $K.n$ be the subset of H defined recursively by $K.0 = \emptyset$ and

$$h \in K.(n+1) \quad \equiv \quad \mathbf{body}.h \in (S \cup K.n)^{\odot} \ .$$

Prove that $wa_e.h = wb_e.h$ for all $h \in (\bigcup n :: K.n)$.

Exercise 3. Prove that for v, $w \in MT^H$ and $e \in \{0,1\}$

$$v \le w \quad \Rightarrow \quad (\forall r \in A^{\odot} :: v^e.r \le w^e.r) \ .$$

Exercises of Section 4.5.

Exercise 0. Show that MU^H is inf–closed in MT^H, cf. (28).

Exercises of Section 4.6.

Exercise 0. Verify that $wb_1 \in WT$ (this should be very easy).

Exercise 1. Let $v \in MT^H$ and $w \in MC^H$ be such that

$$(\forall h \in H, p \in \mathbb{P} :: v.h.p = v.h.true \wedge w.h.p) .$$

Prove that, for $e \in \{0,1\}$,

$$(\forall r \in A^{\odot}, p \in \mathbb{P} :: v^e.r.p = v^e.r.true \wedge w^e.r.p) .$$

Does the proof generalize to the case where the equal signs '=' are replaced by '≥'?

Exercise 2. Prove that $wp.h.p = wp.h.true \wedge v.h.p$ for every fixpoint v of D_e in MU^H.

Exercises of Section 4.9.

Exercise 0. ♡ Let $p \in \mathbb{P}$. Let C be a subset of A such that

$$(\forall s \in S \cap C :: [p \Rightarrow wlp.s.p]) \quad \text{and}$$
$$(\forall h \in H \cap C :: \mathbf{body}.h \in C^{\odot}) ,$$

where $C^{\odot}$ is the subset of $A^{\odot}$ that consists of the nonempty sets of strings over C. Prove that $[p \Rightarrow wlp.c.p]$ for all $c \in C^{\odot}$.

Exercise 1. Give a complete proof of the version of Theorem (45) suggested in the remark.

CHAPTER 5

RAMIFICATIONS

5.0. In this chapter we present a number of more or less isolated extensions of the fundamental concepts. They broaden the view but have no high priority. We do not need the theory of Chapter 4.

In Section 5.1 we give our version of refinement of commands. Refinement is a very important concept in programming methodology. In this book it plays a less prominent rôle. It occurs in some exercises and it comes again to the fore in Chapter 12. Section 5.2 contains an example where a refinement between procedures is proved by means of the induction rules of Section 2.7.

In Section 5.3 we introduce the calculational method of insertion of guards. This method can be regarded as an alternative to annotation. It is especially useful for proofs of semantic equality. In Section 5.4 this method is used to handle a complicated example that is needed in Chapter 12.

Section 5.5 contains a discussion of strongest postconditions.

In Section 5.6 we prepare the ground for an extension of the termination argument used in Theorem 2(16). The harvest is reaped in Section 5.7, where we present a generalization of Theorem 2(16) and a Necessity Rule for *wlp*.

5.1 Refinement and relative refinement

The function of a compiler is to transform programs written in some high–level programming language, say Pascal, into machine instructions. This transformation has many different aspects: names are replaced by machine addresses, values are replaced by bit strings, the flow of command is represented by jumps and branches, comments and types are removed, etc.

We focus on one aspect of the transformation, namely that it should preserve the meaning of the program. For this purpose, we have introduced semantic equality, cf. 1(7). Actually, the compiler need not preserve the semantics completely. It may reduce the amount of nondeterminacy. It may, for instance, replace command ($x := 0 \,[\!]\, x := 1$) by ($x := 1$). In that case, we speak of refinement or implementation.

We say that command c is *refined* by command d (notation $c \sqsubseteq d$) if and only if command d satisfies all Hoare triples of c:

(0) $$\begin{array}{l} c \sqsubseteq d \;\equiv \\ (\forall p, q :: (\{p\}\, c\, \{q\} \;\Rightarrow \{p\}\, d\, \{q\}\,) \\ \wedge \;\; (p\,\{c\}\,q \Rightarrow p\,\{d\}\,q))\,. \end{array}$$

We claim that

(1) $$c \sqsubseteq d \;\equiv\; (\forall q :: [\,wp.c.q \Rightarrow wp.d.q\,] \wedge [\,wlp.c.q \Rightarrow wlp.d.q\,])\,.$$

This is proved by observing that for any predicate q

$$\begin{array}{ll} & (\forall p ::\; \{p\}\, c\, \{q\} \;\Rightarrow\; \{p\}\, d\, \{q\}\,) \\ \equiv & \{2(0)\} \\ & (\forall p ::\; [\,p \Rightarrow wp.c.q\,] \Rightarrow [\,p \Rightarrow wp.d.q\,]) \\ \equiv & \{\text{predicate calculus}\} \\ & [\,wp.c.q \Rightarrow wp.d.q\,])\,, \end{array}$$

and a similar calculation for formula 2(1) and function *wlp*.

It often happens that a command d implements c only under specific circumstances, i.e., if a certain precondition r is satisfied. This can be formalized in the relative refinement relation '$\sqsubseteq_r$' given by

(2) $$\begin{array}{l} c \sqsubseteq_r d \;\equiv \\ (\forall p, q :: (\{r \wedge p\}\, c\, \{q\} \;\Rightarrow \{r \wedge p\}\, d\, \{q\}\,) \\ \wedge \;\; ((r \wedge p\,\{c\}\,q) \Rightarrow (r \wedge p\,\{d\}\,q)))\,. \end{array}$$

In the exercises, it is shown that both refinement relations can be expressed in terms of '$\cong$', '$[\!]$' and '$;$'.

Remark. Notice that every command is refined by *miracle*. More generally, in using refinement one may lose totality.

Definitions (0) and (1) are debatable. We include the second conjunct since we regard some possibly nonterminating commands as useful. Authors dealing with refinements (cf. [Morris 1987], [Back-von Wright 1989a], [Morgan-Gardiner 1990]) often treat partial correctness as totally insufficient, and therefore omit the second conjuncts in formulae (0) and (1). This has the effect that for instance *skip* $[\!]$ *abort* is refined by ($v := v - 1$).

It should also be mentioned that [Nelson 1989] writes $c \sqsubseteq d$ to denote the condition

$$(\forall q :: [\,wp.c.q \Rightarrow wp.d.q\,] \wedge [\,wlp.c.q \Leftarrow wlp.d.q\,])\,.$$

This order is not refinement but approximation. It can be used for a least fixpoint definition of the semantics of recursion. (End of remark)

5.2 Refinement of procedures

In this Section, we give an example in which the induction rules of Section 2.7 are used to prove that procedures h_0 and h_1 satisfy $h_0 \sqsubseteq h_1$ under certain assumptions on their bodies. Let h_0 and h_1 be declared by

$$\mathbf{body}.h_i \quad = \quad (r_i \parallel s_i; h_i; t_i)$$

for $i = 0$ or 1, where r_i, s_i, $t_i \in S^{\odot}$ are commands for $i = 0$ or 1, such that

$$r_0 \sqsubseteq r_1 \quad , \quad s_0 \sqsubseteq s_1 \quad , \quad t_0 \sqsubseteq t_1 \ .$$

We claim that this implies $h_0 \sqsubseteq h_1$. This would be an easy application of the theory of Chapter 12, but it can already be proved by means of the results of 2.7. By Formula (1), we have to prove

$$[\, wg.h_0.q \;\Rightarrow\; wg.h_1.q \,]$$

where q ranges over $\mathbb{P}$ and wg ranges over wp and wlp.

We first treat the case $wg = wp$. In this case our proof obligation fits Necessity Rule 2(26) with $I = \mathbb{P}$ and for $q \in \mathbb{P}$:

$$h.q = h_0 \quad , \quad q.q = q \quad , \quad p.q = wp.h_1.q \ .$$

In fact, by Rule 2(26), it suffices to prove that for every $w \in WP$

$$(\forall q \in \mathbb{P} :: [\, w.h_0.q \Rightarrow wp.h_1.q \,]) \qquad \{\text{ind. hyp.}\}$$
$$\Rightarrow \quad (\forall q \in \mathbb{P} :: [\, w.(\mathbf{body}.h_0).q \Rightarrow wp.h_1.q \,]) \ .$$

This is proved by observing that for every $q \in \mathbb{P}$

$$\begin{array}{ll}
& w.(\mathbf{body}.h_0).q \\
= & \{\text{declaration } h_0\} \\
& w.(r_0 \parallel s_0; h_0; t_0).q \\
= & \{w \text{ is a homomorphism}\} \\
& w.r_0.q \;\;\wedge\;\; w.s_0.(w.h_0.(w.t_0.q)) \\
= & \{2(22) \text{ and } r_0, s_0, t_0 \in S^{\odot}\} \\
& wp.r_0.q \;\;\wedge\;\; wp.s_0.(w.h_0.(wp.t_0.q)) \\
\Rightarrow & \{\text{ind. hyp. with } q := wp.t_0.q, \\
& \quad \text{and monotony of } wp.s_0\} \\
& wp.r_0.q \;\;\wedge\;\; wp.s_0.(wp.h_1.(wp.t_0.q)) \\
\Rightarrow & \{\text{monotony and data concerning } r_0,\, r_1, \text{ etc.}\} \\
& wp.r_1.q \;\;\wedge\;\; wp.s_1.(wp.h_1.(wp.t_1.q)) \\
= & \{\text{same calculation as in the first two steps}\}
\end{array}$$

$$\begin{array}{ll} & wp.(\mathbf{body}.h_1).q \\ = & \{2(14)\} \\ & wp.h_1.q \ . \end{array}$$

The case $wg = wlp$ is proved by means of Hoare's Induction Rule 2(23) and a similar calculation.

5.3 Insertion of guards, and calculus

Guards are not only useful as elementary building blocks of conditional combinations, they are equally useful as commands that can represent pre– and postconditions. The fundamental result in this direction is that for any command c and any predicate q

(3) $\qquad c \cong c\,;?q \;\equiv\; [\,wlp.c.q\,]$.

The proof of this result is rather delicate. First, the semantic equality is expressed by means of wp and wlp. Termination Rule 3(3) and definition 1(8) are used to eliminate the wp–part. The remainder of the proof is by mutual implication. So, we first observe that

$$\begin{array}{lll} & & c \;\cong\; c;?q \\ & \equiv & \{\text{definition 1(7) and Termination Rule 3(3)}\} \\ & & wp.c.true \;=\; wp.(c;?q).true \quad\wedge\quad wlp.c \;=\; wlp.(c;?q) \\ & \equiv & \{1(8) \text{ and } 1(13)\} \\ & & wp.c.true \;=\; wp.c.(q \Rightarrow true) \quad\wedge\quad wlp.c \;=\; wlp.(c;?q) \\ & \equiv & \{\text{calculus}\} \\ (*) & & wlp.c \;=\; wlp.(c;?q) \\ & \Rightarrow & \{\text{application to } q;\ 1(8) \text{ and } 1(13)\} \\ & & wlp.c.q \;=\; wlp.c.(q \Rightarrow q) \\ & \equiv & \{\text{calculus, } 3(5)\} \\ & & [\,wlp.c.q\,] \ . \end{array}$$

For the other implication, it remains to prove that $[\,wlp.c.q\,]$ implies formula (*). This is proved by observing that for any predicate p

$$\begin{array}{ll} & wlp.c.p \;=\; wlp.(c;?q).p \\ \equiv & \{1(8) \text{ and } 1(13)\} \\ & wlp.c.p \;=\; wlp.c.(q \Rightarrow p) \\ \equiv & \{\text{use } [\,wlp.c.q\,]\} \\ & wlp.c.p \wedge wlp.c.q \;=\; wlp.c.(q \Rightarrow p) \wedge wlp.c.q \\ \equiv & \{wlp.c \text{ is conjunctive by 3(4) and } p \wedge q = (q \Rightarrow p) \wedge q\} \end{array}$$

true .

Formula (3) is rather abstract. In most applications we need the following version:

(4) **Theorem.** For any command c and predicates p and q

$$?p; c \cong ?p; c; ?q \quad \equiv \quad [p \Rightarrow wlp.c.q] \ .$$

Proof. This formula follows from (3) by the observation that, by 1(8) and 1(13),

$$wlp.(?p; c).q \quad = \quad (p \Rightarrow wlp.c.q) \ .$$

(End of proof)

Remark. The importance of Theorem (4) is that it enables us to give linear proofs of semantic equalities. We illustrate the method by means of an abstract example. In Section 5.4 the method is used again, but there for a highly specific purpose. (End of remark)

Example. Consider predicates p, q and r, and commands c, d and e. Assume that $[p \Rightarrow wlp.c.q]$ and $q \wedge r = false$. Then we have

$$?p; c; (?q; d \,[\!]\, ?r; e)$$
$$\cong \quad \{\text{Theorem (4) and assumption}\}$$
$$?p; c; ?q; (?q; d \,[\!]\, ?r; e)$$
$$\cong \quad \{\text{distributivity 3(7); composition of guards}\}$$
$$?p; c; (?(q \wedge q); d \,[\!]\, ?(q \wedge r); e)$$
$$\cong \quad \{\text{calculus}\}$$
$$?p; c; (?q; d \,[\!]\, ?false; e)$$
$$\cong \quad \{\text{exercise 1.4.4}\}$$
$$?p; c; ?q; d$$
$$\cong \quad \{\text{Theorem (4) and assumption}\}$$
$$?p; c; d \ .$$

In calculations of this form, we often combine steps where distributivity, composition of guards and exercise 1.1.4 are used. Such arguments are referred to as 'calculus with guards'. (End of example)

5.4 The commutation problem

Let s be a total command such that

(5) $\qquad s; c \ \cong \ c; s \ ,$

(6) $\qquad s; ?b \ \cong \ ?b; s \ \wedge \ s; ?\neg b \ \cong \ ?\neg b; s \ .$

In this situation, one might expect that repetition $L = (\textbf{while } b \textbf{ do } c \textbf{ od})$, cf. 2(27), satisfies

(7) $\quad s; L \;\cong\; L; s$,

as we conjectured in [Hesselink 1990] Section 6.5. In exercise 11.3.0 below, we show that formula (7) holds under a mild restriction on command s. Here we give an example to refute the general conjecture.

This example also shows that the results of Section 5.3 can be used to handle nasty case distinctions in a systematic way.

Example. Let v be an integer program variable. Let the commands s and c be defined by

$$s \;=\; (?(\mathrm{v} \geq 0) \;[\!]\; ?(\mathrm{v} < 0); (\;[\!]\; m : m > 0 : \mathrm{v} := m))\ ,$$
$$c \;=\; (?(\mathrm{v} < 0) \;[\!]\; ?(\mathrm{v} \leq 0); \mathrm{v} := 0 \;[\!]\; ?(\mathrm{v} > 0); \mathrm{v} := \mathrm{v} - 1)\ .$$

We first prove that formula (5) holds. To this end, we observe

$$
\begin{array}{ll}
 & c; s \\
\cong & \{\text{definition of } c\text{; Theorem (4); distributivity}\} \\
 & ?(\mathrm{v} < 0); s \\
 & [\!]\; ?(\mathrm{v} \leq 0); \mathrm{v} := 0; ?(\mathrm{v} = 0); s \\
 & [\!]\; ?(\mathrm{v} > 0); \mathrm{v} := \mathrm{v} - 1; ?(\mathrm{v} \geq 0); s \\
\cong & \{\text{definition of } s\text{; calculus with guards; Theorem (4)}\} \\
 & ?(\mathrm{v} < 0); (\;[\!]\; m : m > 0 : \mathrm{v} := m) \\
 & [\!]\; ?(\mathrm{v} \leq 0); \mathrm{v} := 0 \\
 & [\!]\; ?(\mathrm{v} > 0); \mathrm{v} := \mathrm{v} - 1\ .
\end{array}
$$

We now start from the other end:

$$
\begin{array}{ll}
 & s; c \\
\cong & \{\text{definition of } s\text{; Theorem (4); distributivity}\} \\
 & ?(\mathrm{v} < 0); (\;[\!]\; m : m > 0 : \mathrm{v} := m; ?(\mathrm{v} > 0); c) \\
 & [\!]\; ?(\mathrm{v} \geq 0); c \\
\cong & \{\text{definition of } c\text{; calculus with guards}\} \\
 & ?(\mathrm{v} < 0); (\;[\!]\; m : m \geq 0 : \mathrm{v} := m) \\
 & [\!]\; ?(\mathrm{v} = 0); \mathrm{v} := 0 \\
 & [\!]\; ?(\mathrm{v} > 0); \mathrm{v} := \mathrm{v} - 1 \\
\cong & \{\text{calculus}\} \\
 & ?(\mathrm{v} < 0); (\;[\!]\; m : m > 0 : \mathrm{v} := m) \\
 & [\!]\; ?(\mathrm{v} \leq 0); \mathrm{v} := 0 \\
 & [\!]\; ?(\mathrm{v} > 0); \mathrm{v} := \mathrm{v} - 1 \\
\cong & \{\text{above calculation}\}
\end{array}
$$

$c; s$.

This concludes the proof of formula (5). It is clear that command s is total. We choose guard b of repetition L as $b = (\mathrm{v} \neq 0)$. An easy verification shows that formula (6) holds. It remains to refute formula (7), i.e. to show that $(s; L)$ and $(L; s)$ are not semantically equivalent. To this end, we first observe that

$$\begin{aligned} wp.L.true &= (\mathrm{v} \geq 0) \text{ , see exercise 2.8.3,} \\ wp.s.(\mathrm{v} \geq 0) &= true \text{ .} \end{aligned}$$

It follows that

$$\begin{aligned} wp.(s; L).true &= true \quad \text{and} \\ wp.(L; s).true &= (\mathrm{v} \geq 0) \text{ .} \end{aligned}$$

This shows that $s; L \not\equiv L; s$. (End of example)

5.5 Strongest postconditions

Let c be a command and p a predicate. Let a predicate q be called a *postcondition for* command c and precondition p if and only if $[p \Rightarrow wlp.c.q]$. We claim that there is a strongest postcondition for c and p. If this is true, then clearly this strongest postcondition is equivalent to the conjunction of all postconditions for c and p. This conjunction is

(8) $\qquad sp.c.p \;=\; (\forall q \in \mathbb{P} : [p \Rightarrow wlp.c.q] : q)$.

We claim that, indeed, $sp.c.p$ is the strongest postcondition for c and p. It is clear that $sp.c.p$ implies every postcondition for c and p. Therefore, it suffices to observe that $sp.c.p$ is a postcondition for c and p:

(9)
$$\begin{aligned} & [p \Rightarrow wlp.c.(sp.c.p)] \\ \equiv \;\; & \{\text{definition (8) and law 3(4)}\} \\ & [p \Rightarrow (\forall q \in \mathbb{P} : [p \Rightarrow wlp.c.q] : wlp.c.q)] \\ \equiv \;\; & \{\text{exercise 1.1.4}\} \\ & (\forall q \in \mathbb{P} : [p \Rightarrow wlp.c.q] : [p \Rightarrow wlp.c.q]) \\ \equiv \;\; & \{\text{calculus}\} \\ & \text{true .} \end{aligned}$$

We now observe that for every predicate q

$$\begin{aligned} & [p \Rightarrow wlp.c.q] \\ \Rightarrow \;\; & \{\text{definition (8)}\} \\ & [sp.c.p \Rightarrow q] \\ \Rightarrow \;\; & \{\text{monotony of } wlp.c\} \\ & [wlp.c.(sp.c.p) \Rightarrow wlp.c.q] \end{aligned}$$

$$\Rightarrow \quad \{\text{transitivity and (9)}\}$$
$$[\, p \Rightarrow wlp.c.q \,] \; .$$

This cycle of implications proves that for all predicates p and q

(10) $\quad [\, p \Rightarrow wlp.c.q \,] \quad \equiv \quad [\, sp.c.p \Rightarrow q \,] \; .$

In category theory, formula (10) can be expressed by saying that $sp.c$ is the right adjoint of $wlp.c$, see [Hoare 1989] p. 281.

The strongest postcondition of a sequential composition $(c; d)$ can be determined in the following way. We observe that for all predicates p and q

$$[\, sp.(c;d).p \Rightarrow q \,]$$
$$\equiv \quad \{(10) \text{ and } 1(13)\}$$
$$[\, p \Rightarrow wlp.c.(wlp.d.q) \,]$$
$$\equiv \quad \{(10) \text{ with } q := wlp.d.q\}$$
$$[\, sp.c.p \Rightarrow wlp.d.q \,]$$
$$\equiv \quad \{(10) \text{ with } p := sp.c.p\}$$
$$[\, sp.d.(sp.c.p) \Rightarrow q \,] \; .$$

By exercise 1.1.5, this implies that for all predicates p

$$sp.(c;d).p = sp.d.(sp.c.p) \; .$$

By a similar calculation, one can prove that for any nonempty set C of commands and any predicate p

(11) $\quad sp.(\, [\!] \, c \in C :: c).p = (\exists c \in C :: sp.c.p) \; .$

Remark. For the relational interpretation of the strongest postcondition we refer to exercise 6.4.2 below. The ideas of this section were inspired by [von Wright 1990] Chapter 6. The strongest postcondition itself goes back to [de Bakker-Meertens 1975]. (End of remark)

5.6 Termination and well-founded triples

Termination arguments for repetitions and recursive procedures are usually based on the fact that every decreasing sequence of natural numbers terminates. Sometimes a lexical order is needed, for example in the unification algorithm (cf. [Galllier 1987] p.391).

Actually, we do not even need a partial ordering, cf. [Dijkstra–Scholten 1990] p. 174. Quite generally, let '$<$' be a binary relation on a set Z. If S is a subset of Z, an element z is called a *minimal* element of S if and only if

(12) $\quad z \in S \quad \wedge \quad (\forall y : y < z : y \notin S) \; .$

A subset N of Z is said to be *well-founded* with respect to $<$ if and only if every nonempty subset of N has a minimal element. In that case, we also say that $\langle Z, <, N\rangle$ is a *well-founded triple*.

The standard example is the triple $\langle \mathbb{Z}, <, \mathbb{N}\rangle$ where $\mathbb{Z}$ is the set of the integers, $\mathbb{N}$ the set of the natural numbers and $<$ the usual "less than" relation.

Well-foundedness is equivalent to the validity of mathematical induction. We need this result in the following —slightly unusual— form.

(13) **Theorem.** Subset N is well-founded with respect to $<$ if and only if, for every predicate f on Z,

(14) $\quad (\forall z : z \notin N \vee (\forall y : y < z : f.y) : f.z) \quad \Rightarrow \quad (\forall z :: f.z)$,

where the dummies z and y range over Z.

Proof. We need six bold steps:

$$
\begin{array}{l}
\quad N \text{ is well-founded with respect to } < \\
\equiv \quad \{\text{definition and (12)}\} \\
\quad (\forall S : S \subset N \ \wedge \ (\exists z :: z \in S) : \\
\qquad (\exists z :: z \in S \ \wedge \ (\forall y : y < z : y \notin S))) \\
\equiv \quad \{\text{let predicate } f \text{ on } Z \text{ be related to subset } S \text{ of } Z \text{ by } f.z \equiv z \notin S\} \\
\quad (\forall f : (\forall z : \neg f.z : z \in N) \ \wedge \ (\exists z :: \neg f.z) : \\
\qquad (\exists z :: \neg f.z \ \wedge \ (\forall y : y < z : f.y))) \\
\equiv \quad \{\text{trading}\} \\
\quad (\forall f : (\forall z : z \notin N : f.z) \ \wedge \ (\exists z :: \neg f.z) : \\
\qquad (\exists z : (\forall y : y < z : f.y) : \neg f.z)) \\
\equiv \quad \{\text{De Morgan}\} \\
\quad (\forall f : (\forall z : z \notin N : f.z) \ \wedge \ \neg(\forall z :: f.z) : \\
\qquad \neg(\forall z : (\forall y : y < z : f.y) : f.z)) \\
\equiv \quad \{\text{trading}\} \\
\quad (\forall f : (\forall z : z \notin N : f.z) \ \wedge \ (\forall z : (\forall y : y < z : f.y) : f.z) : \\
\qquad (\forall z :: f.z)) \\
\equiv \quad \{\text{range union}\} \\
\quad (\forall f : (\forall z : z \notin N \vee (\forall y : y < z : f.y) : f.z) : \\
\qquad (\forall z :: f.z)) \ .
\end{array}
$$

(End of proof)

The above theorem is applied to yield the next lemma on predicates.

(15) **Lemma.** Let $\langle Z, <, N \rangle$ be a well-founded triple. Let $(i \in I :: r.i)$ be a family of predicates and $(i \in I :: vf.i)$ a family of Z-valued state functions such that for all $m \in Z$

$$\begin{aligned} &(\forall i :: [\, vf.i < m \wedge m \in N \Rightarrow r.i\,]) \\ \Rightarrow \quad &(\forall i :: [\, vf.i = m \Rightarrow r.i\,]) \;. \end{aligned}$$

Then $[\, r.i\,]$ for all $i \in I$.

Proof. We observe that

$$\begin{aligned} &(\forall i :: [\, r.i\,]) \\ \equiv \quad &\{vf.i \text{ is defined everywhere}\} \\ &(\forall i :: [\,(\exists z :: vf.i = z) \Rightarrow r.i\,]) \\ \equiv \quad &\{\text{calculus}\} \\ &(\forall i :: (\forall z :: [\, vf.i = z \Rightarrow r.i\,])) \\ \equiv \quad &\{\text{interchange, definition (16) below}\} \\ &(\forall z :: f.z) \end{aligned}$$

where predicate f on Z is defined by

(16) $\quad f.z \;\equiv\; (\forall i :: [\, vf.i = z \Rightarrow r.i\,])$.

We now have to prove $(\forall z :: f.z)$. Since $\langle Z, <, N \rangle$ is a well-founded triple, this follows from Theorem (13) if the antecedent of Formula (14) holds. This is proved by observing that for any $z \in Z$

$$\begin{aligned} &z \notin N \;\vee\; (\forall y : y < z : f.y) \\ \equiv \quad &\{(16) \text{ with } z := y\} \\ &z \notin N \;\vee\; (\forall y : y < z : (\forall i :: [\, vf.i = y \Rightarrow r.i\,])) \\ \equiv \quad &\{\text{calculus}\} \\ &z \notin N \;\vee\; (\forall i :: [\,(\exists y : y < z : vf.i = y) \Rightarrow r.i\,]) \\ \equiv \quad &\{\text{calculus}\} \\ &(\forall i :: z \notin N \vee [\, vf.i < z \Rightarrow r.i\,]) \\ \equiv \quad &\{\text{calculus}\} \\ &(\forall i :: [\, z \notin N \vee (vf.i < z \Rightarrow r.i)\,]) \\ \equiv \quad &\{\text{calculus}\} \\ &(\forall i :: [\, vf.i < z \wedge z \in N \Rightarrow r.i\,]) \\ \Rightarrow \quad &\{\text{assumption of the lemma with } m := z\} \\ &(\forall i :: [\, vf.i = z \Rightarrow r.i\,]) \\ \equiv \quad &\{(16)\} \\ &f.z \;. \end{aligned}$$

(End of proof)

5.7 Two new recursion theorems

The results of the previous section are used to prove a generalization of Theorem 2(16) and a necessity rule for *wlp*.

(17) **Theorem.** Let $\langle Z, <, N \rangle$ be a well-founded triple. Let $(i \in I :: vf.i)$ be a family of Z–valued state functions such that for every $m \in Z$

$$(\forall i \in I :: \ \{p.i \ \wedge \ vf.i < m \ \wedge \ m \in N\} \ h.i \ \{q.i\} \ ) \\ \Rightarrow \quad (\forall i \in I :: \{p.i \ \wedge \ vf.i = m\} \ \mathbf{body}.(h.i) \ \{q.i\} \ ) \ .$$

Then $\{p.i\} \ h.i \ \{q.i\}$ for all $i \in I$.

Proof. It follows from 2(0) that the proof obligation is equivalent to $(\forall i :: [\, r.i \,])$ where

$$r.i \quad = \quad (p.i \Rightarrow wp.(h.i).(q.i)) \qquad \text{for all } i \in I.$$

In view of 2(0) and 2(14), the assumption of the theorem is equivalent to the assumption that for all $m \in Z$

$$(\forall i :: [\, vf.i < m \wedge m \in N \wedge p.i \ \Rightarrow \ wp.(h.i).(q.i) \,]) \\ \Rightarrow \quad (\forall i :: [\, vf.i = m \wedge p.i \ \Rightarrow \ wp.(h.i).(q.i) \,]) \ .$$

Since $[\, p \wedge q \Rightarrow r \,]$ equivales $[\, p \Rightarrow (q \Rightarrow r) \,]$ for all predicates p, q and r, this means

$$(\forall i :: [\, vf.i < m \wedge m \in N \ \Rightarrow \ r.i \,]) \\ \Rightarrow \quad (\forall i :: [\, vf.i = m \ \Rightarrow \ r.i \,]) \ .$$

The theorem now follows from Lemma (15). (End of proof)

The separation of Lemma (15) from the proof of Theorem (17) is also motivated by the next result, a Necessity Rule for *wlp*, which can be compared to the Necessity Rule 2(26) for *wp*.

(18) **Theorem.** Let $\langle Z, <, N \rangle$ be a well-founded triple. Let $(i \in I :: vf.i)$ be a family of Z-valued state functions such that for every $m \in Z$

$$(\forall i :: [\, vf.i < m \wedge m \in N \wedge wlp.(h.i).(q.i) \ \Rightarrow \ p.i \,]) \\ \Rightarrow \quad (\forall i :: [\, vf.i = m \wedge wlp.(\mathbf{body}.(h.i)).(q.i) \ \Rightarrow \ p.i \,]) \ .$$

Then $[\, wlp.(h.i).(q.i) \ \Rightarrow \ p.i \,]$ for all i.

Proof. The proof is completely analogous to the proof of (17), but based on postulate 2(15). It follows from Lemma (15) by means of the substitution

$$r.i \quad = \quad (wlp.(h.i).(q.i) \Rightarrow p.i) \ .$$

(End of proof)

Example. Let v be an integer program variable and let procedure h be declared by

$$\mathbf{body}.h \quad = \quad (skip \,[\!]\, \mathrm{v} := \mathrm{v} - 1\,;\ h\,;\ \mathrm{v} := \mathrm{v} + 2)\ .$$

Operationally, it is clear that h need not terminate and that if h terminates the value of v may be arbitrarily large. The second assertion is formalized in

$$(\forall i \in \mathbb{Z} :: [\neg wlp.h.(\mathrm{v} < i)])\ .$$

This formula can be proved by means of Theorem (18) with $h.i = h$ and $p.i = false$ and $q.i = (\mathrm{v} < i)$ for all $i \in \mathbb{Z}$. We use the standard well-founded triple $\langle \mathbb{Z}, <, \mathbb{N} \rangle$. By (18) it suffices to give a family of $\mathbb{Z}$-valued state functions $vf.i$ such that for every $m \in \mathbb{Z}$ the induction hypothesis

$$(\forall i \in \mathbb{Z} :: [\, vf.i < m \wedge m \in \mathbb{N} \wedge wlp.h.(\mathrm{v} < i) \Rightarrow false\,])$$

implies for every i

$$[\, vf.i = m \quad \wedge \quad wlp.(\mathbf{body}.h).(\mathrm{v} < i) \quad \Rightarrow \quad false\,]\ .$$

To this end we first observe that the induction hypothesis is equivalent to

(19) $$(\forall i \in \mathbb{Z} :: [\, wlp.h.(\mathrm{v} < i) \Rightarrow \neg(vf.i < m \wedge m \in \mathbb{N})\,])\ .$$

Now our proof obligation is fulfilled by

$$
\begin{array}{ll}
 & vf.i = m \quad \wedge \quad wlp.(\mathbf{body}.h).(\mathrm{v} < i) \\
= & \{\text{declaration of } h\} \\
 & vf.i = m \quad \wedge \quad \mathrm{v} < i \quad \wedge \quad wlp.(\mathrm{v} := \mathrm{v} - 1\,;\ h\,;\ \mathrm{v} := \mathrm{v} + 2).(\mathrm{v} < i) \\
= & \{\text{calculus}\} \\
 & vf.i = m \quad \wedge \quad \mathrm{v} < i \quad \wedge \quad wlp.(\mathrm{v} := \mathrm{v} - 1\,;\ h).(\mathrm{v} < i - 2) \\
\Rightarrow & \{(19) \text{ with } i := i - 2;\ \text{monotony}\} \\
 & vf.i = m \quad \wedge \quad \mathrm{v} < i \quad \wedge \\
 & wlp.(\mathrm{v} := \mathrm{v} - 1).(\neg(vf.(i-2) < m \wedge m \in \mathbb{N})) \\
\Rightarrow & \{\text{choose } vf.i = i - \mathrm{v}, \text{ then first two conjuncts} \\
 & \quad \text{imply } m > 0 \text{ and hence } m \in \mathbb{N}; \\
 & \quad \text{since } m \text{ is constant, this can be used in third conjunct}\} \\
 & i - \mathrm{v} = m \quad \wedge \quad wlp.(\mathrm{v} := \mathrm{v} - 1).(\neg(i - 2 - \mathrm{v} < m)) \\
= & \{\text{calculus}\} \\
 & i - \mathrm{v} = m \quad \wedge \quad i - 2 - (\mathrm{v} - 1) \geq m \\
= & \{\text{calculus}\} \\
 & false\ .
\end{array}
$$

Notice that we delayed the choice of the state functions $vf.i$ until the point where the expression indicated a useful choice. (End of example)

Remark. According to [Apt–Plotkin 1986] the usage of well–founded sets for proofs of total correctness goes back to [Manna–Pnueli 1974]. (End of remark)

5.8 Exercises

Exercises of Section 5.1.

Exercise 0. Prove that $c \sqsubseteq d \;\equiv\; c \cong c \,[\!]\, d$.

Exercise 1. Prove that

$$c \sqsubseteq_r d \;\equiv\; (\forall q :: [\, r \wedge wp.c.q \Rightarrow wp.d.q \,] \wedge [\, r \wedge wlp.c.q \Rightarrow wlp.d.q \,])\ .$$
$$c \sqsubseteq_r d \;\equiv\; c \sqsubseteq (?r; d)\ .$$

Exercise 2. Prove that, if $c \sqsubseteq c'$ and $d \sqsubseteq d'$, then

$$c \,[\!]\, d \sqsubseteq c' \,[\!]\, d' \quad \text{and} \quad c; d \sqsubseteq c'; d'\ .$$

Exercise 3. Prove that $c \cong d \;\equiv\; c \sqsubseteq d \;\wedge\; d \sqsubseteq c$.

Exercise 4. ♡ Let c be a command and p and q predicates. Prove that

(a) $\quad ?p; c \sqsubseteq c; ?q \;\equiv\; [\, p \vee wp.c.(\neg q) \,]$,

(b) $\quad c; ?p \sqsubseteq ?q; c \;\equiv\; [\, q \Rightarrow wlp.c.p \,]$ (use exercise 3.3.1).

Exercises of Section 5.2.

Exercise 0. Treat the case of $wg = wlp$.

Exercises of Section 5.3.

Exercise 0. (a) Prove that Theorem (4) remains valid if command $?p$ is replaced by $!\,p$.

(b) Prove that, in (3) and (4), command $?q$ can be replaced by $!\,q$ (compare Theorem 4.2(ii) of Chapter 9 of [Dijkstra 1990], that asserts that $[\, p \Rightarrow wp.c.q \,]$ implies $wp.(!\,p; c) = wp.(!\,p; c; !\,q)$).

Exercises of Section 5.4.

Exercise 0. Prove the two formulae of (6) in the example of 5.4.

Exercises of Section 5.5.

Exercise 0. Prove that the existence of a strongest postcondition function $sp.c$ that satisfies property (10) implies the universal conjunctivity of $wlp.c$, cf. law 3(4).

Exercise 1. Prove formula (11).

Exercises of Section 5.6.

Exercise 0. Let $\langle Z, <, N\rangle$ be a well-founded triple. Let $f \in Y \to Z$ be a function. Define the subset M of Y and the relation $<$ on Y by

$$y \in M \equiv f.y \in N ,$$
$$x < y \equiv f.x < f.y .$$

Prove that $\langle Y, <, N\rangle$ is a well-founded triple.

Exercise 1. Let prime be the set of prime numbers. For natural number x and prime p, let $x \,\%\, p$ be the number of factors p of x given by

$$x \,\%\, p = (\text{MAX } n, y \in \mathbb{N} : x = y \cdot p^n : n) ,$$

so that $0 \,\%\, p = \infty$. Let relation $\prec$ on $\mathbb{N}$ be defined by

$$x \prec y \equiv$$
$$(\exists p \in \text{prime} :: x \,\%\, p < y \,\%\, p$$
$$\wedge (\forall q \in \text{prime} : p < q : x \,\%\, q = y \,\%\, q)) .$$

Prove that relation $\prec$ on $\mathbb{N}$ is well-founded.

Exercises of Section 5.7.

Exercise 0. Let procedure h be declared by

$$\textbf{body}.h = (\mathit{skip} \,[\!]\, \mathrm{v} := \mathrm{v}+1 \,;\, h \,;\, \mathrm{v} := \mathrm{v}-2 \,;\, h) .$$

Prove that $[\neg \mathit{wlp}.h.(\mathrm{v} > i)]$ for all integer values i.

CHAPTER 6

RELATIONAL SEMANTICS

6.0. In this chapter, we start again from scratch. Now the meaning of a command is not defined by means of the functions *wp* and *wlp*, but by means of the input–output relation of a command. This point of view is closer to the intuitive ideas of most programmers, but —in our view— it is less adequate for program development.

The relational point of view is useful for the analysis of special properties of commands such as totality, termination and determinacy. It provides easy definitions or characterizations of composition, nondeterminate choice, guards and assertions. All these concepts can therefore be treated in this chapter.

When the relational point of view is used in the analysis of repetitions or recursive procedures, one needs to consider finite and infinite sequences of states, usually accompanied by many case distinctions. Such operational reasoning can be useful or necessary, but it is preferable to avoid it whenever possible. We introduce some of the necessary techniques in Chapter 9. It is used only in Chapters 14 and 15.

Although we use the definitions of Section 1.1 and some other concepts introduced in Chapters 1 and 3, this chapter is largely independent of the previous chapters. In fact, it can be read to support them.

In Section 6.1, we introduce (input–output) relations and their weakest preconditions, and we show that relations when interpreted as commands satisfy the healthiness laws introduced in Section 3.2. In Section 6.2, we give the relational interpretation of guards, sequential composition and nondeterminate choice. In Section 6.3, we present relational justifications of the axiomatic definitions of totality and termination.

In Section 6.4 we show that the expressive power of relational semantics equals the expressive power of the predicate–transformation semantics of Chapter 1, under assumption of the healthiness laws of Section 3.2.

6.1 Relations as an alternative specification method

The central concept of relational semantics is that of the *input–output relation* or *relation*, which says whether or not a given state can be the result of a computation that started in a second state. Since we allow nontermination, we need a formal symbol $\infty \notin X$ to stand for the 'result" of a nonterminating computation. It is convenient to treat the (input–output) relation as a curried function

$$R \in X_+ \to (X \to \mathbb{B})$$

where X_+ stands for the union $X \cup \{\infty\}$. Relation R is to be interpreted as follows:

(0) $R.\infty.x \equiv$ the computation if started in x need not terminate,

$R.y.x \equiv$ the computation if started in x may terminate in y.

Here, and henceforth, we use dummies x, y (and z) to range over states in X.

Remark. In relational semantics, one usually writes xRy instead of our $R.y.x$. We prefer the notation $R.y.x$, since it often enables the elimination of x. It gives a closer connection to the functions *wp* and *wlp*. Moreover, we do not like a variable like R to play the rôle of an infix operator. (End of remark)

Let R be an (input–output) relation. Recall from Section 1.1 that a predicate p is a function $p \in X \to \mathbb{B}$. Let x be a state. By Section 1.2, the truth of $wlp.R.p.x$ should mean that every state y that results from the initial state x satisfies $p.y$; the truth of $wp.R.p.x$ should also express that ∞ is not a resulting state. In this way, we arrive at the formal definitions

(1) $$wlp.R.p.x \equiv (\forall y \in X : R.y.x : p.y) ,$$

$$wp.R.p.x \equiv \neg R.\infty.x \;\wedge\; wlp.R.p.x .$$

Example. For a program variable v and a state function f, the assignment $v := f$ can be regarded as the relation given by

$$(v := f).y.x \equiv y = (v \leftarrow f).x ,$$

$$(v := f).\infty.x \equiv \text{false} ,$$

where $(v \leftarrow f).x$ is defined in 1(23). Now one part of formula 1(24) is proved in

$$\begin{aligned} & wlp.(v := f).p.x \\ = \; & (\forall y : y = (v \leftarrow f).x : p.y) \\ = \; & p.((v \leftarrow f).x) . \end{aligned}$$

The other case of 1(24) follows as well. (End of example)

By trading and application of definition 1(1), one can eliminate state x from the formulae of (1). In fact, they are equivalent to

(2) $wlp.R.p \;=\; (\forall y \in X : \neg p.y : \neg R.y)$,
$wp.R.p \;=\; \neg R.\infty \;\wedge\; wlp.R.p$.

It follows from (2) that

(3) $wlp.R.true \;=\; true$,
$wp.R.true \;=\; \neg R.\infty$.

This proves that

$$wp.R.p \;=\; wp.R.true \;\wedge\; wlp.R.p \;.$$

So, if relation R is interpreted as a command it satisfies termination law 3(3).

If U is a set of predicates, the conjunction $(\forall p \in U :: p)$ is a predicate with, for all states x,

$wlp.R.(\forall p \in U :: p).x$
$\equiv$ {(1)}
$(\forall y : R.y.x : (\forall p \in U :: p).y)$
$\equiv$ {definition 1(1)}
$(\forall y : R.y.x : (\forall p \in U :: p.y))$
$\equiv$ {interchange of quantifications}
$(\forall p \in U :: (\forall y : R.y.x : p.y))$
$\equiv$ {(1) followed by definition 1(1)}
$(\forall p \in U :: wlp.R.p).x$.

This proves that

$$wlp.R.(\forall p \in U :: p) \;=\; (\forall p \in U :: wlp.R.p) \;.$$

So, $wlp.R$ is universally conjunctive, cf. definition 3(1). This proves that every relation R (interpreted as a command) satisfies the healthiness laws 3(3) and 3(4).

6.2 The relational view of guards, composition and choice

More or less independently of Section 1.3, we now introduce the relational concepts corresponding to guards, assertions, composition and choice.

Let b be a predicate. The relation $(?b)$ is defined by

(4) $(?b).y.x \;\equiv\; (x = y) \wedge b.x$,
$(?b).\infty.x \;\equiv\;$ false .

It is easy to calculate $wlp.(?b)$ and $wp.(?b)$. In fact, for every predicate p and state x we have

$wlp.(?b).p.x$
$\equiv$ {(4) and (1)}
$(\forall y : (x = y) \wedge b.x : p.y)$

$\equiv$ {calculus}

$b.x \Rightarrow p.x$

$\equiv$ {1(0)}

$(b \Rightarrow p).x$.

This proves that

$$wlp.(?b).p \quad = \quad (b \Rightarrow p) \; .$$

Since $(?b).\infty = \mathit{false}$, it follows with formula (2) that $wp.(?b).p \; = \; (b \Rightarrow p)$. This proves that relation $(?b)$ corresponds to command $?b$ introduced in 1(8).

Similarly, relation $(!b)$ is defined by

(5) $$(!b).y.x \quad \equiv \quad x = y \wedge b.x \; ,$$
$$(!b).\infty.x \quad \equiv \quad \neg b.x \; .$$

It is left to the reader to verify that relation $(!b)$ corresponds to command $!b$ introduced in 1(8).

The informal interpretation of the sequential composition $(R; S)$ of relations R and S is as follows. The composition $(R; S)$ can give an output state y if and only if relation R has an output state z with $S.y.z$. The composition need not terminate if and only if R need not terminate or may yield an output state z with $S.\infty.z$. Therefore, formally, we define the composition $(R; S)$ by

(6) $$(R; S).y \quad = \quad (\exists z : S.y.z : R.z) \; ,$$
$$(R; S).\infty \quad = \quad R.\infty \quad \vee \quad (\exists z : S.\infty.z : R.z) \; .$$

Now one can prove that, for every predicate p and for $wg \in \{wp, wlp\}$,

(7) $$wg.(R; S).p \quad = \quad wg.R.(wg.S.p) \; .$$

This shows that definition (6) is in agreement with the definition 1(13). The proof of (7) is left as an exercise for the reader.

If Φ is a set of input–output relations, we write $(\, [\!] \, R \in \Phi :: R)$ to denote the choice relation given by

(8) $$(\, [\!] \, R \in \Phi :: R).u \quad = \quad (\exists R \in \Phi :: R.u) \qquad \text{for all } u \in X_+ \; .$$

This definition corresponds to definition 1(16), in the sense that, for predicate p and $wg \in \{wp, wlp\}$,

(9) $$wg(\, [\!] \, R \in \Phi :: R).p \quad = \quad (\forall R \in \Phi :: wg.R.p) \; .$$

Again the proof is left to the reader (see the exercises).

6.3 Termination and totality

In Section 1.3 we gave the axiomatic definition of termination and totality. These concept are based on the operational intuition and are, therefore, easily translated into relational semantics. Actually, for termination, the translation itself is based on the intuition. For if relation R is interpreted as a command we have (as expected):

$$
\begin{aligned}
& R \text{ is necessarily terminating} \\
\equiv \quad & \{\text{definition } 1(11)\} \\
& [\,wp.R.true\,] \\
\equiv \quad & \{(3) \text{ and } 1(2)\} \\
& (\forall x \in X :: \neg R.\infty.x)\ .
\end{aligned}
$$

Totality is slightly more difficult:

$$
\begin{aligned}
& R \text{ is total} \\
\equiv \quad & \{1(12)\} \\
& [\,\neg wp.R.false\,] \\
\equiv \quad & \{(1) \text{ and } 1(2)\} \\
& (\forall x :: \neg(\neg R.\infty.x \wedge (\forall y : R.y.x : \text{false}))) \\
\equiv \quad & \{\text{De Morgan}\} \\
& (\forall x :: R.\infty.x \vee (\exists y :: R.y.x)) \\
\equiv \quad & \{\text{alternatively}\} \\
& (\forall x \in X :: (\exists u \in X_+ :: R.u.x))\ .
\end{aligned}
$$

This proves that relation R is total if and only if every initial state admits at least one resulting state (possibly ∞), as suggested in Section 1.3.

6.4 From commands to relations

The next step is to associate to every command c in the sense of Chapter 1 an input–output relation $[\![c]\!]$. This requires the introduction of point predicates. For every state $y \in X$, we define the *point predicate* $d.y \in \mathbb{P}$ by

(10) $\qquad d.y.x \ \equiv\ (y = x)\ .$

The letter d is chosen for the analogy with the Kronecker symbol δ_{ij} and the Dirac function δ.

For a command c, relation $[\![c]\!]$ is defined by

(11) $\qquad [\![c]\!].\infty \ =\ \neg wp.c.true\ ,$

$\qquad\quad [\![c]\!].y \ =\ \neg wlp.c.(\neg d.y) \quad \text{for } y \in X.$

According to interpretation (0), the first formula says that the computation of c need not terminate if started in a state where $wp.c.true$ does not hold. The second formula says that state y is a possible result if command c is started in a state where $wlp.c.(\neg d.y)$ does not hold, i.e., where not all resulting states differ from y. This shows that the definition of $[\![c]\!]$ agrees with the interpretation of wp and wlp, cf. Section 1.2.

By formula (1), every input–output relation R has a weakest precondition and a weakest liberal precondition, can therefore be interpreted as a command and hence yields an associated relation $[\![R]\!]$. We claim that

(12) $\quad [\![R]\!] \;=\; R\,.$

In order to prove formula (12), it suffices to observe that

$$\begin{array}{ll} & [\![R]\!].\infty \\ = & \{(11)\}\quad \neg wp.R.true \\ = & \{(3)\}\quad R.\infty \end{array}$$

and that for any state y

$$\begin{array}{ll} & [\![R]\!].y \\ = & \{(11)\}\quad \neg wlp.R.(\neg d.y) \\ = & \{(2)\}\quad \neg(\forall z : \neg(\neg d.y).z : \neg R.z) \\ = & \{(10)\}\quad \neg(\forall z : y = z : \neg R.z) \\ = & \{\text{calculus}\}\quad R.y\,. \end{array}$$

On the other hand, for every command c that satisfies the healthiness laws 3(3) and 3(4), we claim that

(13) $\quad c \;\cong\; [\![c]\!]\,,$

i.e., c and $[\![c]\!]$ have the same wp and wlp, cf. definition 1(7). We begin with the proof for wlp. For any predicate p we observe

$$\begin{array}{ll} & wlp.[\![c]\!].p \\ = & \{(2)\}\quad (\forall y : \neg p.y : \neg[\![c]\!].y) \\ = & \{(11)\}\quad (\forall y : \neg p.y : wlp.c.(\neg d.y)) \\ = & \{wlp \text{ is universally conjunctive by } 3(4)\} \\ & wlp.c.(\forall y : \neg p.y : \neg d.y) \\ = & \{\text{remaining proof obligation } (14)\} \\ & wlp.c.p\,. \end{array}$$

It remains to prove that

(14) $\quad (\forall y : \neg p.y : \neg d.y) \;=\; p\,.$

This is proved by observing that for any state x

$$\begin{array}{ll} & (\forall y : \neg p.y : \neg d.y).x \\ \equiv & \{1(1)\} \\ & (\forall y : \neg p.y : \neg d.y.x) \end{array}$$

$$\equiv \quad \{\text{trading and (10)}\}$$
$$(\forall y : x = y : p.y)$$
$$\equiv \quad \{\text{one point rule}\}$$
$$p.x\ .$$

This proves

(15) $\quad wlp.([\![c]\!]) \quad = \quad wlp.c\ .$

For *wp* we observe

$$wp.([\![c]\!]).p$$
$$= \quad \{(2)\}$$
$$\neg[\![c]\!].\infty \wedge wlp.[\![c]\!].p$$
$$= \quad \{(11) \text{ and } (15)\}$$
$$wp.c.true \wedge wlp.c.p$$
$$= \quad \{3(3)\}$$
$$wp.c.p\ .$$

This proves $wp.([\![c]\!]) = wp.c$, thus concluding the proof of formula (13).

Formulae (12) implies that predicate–transformation semantics is at least as expressive as relational semantics. The combination of (12) and (13) implies that, under assumption of the healthiness laws 3(3) and 3(4), predicate–transformation semantics and relational semantics are equivalent.

6.5 Exercises

Exercises of Section 6.2

Exercise 0. Prove that relation $(!b)$ has the same *wp* and *wlp* as command $!b$ introduced in 1(8).

Exercise 1. Prove formulae (7) and (9).

Exercises of Section 6.4

Exercise 0. Consider the refinement relation '$\sqsubseteq$' defined in 5(1). Use 1(4), 1(5) and 1(6) to prove that $c \sqsubseteq [\![c]\!]$ for every command c, independently of the healthiness laws.

Exercise 1. For relations R and S, we define

$$R \supset S \quad \equiv \quad (\forall u \in X_+ :: [\, R.u \Leftarrow S.u\,])\ .$$

(a) Prove that, for relations R and S

$$R \supset S \quad \Rightarrow \quad R \sqsubseteq S\ .$$

(b) Prove that for commands c and d

$$c \sqsubseteq d \;\Rightarrow\; [\![c]\!] \supset [\![d]\!] \;.$$

(c) Prove that, independently of the healthiness laws, for a command c and a relation R

$$c \sqsubseteq R \;\equiv\; [\![c]\!] \supset R \;.$$

Exercise 2. ♡ Prove that the strongest postcondition *sp.c* of a command c (cf. Section 5.5) satisfies, for every $p \in \mathbb{P}$, $y \in X$:

$$sp.c.p.y \;\equiv\; (\exists x \in X : [\![c]\!].y.x : p.x) \;.$$

CHAPTER 7

DETERMINACY AND DISJUNCTIVITY

7.0 In this chapter we investigate determinacy of commands and disjunctivity of the associated predicate transformers. It turns out that these concepts are closely related.

7.1 Determinacy

Determinacy of commands has not yet been defined. For the mathematical theory, it is an important concept, both conceptually and historically. Its importance stems from the popularity of the simplest mathematical model of computation, where the output is a (partial) function of the input. In programming methodology, determinacy is not so important. A program must establish a specific postcondition, but uniqueness of the result is irrelevant.

Nevertheless, determinacy is interesting. The more so, since its very definition in predicate–transformation semantics is subject to some debate. Our definition differs from the definitions in [Dijkstra-Scholten 1990] and [Back-von Wright 1989b], and was proposed by C.S. Scholten and J.C.S.P. van der Woude.

Both conceptually and mathematically, it is useful to distinguish two aspects of determinacy: termination and the actual result. We thus arrive at the following definitions.

A command c is called *liberally determinate* if and only if every initial state admits termination in at most one final state, i.e.

(0) $\qquad (\forall x, y, z \in X : [\![c]\!].y.x \wedge [\![c]\!].z.x : y = z)$.

Command c is called *termination determinate* if and only if at every initial state where c need not terminate it cannot terminate, i.e.

(1) $\qquad (\forall x \in X :: [\![c]\!].\infty.x \Rightarrow (\forall y \in X :: \neg[\![c]\!].y.x))$.

Command c is called *determinate* if and only if it is both liberally determinate and termination determinate.

(2) **Lemma.** Command c is liberally determinate if and only if

$$[\,wlp.c.(\neg p) \vee wlp.c.p\,] \qquad \text{for every predicate } p.$$

Proof. By definition (0), it suffices to verify that for every state x

$$\begin{array}{ll}
 & (\forall p :: wlp.c.(\neg p).x \vee wlp.c.p.x) \\
\equiv & \{6(13) \text{ and } 6(1);\ \text{let } y,\ z \text{ range over } X\} \\
 & (\forall p :: (\forall y : [\![c]\!].y.x : \neg p.y) \vee (\forall z : [\![c]\!].z.x : p.z)) \\
\equiv & \{\text{distribution of } \vee \text{ over } \forall\} \\
 & (\forall p :: (\forall y, z : [\![c]\!].y.x \wedge [\![c]\!].z.x : \neg p.y \vee p.z)) \\
\equiv & \{\text{calculus}\} \\
 & (\forall y, z : [\![c]\!].y.x \wedge [\![c]\!].z.x : (\forall p :: p.y \Rightarrow p.z)) \\
\equiv & \{\text{calculus, use } p := d.y \text{ for the downward implication}\} \\
 & (\forall y, z : [\![c]\!].y.x \wedge [\![c]\!].z.x : y = z)\ .
\end{array}$$

(End of proof)

(3) **Lemma.** Command c is termination determinate if and only if

$$[\,wlp.c.\mathit{false} \vee wp.c.\mathit{true}\,]\ .$$

Proof. By definition (1), it suffices to verify that for every state x

$$\begin{array}{ll}
 & wlp.c.\mathit{false}.x \vee wp.c.\mathit{true}.x \\
\equiv & \{6(13),\ 6(1),\ 6(3)\} \\
 & (\forall y : [\![c]\!].y.x : \mathit{false}.y) \vee \neg[\![c]\!].\infty.x \\
\equiv & \{\text{calculus}\} \\
 & [\![c]\!].\infty.x \quad \Rightarrow \quad (\forall y :: \neg[\![c]\!].y.x)\ .
\end{array}$$

(End of proof)

(4) **Theorem.** Command c is determinate if and only if

$$[\,wlp.c.(\neg p) \vee wp.c.p\,] \qquad \text{for every predicate } p.$$

Proof. We first observe that for every predicate p

$$\begin{array}{ll}
 & [\,wlp.c.(\neg p) \vee wp.c.p\,] \\
\equiv & \{\text{termination rule } 3(3)\} \\
 & [\,wlp.c.(\neg p) \vee (wp.c.\mathit{true} \wedge wlp.c.p)\,] \\
\equiv & \{\text{distributivity}\} \\
 & [\,(wlp.c.(\neg p) \vee wp.c.\mathit{true}) \wedge (wlp.c.(\neg p) \vee wlp.c.p)\,] \\
\equiv & \{\wedge \text{ distributes over } [\;]\} \\
 & [\,wlp.c.(\neg p) \vee wp.c.\mathit{true}\,] \wedge [\,wlp.c.(\neg p) \vee wlp.c.p\,]\ .
\end{array}$$

We now conclude by

$$(\forall p :: [\,wlp.c.(\neg p) \vee wp.c.p\,])$$

$\equiv$ {above calculation}
$(\forall p :: [\, wlp.c.(\neg p) \vee wp.c.true\,]) \wedge (\forall p :: [\, wlp.c.(\neg p) \vee wlp.c.p\,])$
$\equiv$ {$wlp.c$ is monotone}
$[\, wlp.c.false \vee wp.c.true\,] \wedge (\forall p :: [\, wlp.c.(\neg p) \vee wlp.c.p\,])$
$\equiv$ {Lemmas (2) and (3)}
c is termination determinate and liberally determinate
$\equiv$ {definition}
c is determinate .

(End of proof)

Remark. By Theorem (4), command c is determinate if and only if

$$[\neg wlp.c.(\neg p) \Rightarrow wp.c.p] \qquad \text{for all } p.$$

In exercise 3.3.2 it is proved that command c is total if and only if

$$[\neg wlp.c.(\neg p) \Leftarrow wp.c.p] \qquad \text{for all } p.$$

In [Dijkstra-Scholten 1990], all commands are postulated to be total. Therefore, determinism of c is defined in loc. cit. by the condition that

$$[\neg wlp.c.(\neg p) \equiv wp.c.p] \qquad \text{for all } p.$$

(End of remark)

7.2 Disjunctivity properties

In the remainder of this chapter, we consider various disjunctivity properties of weakest preconditions of commands. We concentrate on semantic properties. An investigation of syntactic criteria that imply these semantic properties is given in Chapter 8.

Analogously to the conjunctivity properties in Section 3.1, we consider the following disjunctivity properties. A predicate transformer $h \in \mathbb{P} \to \mathbb{P}$ is called *finitely disjunctive* if and only if for all predicates p and q

(5) $\quad h.(p \vee q) \;=\; h.p \vee h.q$.

It is called *universally disjunctive* if and only if for every subset U of $\mathbb{P}$

(6) $\quad h.(\exists p \in U :: p) \;=\; (\exists p \in U :: h.p)$.

It is called *positively disjunctive* if and only formula (6) holds for all nonempty sets U. It is called $\{\emptyset\}$*-disjunctive* if and only if formula (6) holds for $U = \emptyset$. Since $(\exists p \in \emptyset :: p) = false$, function h is $\{\emptyset\}$–disjunctive if and only if

(7) $\quad h.false \;=\; false$.

Therefore, by 1(12), a command c is total if and only if $wp.c$ is $\{\emptyset\}$–disjunctive.

Another disjunctivity property is upper continuity, defined as follows. A set of predicates $U \subset \mathbb{P}$ is called a *chain* if and only if

$$(\forall p, q \in U :: [p \Rightarrow q] \vee [q \Rightarrow p]) .$$

More generally, a partially ordered set $\langle L, \leq \rangle$ is called a *chain* if and only if

(8) $$(\forall x, y \in L :: x \leq y \vee y \leq x) .$$

Predicate transformer h is called *upper continuous* if and only if formula (6) holds for every nonempty chain $U \subset \mathbb{P}$.

7.3 Determinacy and disjunctivity

In this section, we show that positive disjunctivity of *wlp.c* is equivalent to liberal determinacy of command c, cf. Section 7.1.

(9) **Theorem.** Command c is liberally determinate if and only if *wlp.c* is positively disjunctive.

Proof. One implication is contained in

wlp.c is positively conjunctive

$\Rightarrow$ {special case}

$(\forall p \in \mathbb{P} :: wlp.c.(\neg p) \vee wlp.c.p = wlp.c.true)$

$\equiv$ {3(5) and 1(2)}

$(\forall p \in \mathbb{P} :: [\, wlp.c.(\neg p) \vee wlp.c.p])$

$\equiv$ {Lemma (2)}

c is liberally determinate.

Conversely, let c be liberally determinate. In order to show that *wlp.c* is positively disjunctive, it suffices to observe that for every nonempty set U of predicates and every state x

$wlp.c.(\exists p \in U :: p).x$

$\equiv$ {6(13) and 6(1)}

$(\forall y : [\![c]\!].y.x : (\exists p \in U :: p).y)$

$\equiv$ {1(1)}

$(\forall y : [\![c]\!].y.x : (\exists p \in U :: p.y))$

$\equiv$ {(0): if y exists it is unique}

$(\exists y :: [\![c]\!].y.x) \Rightarrow (\exists y : [\![c]\!].y.x : (\exists p \in U :: p.y))$

$\equiv$ {calculus; U is nonempty}

$(\exists p \in U :: (\exists y :: [\![c]\!].y.x) \Rightarrow (\exists y : [\![c]\!].y.x : p.y))$

$\equiv$ {(0): if y exists it is unique}

$$(\exists p \in U :: (\forall y : [\![c]\!].y.x : p.y))$$
$$\equiv \quad \{6(13),\ 6(1),\ 1(1)\}$$
$$(\exists p \in U :: wlp.c.p).x \ .$$

(End of proof)

7.4 Disjunctivity of *wp*

Let a command c be called *disjunctive* if and only if $wp.c$ is positively disjunctive.

Remark. The weakest *liberal* precondition of a disjunctive command need not be (finitely) disjunctive. For example, if `i` is an integer program variable, the choice

$$q \quad = \quad (\texttt{i} := 0 \ [\!] \ \texttt{i} := 1 \ [\!] \ abort)$$

is disjunctive, since $wp.q.p = false$ for every predicate p. Its weakest liberal precondition is not disjunctive, since

$$wlp.q.(\texttt{i} = 0 \vee \texttt{i} = 1) \quad = \quad true \ ,$$
$$wlp.q.(\texttt{i} = 0) \vee wlp.q.(\texttt{i} = 1) \quad = \quad false \ .$$

This example also shows that disjunctive commands need not be liberally determinate. (End of remark)

Using Theorem (9) and the termination rule, one can show that every liberally determinate command is disjunctive. It is possible to prove that a command c is disjunctive if and only if

$$(\forall x, y, z \in X : \neg [\![c]\!].\infty.x \wedge [\![c]\!].y.x \wedge [\![c]\!].z.x : y = z) \ .$$

7.5 Finite nondeterminacy

A command c is defined to be *finitely nondeterminate* if and only if for all states $x \in X$

(10) $\quad [\![c]\!].\infty.x \quad \vee \quad (\texttt{FIN}\ \ y \in X :: [\![c]\!].y.x) \ ,$

where for a predicate q the quantification $(\texttt{FIN}\ \ y :: q.y)$ says that the set of elements y with $q.y$ is finite. The following result is presumably well–known, cf. [Hesselink 1990] Theorem 4(15).

(11) **Theorem.** Command c is finitely nondeterminate if and only if $wp.c$ is upper continuous.

Proof. For any state x, and any nonempty chain L of predicates, we have, with p ranging over L

$$(wp.c.(\exists p :: p).x \equiv (\exists p :: wp.c.p).x)$$
$$\equiv \quad \{6(13) \text{ and } 6(11); \text{ let } y \text{ range over the states with } [\![c]\!].y.x\}$$
$$(\neg [\![c]\!].\infty.x \wedge (\forall y :: (\exists p :: p).y) \quad \equiv \quad (\exists p :: \neg [\![c]\!].\infty.x \wedge (\forall y :: p.y)))$$
$$\equiv \quad \{\text{predicate calculus}\}$$
$$[\![c]\!].\infty.x \quad \vee \quad ((\forall y :: (\exists p :: p.y)) \equiv (\exists p :: (\forall y :: p.y))) .$$

Now letting L ranging over all nonempty chains of predicates, we get

$$(\forall L :: wp.c.(\exists p :: p).x \equiv (\exists p :: wp.c.p).x)$$
$$\equiv \quad \{\text{above calculation and distribution of } \vee \text{ over } \forall\}$$
$$[\![c]\!].\infty.x \quad \vee \quad (\forall L :: (\forall y :: (\exists p :: p.y)) \equiv (\exists p :: (\forall y :: p.y)))$$
$$\equiv \quad \{\text{making the range of } y \text{ explicit; Lemma (12) below}\}$$
$$[\![c]\!].\infty.x \quad \vee \quad (\texttt{FIN} \; y :: [\![c]\!].y.x) .$$

Now quantifying over x, we get

$$(\forall L :: \; wp.c.(\exists p :: p) \; = \; (\exists p :: wp.c.p))$$
$$\equiv \quad (\forall x :: [\![c]\!].\infty.x \quad \vee \quad (\texttt{FIN} \; y :: [\![c]\!].y.x)) .$$

By definition (10) and the definition of upper continuity in Section 7.2, this proves the assertion. (End of proof)

It remains to verify

(12) **Lemma.** A subset Y of X is finite if and only if for every nonempty chain L of predicates

$$(\forall y \in Y :: (\exists p \in L :: p.y)) \quad \equiv \quad (\exists p \in L :: (\forall y \in Y :: p.y)) .$$

Proof. If Y is finite and L is a nonempty chain of predicates, then

$$(\forall y \in Y :: (\exists p \in L :: p.y))$$
$$\equiv \quad \{\text{axiom of choice for finite } Y\}$$
$$(\exists f \in Y \to L :: (\forall y \in Y :: f.y.y))$$
$$\equiv \quad \{Y \text{ finite, } L \text{ a nonempty chain; take } p = (\texttt{MAX} \; y :: f.y) \text{ in } L$$
$$\text{so that } [f.y \Rightarrow p] \text{ for all } y \in Y.$$
$$\text{For the upward implication, take } f.y = p \text{ for all } y.\}$$
$$(\exists p \in L :: (\forall y \in Y :: p.y)) .$$

For the converse implication we proceed as follows. It suffices to assume that Y is infinite and to construct a nonempty chain of predicates for which the equivalence is false. Since Y is infinite, we can choose a sequence $(i \in \mathbb{N} :: u.i)$ of different elements of Y. Thus, $u.i \neq u.j$ whenever $i \neq j$. For $k \in \mathbb{N}$, let predicate $q.k$ be defined by

$$q.k.x \equiv (\forall i : k < i : x \neq u.i) \ .$$

Then $[q.k \Rightarrow q.n]$ whenever $k \leq n$. Therefore, the family $L = (k \in \mathbb{N} :: q.k)$ is a nonempty chain of predicates. The equivalence in the assertion evaluates to false, since we have

$$\begin{array}{l} (\forall y :: (\exists p \in L :: p.y)) \\ \equiv \quad \{\text{definitions}\} \\ (\forall y :: (\exists k :: (\forall i : k < i : y \neq u.i))) \\ \equiv \quad \{\text{all } u.i \text{ are different}\} \\ \text{true} \ , \end{array}$$

and on the other hand

$$\begin{array}{l} (\exists p \in L :: (\forall y :: p.y)) \\ \equiv \quad \{\text{definitions}\} \\ (\exists k :: (\forall y :: (\forall i : k < i : y \neq u.i))) \\ \equiv \quad \{\text{take } y = u.(k+1)\} \\ \text{false} \ . \end{array}$$

(End of proof)

7.6 Exercises

Exercises of Section 7.1.

Exercise 0. Prove that every assignment and every guard is determinate.

Exercise 1. Let i be an integer program variable. Use the axiomatic characterizations (2) and (3) to prove that

$$\mathtt{i} := 0 \ [] \ abort$$

is liberally determinate and not determinate, and that

$$\mathtt{i} := 0 \ [] \ \mathtt{i} := 1$$

is termination determinate and not determinate.

Exercises of Section 7.4.

Exercise 0. Prove that every liberally determinate command is disjunctive.

Exercise 1. Prove that $wp.c$ is positively disjunctive if and only $wp.c$ is finitely disjunctive.

Exercise 2. Prove the last assertion of Section 7.4.

CHAPTER 8

SYNTACTIC CRITERIA

8.0. In this chapter, we develop syntactic criteria on commands, which imply disjunctivity properties for their weakest preconditions. We suppose that the disjunctivity properties of the simple commands are known and try to generalize these properties to procedures and composite commands. From this chapter onward, the theory of Chapter 4 is indispensable.

In Section 8.1 we introduce, for a given set R of predicate transformers, a set of commands called the syntactic reflection $Sy.R$ of R. The main property is that $wp.q \in R$ for all $q \in Sy.R$. In Section 8.2 we provide methods to prove that a command belongs to the syntactic reflection.

In Section 8.3 the theory is specialized to the case that R is characterized by a disjunctivity property. Section 8.4 contains the next specialization, namely to the classes of total commands, of disjunctive commands, and of finitely nondeterminate commands. For our purposes the first two classes merely serve as examples or test cases. Our real aim is the class of the finitely nondeterminate commands. It is this class, or rather its syntactic reflection, that plays a key rôle in Chapters 11 and 13.

8.1 Syntactic reflection of semantic properties

Throughout this section we let R be a sup–closed subset of MT. We are interested in syntactic criteria on commands $c \in A^{\odot}$ that imply $wp.c \in R$. Our solution consists of an algebraic definition of a subset $Sy.R$ of $A^{\odot}$ with $wp.q \in R$ for all $q \in Sy.R$. The set $Sy.R$ can be regarded as the biggest set of commands q for which a specific way of fixpoint induction is powerful enough to prove $wp.q \in R$, under the assumption that it is known for which elements c of S the property $wp.c \in R$ holds. In the proofs of the properties of $Sy.R$, we need a related set $Sx.R$ of procedure names, and a set $Wp.R$ of functions $w \in MT^H$.

We first give some auxiliary definitions. Recall that in 4(33) the subset WT of MT^H is defined by

$$w \in WT \quad \equiv \quad (\forall h \in H, p \in \mathbb{P} :: w.h.p = w.h.true \wedge wlp.h.p) .$$

We define an *R–adapted pair* to be a pair $\langle K, Q\rangle$ of sets $K \subset H$ and $Q \subset A^{\odot}$ such that

(0) $\quad (\forall h \in K :: \mathbf{body}.h \in Q) \quad$ and

(1) $\quad (\forall w \in WT ::$

$$(\forall h \in K :: w.h \in R) \quad \Rightarrow \quad (\forall q \in Q :: w^0.q \in R)) ,$$

where w^0 is as defined in 4(25).

Letting $\langle K, Q\rangle$ range over all R–adapted pairs, we define the unions

(2)
$$Sx.R \;=\; (\bigcup \langle K, Q\rangle :: K) \;\subset\; H ,$$
$$Sy.R \;=\; (\bigcup \langle K, Q\rangle :: Q) \;\subset\; A^{\odot} .$$

The set $Sy.R$ is called the *syntactic reflection* of R. For technical convenience, we also introduce the subset $Wp.R$ of MT^H given by

(3) $\quad w \in Wp.R \;\equiv\; w \in WT \;\wedge\; (\forall h \in Sx.R :: w.h \in R) .$

The main results of the section are contained in

(4) **Theorem.** (a) The pair $\langle Sx.R, Sy.R\rangle$ is R–adapted.
(b) The subset $Wp.R$ of MT^H is sup–closed and D_0–invariant.
(c) $wp.q \in R$ for every command $q \in Sy.R$.

Remark. Primarily, parts (a) and (b) are stepping stones to reach the main assertion (c). They are stated explicitly, since they have some independent interest.

Proof. (a) Condition (0) is verified by observing that for every h

$$
\begin{array}{ll}
 & h \in Sx.R \\
\equiv & \{(2)\} \\
 & (\exists \langle K, Q\rangle : R\text{–adapted} : h \in K) \\
\Rightarrow & \{(0)\} \\
 & (\exists \langle K, Q\rangle : R\text{–adapted} : \mathbf{body}.h \in Q) \\
\equiv & \{(2)\} \\
 & \mathbf{body}.h \in Sy.R .
\end{array}
$$

Condition (1) is proved by observing that for every $w \in WT$

$$
\begin{array}{ll}
 & (\forall h \in Sx.R :: w.h \in R) \\
\equiv & \{(2)\} \\
 & (\forall \langle K, Q\rangle : R\text{–adapted} : (\forall h \in K :: w.h \in R)) \\
\Rightarrow & \{(1)\} \\
 & (\forall \langle K, Q\rangle : R\text{–adapted} : (\forall q \in Q :: w^0.q \in R))
\end{array}
$$

$$\equiv \quad \{(2)\}$$
$$(\forall q \in Sy.R :: w^0.q \in R) \ .$$

This proves that $\langle Sx.R, Sy.R \rangle$ is an R–adapted pair. Notice that definition (3) now allows to reformulate (1) for this special case into

(5) $$(\forall w \in Wp.R, q \in Sy.R :: w^0.q \in R) \ .$$

(b) The set $Wp.R$ is sup–closed in MT^H since for every subset U of MT^H

$$
\begin{array}{ll}
 & (\sup U) \in Wp.R \\
\equiv & \{(3)\} \\
 & (\sup U) \in WT \quad \wedge \quad (\forall h \in Sx.R :: (\sup U).h \in R) \\
\Leftarrow & \{4(37) \text{ and } 4(3)\} \\
 & U \subset WT \quad \wedge \quad (\forall h \in Sx.R :: (\sup w \in U :: w.h) \in R) \\
\Leftarrow & \{R \text{ is sup–closed}\} \\
 & U \subset WT \quad \wedge \quad (\forall h \in Sx.R, w \in U :: w.h \in R) \\
\equiv & \{(3)\} \\
 & U \subset Wp.R \ .
\end{array}
$$

The set $Wp.R$ is D_0–invariant since for every $w \in MT^H$

$$
\begin{array}{ll}
 & D_0.w \in Wp.R \\
\equiv & \{(3)\} \\
 & D_0.w \in WT \quad \wedge \quad (\forall h \in Sx.R :: D_0.w.h \in R) \\
\Leftarrow & \{4(35) \text{ and } 4(26)\} \\
 & w \in WT \quad \wedge \quad (\forall h \in Sx.R :: w^0.(\mathbf{body}.h) \in R) \\
\Leftarrow & \{\text{part (a)(0)}\} \\
 & w \in WT \quad \wedge \quad (\forall q \in Sy.R :: w^0.q \in R) \\
\Leftarrow & \{(3), (5)\} \\
 & w \in Wp.R \ .
\end{array}
$$

(c) It remains to verify that

$$
\begin{array}{ll}
 & (\forall q \in Sy.R :: \mathrm{wp}.q \in R) \\
\equiv & \{\mathrm{wp} = (\mathrm{wp}|H)^0\} \\
 & (\forall q \in Sy.R :: (\mathrm{wp}|H)^0.q \in R) \\
\Leftarrow & \{(5)\} \\
 & \mathrm{wp}|H \in Wp.R \\
\Leftarrow & \{\mathrm{wp}|H \text{ is least fixpoint of } D_0 \text{ in } MT^H \text{ and Theorem 4(8)(a)}\} \\
 & Wp.R \text{ is sup–closed and } D_0\text{–invariant} \\
\equiv & \{\text{part (b)}\} \\
 & \text{true} \ .
\end{array}
$$

(End of proof)

In view of Theorem (4), it is important to obtain a more concrete characterization of $Sy.R$. As a first step, we claim that $Sy.R$ equals the set of commands Q given by

$$q \in Q \quad \equiv \quad (\forall w \in Wp.R :: w^0.q \in R) \ .$$

This is proved by mutual inclusion in

$$\begin{array}{ll} & Q \subset Sy.R \\ \Leftarrow & \{\text{definition (2)}\} \\ & \langle Sx.R, Q\rangle \text{ is an } R\text{–adapted pair} \\ \equiv & \{(0), (1), (3)\} \\ & (\forall h \in Sx.R :: \mathbf{body}.h \in Q) \quad \wedge \\ & (\forall w \in Wp.R, q \in Q :: w^0.q \in R) \\ \Leftarrow & \{\text{Theorem (4)(a) and definition of } Q\} \\ & Sy.R \subset Q \\ \equiv & \{\text{(5) and definition of } Q\} \\ & \text{true} \ . \end{array}$$

Since $Q = Sy.R$, formula (5) can be strengthened to

(6) $$q \in Sy.R \quad \equiv \quad (\forall w \in Wp.R :: w^0.q \in R) \ .$$

In definition (3), the set $Wp.R$ is expressed in terms of $Sx.R$. In formula (6), the set $Sy.R$ is expressed in terms of $Wp.R$. We close the circle by expressing $Sx.R$ in terms of $Sy.R$. We claim that $Sx.R$ equals the set of procedure names K given by

$$h \in K \quad \equiv \quad h \in H \quad \wedge \quad \mathbf{body}.h \in Sy.R \ .$$

This is proved by mutual inclusion in

$$\begin{array}{ll} & K \subset Sx.R \\ \Leftarrow & \{\text{definition (2)}\} \\ & \langle K, Sy.R\rangle \text{ is an } R\text{–adapted pair} \\ \equiv & \{(0), (1), \text{definition } K\} \\ & (\forall w \in WT :: \\ & \quad (\forall h \in K :: w.h \in R) \quad \Rightarrow \quad (\forall q \in Sy.R :: w^0.q \in R)) \\ \Leftarrow & \{\text{Theorem (4)(a) and (1)}\} \\ & Sx.R \subset K \\ \equiv & \{\text{Theorem (4)(a), (0) and definition } K\} \\ & \text{true} \ . \end{array}$$

The result $K = Sx.R$ means that

(7) $$h \in Sx.R \quad \equiv \quad h \in H \quad \wedge \quad \mathbf{body}.h \in Sy.R \ .$$

Example. The syntactic reflection need not contain all commands with a weakest precondition in R. This is shown as follows.

Let i be an integer program variable. Let procedure h be declared by

$$\textbf{body}.h \;=\; (\mathtt{i} := 0\,;\; h \,\|\, ?(\mathtt{i} \neq 0)\,;\; c)$$

for some command $c \in S^{\odot}$. One can prove (see exercise 2.7.2) that for every predicate p

$$wp.h.p \;=\; \mathit{false}\;,$$
$$wlp.h.p \;=\; (\mathtt{i} = 0 \vee wlp.c.p)\;.$$

We take $H = \{h\}$. Let $w \in MT^H$ be given by

$$w.h.p \;=\; (\mathtt{i} = 0) \quad \text{for every } p.$$

Function w is element of WT since for any predicate p

$$\begin{aligned}
& w.h.p \;=\; w.h.\mathit{true} \wedge wlp.h.p \\
\equiv\;\; & \{\text{see above}\} \\
& (\mathtt{i} = 0) \;=\; (\mathtt{i} = 0 \wedge (\mathtt{i} = 0 \vee wlp.c.p)) \\
\equiv\;\; & \{\text{calculus}\} \\
& \mathrm{true}\;.
\end{aligned}$$

We compute

$$\begin{aligned}
& w^0.(\textbf{body}.h).p \\
=\;\; & \{\text{declaration}\} \\
& wp.(\mathtt{i} := 0).(w.h.p) \;\;\wedge\;\; (\mathtt{i} \neq 0 \Rightarrow wp.c.p) \\
=\;\; & \{\text{definition } w;\ \text{calculus}\} \\
& \mathtt{i} = 0 \;\;\vee\;\; wp.c.p\;.
\end{aligned}$$

We now take R to be the subset of MT given by

$$f \in R \;\equiv\; (\forall p \in \mathbb{P} :: f.p = f.\mathit{true})\;.$$

It is easy to verify that R is sup–closed. We have $wp.h \in R$ and $w.h \in R$. Since $Sx.R \subset \{h\}$, it follows with (3) that $w \in Wp.R$.

We take $c = (\mathtt{i} := 1)$. Using the above computation, it is easy to verify that

$$w^0.(\textbf{body}.h) \notin R\;,$$

so that $\textbf{body}.h \notin Sy.R$ from (6). On the other hand, we have $wp.(\textbf{body}.h) = wp.h \in R$. (End of example)

8.2 Membership of the syntactic reflection

We now introduce the main instrument to prove that a recursive procedure belongs to $Sy.R$. For an arbitrary subset K of H, we define the *saturation* $Sat.R.K$ as the subset of $A^{\odot}$ given by

(8) $q \in Sat.R.K \quad \equiv$
$(\forall w \in WT : (\forall h \in K :: w.h \in R) : w^0.q \in R)$.

The importance of the concept of saturation is due to the facts collected in

(9) **Theorem.** (a) $Sy.R = Sat.R.(Sx.R)$.
(b) If $(\forall h \in K :: \mathbf{body}.h \in Sat.R.K)$ then $Sat.R.K \subset Sy.R$.
(c) $K \subset Sat.R.K$.
(d) If $K0 \subset K$ then $Sat.R.K0 \subset Sat.R.K$.
(e) For all $q \in S^{\odot}$ with $wp.q \in R$, we have $q \in Sat.R.K$.
(f) If the set R is closed under functional composition, then $Sat.R.K$ is closed under sequential composition.
(g) If the set R is closed under nonempty (finite) infima in the lattice MT, then $Sat.R.K$ is closed under (finite) choice.

Proof. (a) This is a reformulation of (6) based on (3) and (8).

(b) By definition (8) the pair $\langle K, Sat.R.K \rangle$ satisfies formula (1). The extra condition gives formula (0), so it implies that the pair is R–adapted, and hence that $Sat.R.K \subset Sy.R$ by definition (2).

(c) and (d) are easy and may be left to the reader.

(e) For $q \in S^{\odot}$ we have

$$
\begin{array}{ll}
& q \in Sat.R.K \\
\Leftarrow & \{\text{definition (8)}\} \\
& (\forall w \in WT :: w^0.q \in R) \\
\Leftarrow & \{q \in S^{\odot} \text{ implies that } w^0.q = wp.q \text{ for all } w \in WT\} \\
& wp.q \in R \;.
\end{array}
$$

(f) For commands q, r and a function $w \in WT$ we have

$$
\begin{array}{ll}
& w^0.(q;r) \in R \\
\equiv & \{w^0 \text{ is a homomorphism by 4(43)}\} \\
& w^0.q \circ w^0.r \in R \\
\Leftarrow & \{R \text{ is closed under functional composition}\} \\
& w^0.q \in R \;\;\wedge\;\; w^0.r \in R \;.
\end{array}
$$

By definition (8), this implies

$$(q;r) \in Sat.R.K \quad \Leftarrow \quad q \in Sat.R.K \quad \wedge \quad r \in Sat.R.K \;.$$

(g) This is proved in the same way as part (f).

(End of proof)

Example. In this example we show how Theorem (9) can be used to prove that a command belongs to $Sy.R$. Assume that R is closed under functional composition and nonempty finite conjunctions. By Theorem (9), the set $Sy.R$ is closed under sequential composition and finite choice. If $q \in S^{\odot}$ satisfies $wp.q \in R$ then $q \in Sy.R$.

Let us now consider a repetition $L =$ **while** b **do** c **od** , and ask for a sufficient condition for $L \in Sy.R$. Repetition L is the procedure declared by

$$\mathbf{body}.L \quad = \quad ?\neg b \,[\!]\, ?b; c; L \ .$$

We use Theorem (9) with $K = Sx.R \cup \{L\}$ and observe

$$
\begin{array}{ll}
 & L \in Sy.R \\
\Leftarrow & \{(9)(c)\} \\
 & Sat.R.K \subset Sy.R \\
\Leftarrow & \{(9)(b)\} \\
 & (\forall h \in K :: \mathbf{body}.h \in Sat.R.K) \\
\equiv & \{\text{by (9)(a,d), we have } Sy.R \subset Sat.R.K\text{; also use (4)(a)}\} \\
 & \mathbf{body}.L \in Sat.R.K \\
\Leftarrow & \{\text{declaration of } L\text{; closure properties of } R\text{; (9)(f,g)}\} \\
 & ?\neg b,\ ?b,\ c,\ L \in Sat.R.K \\
\Leftarrow & \{L \in Sat.R.K \text{ by (9)(c); } Sy.R \subset Sat.R.K \text{ by (9)(a,d)}\} \\
 & ?\neg b,\ ?b,\ c \in Sy.R \ .
\end{array}
$$

So, it is sufficient that the body and the two guards be element of $Sy.R$. (End of example)

8.3 Ψ–disjunctivity

The results of the previous sections are applicable to various disjunctivity properties. Since we do not want to give the same proof several times, we propose the following unifying definition.

Let Ψ be a class of ordered sets. A predicate transformer h is called Ψ–*disjunctive* if and only if h is monotone and for every ordered set $\langle L, \leq \rangle \in \Psi$ and every monotone function $g \in L \to \mathbb{P}$

(10) $\quad h.(\exists x \in L :: g.x) \quad = \quad (\exists x \in L :: h.(g.x))$.

This definition covers the definitions in Section 7.2, since we have the following table:

property of h	Ψ
universally disjunctive	L arbitrary
positively disjunctive	L nonempty
finitely disjunctive	L nonempty finite
$\{\emptyset\}$–disjunctive	L empty
upper continuous	$\langle L, \leq \rangle$ a nonempty chain

We write $Md.\Psi$ to denote the subset of MT of the Ψ–disjunctive predicate transformers. In order to reap the fruits of the previous sections, we verify

(11) $\quad Md.\Psi$ is a sup–closed subset of MT.

Indeed, let U be a subset of $Md.\Psi$. We have to prove that $(\sup U) \in Md.\Psi$. This follows from the observation that for any ordered set $\langle L, \leq \rangle \in \Psi$ and any monotone function $g \in L \to \mathbb{P}$

$$
\begin{array}{ll}
 & (\sup U).(\exists i \in L :: g.i) \\
= & \{4(6)\} \\
 & (\exists h \in U :: h.(\exists i \in L :: g.i)) \\
= & \{(10)\text{: every } h \in Md.\Psi\} \\
 & (\exists h \in U :: (\exists i \in L :: h.(g.i))) \\
= & \{\text{interchange and } 4(6)\} \\
 & (\exists i \in L :: (\sup U).(g.i)) \ .
\end{array}
$$

This proves (11). Now all results of Sections 8.1 and 8.2 are applicable to $Md.\Psi$. In particular, we have

(12) $\quad wp.q \in Md.\Psi$ for every $q \in Sy.(Md.\Psi)$.

With respect to the method of Section 8.2, it is useful to observe

(13) **Theorem.** For any subset K of H, the set of commands $Sat.(Md.\Psi).K$ is closed under sequential composition and deterministic choice.

Proof. It is easy to see that a functional composition of Ψ–disjunctive predicate transformers is Ψ–disjunctive. Thus, $Md.\Psi$ is closed under functional composition. By Theorem (9)(f), it follows that $Sat.(Md.\Psi).K$ is closed under sequential composition.

It remains to consider deterministic choice, cf. Section 1.8. Let $f \in I^X$ be an I–valued state function and let $(t \in I :: q.t)$ be a family of commands $q.t \in$

$Sat.(Md.\Psi).K$. We have to prove that the deterministic choice $q.f$ defined in 1(27) satisfies $q.f \in Sat.(Md.\Psi).K$. By definition (8), this amounts to proving that $w^0.(q.f) \in Md.\Psi$, whenever $w \in WT$ satisfies

$$(\forall h \in K :: w.h \in Md.\Psi) .$$

Now $w^0.(q.f) \in Md.\Psi$ is proved by observing that for any pair $\langle L, \leq \rangle \in \Psi$ and any monotone function $g \in L \to \mathbb{P}$

$$\begin{array}{ll} & w^0.(q.f).(\exists i \in L :: g.i) \\ = & \{\text{Lemma (14) below}\} \\ & (\exists t \in I :: (f = t) \wedge w^0.(q.t).(\exists i \in L :: g.i)) \\ = & \{q.t \in Sat.(Md.\Psi).K, \text{ so that } w^0.(q.t) \in Md.\Psi, \text{ and (10)}\} \\ & (\exists t \in I :: (f = t) \wedge (\exists i \in L :: w^0.(q.t).(g.i))) \\ = & \{\text{predicate calculus}\} \\ & (\exists i \in L :: (\exists t \in I :: (f = t) \wedge w^0.(q.t).(g.i))) \\ = & \{\text{Lemma (14) below}\} \\ & (\exists i \in L :: w^0.(q.f).(g.i)) . \end{array}$$

(End of proof)

(14) **Lemma.** Let $f \in I^X$ be an I–valued state function. Let $(t \in I :: q.t)$ be a family of commands. Then the deterministic choice $q.f$ satisfies, for any $v \in H \to MP$ and any $p \in \mathbb{P}$,

$$\begin{array}{lll} v^0.(q.f).p & = & (\forall t :: (f = t) \Rightarrow v^0.(q.t).p) \text{ , and also} \\ v^0.(q.f).p & = & (\exists t :: (f = t) \wedge v^0.(q.t).p) . \end{array}$$

Proof. By Corollary 4(43), v^0 is a homomorphism. Now the first formula is proved in the same way as 1(28). The second formula follows from the first one, by means of the next lemma. (End of proof)

Lemma. Let $f \in I^X$ be a I–valued state function and let $(t \in I :: p.t)$ be a family of predicates. Then

$$(\forall t :: (f = t) \Rightarrow p.t) \quad \equiv \quad (\exists t :: (f = t) \wedge p.t) .$$

Proof. Using definitions 1(0), 1(1) and 1(20), one can verify that for any state x

$$\begin{array}{ll} & (\forall t :: (f = t) \Rightarrow p.t).x \\ \equiv & (\forall t :: (f.x = t) \Rightarrow p.t.x) \\ \equiv & p.(f.x).x \\ \equiv & (\exists t :: (f.x = t) \wedge p.t.x) \\ \equiv & (\exists t :: (f = t) \wedge p.t).x . \end{array}$$

(End of proof)

This concludes the treatment of Theorem (13).

Example. Let c be a command in $Sy.(Md.\Psi)$ and let $b \in \mathbb{P}$. Then we have

$$\textbf{while } b \textbf{ do } c \textbf{ od } \in Sy.(Md.\Psi) .$$

In fact, the repetition is a procedure L declared by

$$\textbf{body}.L \quad = \quad ?\neg b \,[\!]\, ?b; c; L .$$

We proceed in the same way as in the example of Section 8.2. So we put $K = Sx.R \cup \{L\}$ and observe

$$\begin{array}{ll} & L \in Sy.(Md.\Psi) \\ \Leftarrow & \{\text{just as in the example of 8.2}\} \\ & \textbf{body}.L \in Sat.(Md.\Psi).K \\ \Leftarrow & \{\text{declaration of } L;\ (9)(f);\ (13)\} \\ & c,\ L \in Sat.(Md.\Psi).K \\ \equiv & \{\text{just as in the example of 8.2}\} \\ & c \in Sy.(Md.\Psi) . \end{array}$$

This proves that $L \in Sy.(Md.\Psi)$. (End of proof)

8.4 Totality, disjunctivity and finite nondeterminacy

The theory of Section 8.3 is mainly applied to three classes Ψ:

$\Psi 0$: the empty set

$\Psi 1$: all nonempty sets with arbitrary order

$\Psi 2$: all nonempty chains,

with the corresponding sets of predicate transformers

(15) $Mto = Md.\Psi 0$: $\{\emptyset\}$–disjunctive predicate transformers

$Mdi = Md.\Psi 1$: positively disjunctive predicate transformers

$Muc = Md.\Psi 2$: upper–continuous predicate transformers,

and the corresponding conditions on commands c

$wp.c \in Mto \quad \equiv \quad c$ is total, cf. Section 7.2

$wp.c \in Mdi \quad \equiv \quad c$ is disjunctive, cf. Section 7.4

$wp.c \in Muc \quad \equiv \quad c$ is finitely nondeterminate, cf. Section 7.5.

It is easy to verify that

(16) **Corollary.** (a) All assignments belong to $Sy.Mto$.

(b) All guards and all assignments belong to $Sy.Mdi$.

(c) $Sy.Mdi \subset Sy.Muc$.

The set $Sy.Muc$ requires some further investigation, since it plays an important rôle in the analysis of computational induction. We first need two auxiliary results.

(17) **Lemma** (diagonalization). Let $(i, j \in L :: f.i.j)$ be a family of predicates. Let L be a chain, and assume that $f.i.j$ is monotone in both i and j. Then

$$(\exists i, j :: f.i.j) \;=\; (\exists i :: f.i.i) \text{ , and}$$
$$(\forall i, j :: f.i.j) \;=\; (\forall i :: f.i.i) \text{ .}$$

Proof. We use domain splitting

$$\begin{array}{ll} & (\exists i, j :: f.i.j) \\ = & \{L \text{ is a chain}\} \\ & (\exists i, j : i \le j : f.i.j) \;\vee\; (\exists i, j : j \le i : f.i.j) \\ = & \{\text{monotony of } f \text{ in both } i \text{ and } j\} \\ & (\exists j :: f.j.j) \;\vee\; (\exists i :: f.i.i) \\ = & \{\text{renaming, idempotency of } \vee\} \\ & (\exists i :: f.i.i) \text{ .} \end{array}$$

The second formula is proved in the same way. (End of proof)

We claim that Muc is closed under nonempty finite infima, i.e.

(18) $(\forall f, g \in Muc :: f \wedge g \in Muc)$,

where $f \wedge g = (\inf \{f, g\})$ in MT. This formula is proved by observing that for f, $g \in Muc$ and any nonempty chain U in $\mathbb{P}$

$$\begin{array}{ll} & (f \wedge g).(\exists p \in U :: p) \\ = & \{\text{definition } f \wedge g \text{ in } 4(6)\} \\ & f.(\exists p \in U :: p) \;\wedge\; g.(\exists p \in U :: p) \\ = & \{f,\, g \in Muc \text{ and } U \text{ a nonempty chain, see Section 7.0}\} \\ & (\exists p \in U :: f.p) \;\wedge\; (\exists p \in U :: g.p) \\ = & \{\text{distributivity}\} \\ & (\exists p, q \in U :: f.p \wedge g.q) \\ = & \{f.p \wedge g.q \text{ monotone in both } p \text{ and } q,\ (17)\} \\ & (\exists p \in U :: f.p \wedge g.p) \\ = & \{\text{definition } f \wedge g\} \\ & (\exists p \in U :: (f \wedge g).p) \text{ .} \end{array}$$

By Lemma (9)(g), formula (18) implies

(19) **Theorem**. For any subset K of H, the set $Sat.Muc.K$ is closed under finite choice.

We summarize by presenting a more syntactic rule for proving that commands belong to *Sy.Muc*. For any set of commands $Q \subset A^{\odot}$, let *Fin.Q* be the smallest set of commands that satisfies
(i) $Q \subset Fin.Q$,
(ii) if $q, r \in Fin.Q$ then $(q;r)$, $(q \,[\!]\, r) \in Fin.Q$,
(iii) if $(j \in J :: q.j)$ is a family of commands in *Fin.Q* and f is a J–valued state function the deterministic choice $q.f$ satisfies $q.f \in Fin.Q$.

(20) **Theorem.** (a) If $c \in S^{\odot}$ is of finite nondeterminacy, then $c \in Sy.Muc$.
(b) $Sy.Muc = Fin.(Sy.Muc)$.
(c) If G is a set of procedure names with

$$\textbf{body}.h \in Fin.(G \cup Sy.Muc) \text{ for all } h \in G,$$

then $G \subset Sy.Muc$.

Proof. (a) If $c \in S^{\odot}$ is of finite nondeterminacy, then $wp.c \in Muc$ and hence $c \in Sat.Muc.K$ for every K by (9)(e). Therefore the assertion follows from the application of (9)(a):

(21) $$Sy.Muc = Sat.Muc.(Sx.Muc) \ .$$

(b) By (13) and (19), for every subset K of H, the set $Sat.Muc.K$ is closed under composition, finite choice and deterministic choice, i.e.,

(22) $$Sat.Muc.K = Fin.(Sat.Muc.K) \ .$$

Now again the assertion follows with (21).

(c) This part is proved by

$$\begin{array}{ll}
 & G \subset Sy.Muc \\
\Leftarrow & \{(9)(c)\} \\
 & Sat.Muc.(G \cup Sx.Muc) \subset Sy.Muc \\
\Leftarrow & \{(9)(b)\} \\
 & (\forall h \in G \cup Sx.Muc :: \textbf{body}.h \in Sat.Muc.(G \cup Sx.Muc)) \\
\Leftarrow & \{(4)(a),\ (9)(d) \text{ and } (21)\} \\
 & (\forall h \in G :: \textbf{body}.h \in Sat.Muc.(G \cup Sx.Muc)) \\
\Leftarrow & \{\text{assumption}\} \\
 & Fin.(G \cup Sy.Muc) \subset Sat.Muc.(G \cup Sx.Muc) \\
\Leftarrow & \{Fin \text{ is monotone and } (22)\} \\
 & G \cup Sy.Muc \subset Sat.Muc.(G \cup Sx.Muc) \\
\equiv & \{(9)(c,d) \text{ and } (21)\} \\
 & \text{true} \ .
\end{array}$$

(End of proof)

We conclude this section with an example to show that, if a command is finitely nondeterminate, it need not be element of *Sy.Muc*.

Example. We use a variation of the example of Section 8.1. Just as in that example, we let i be an integer program variable. We let procedure h be declared by

$$\mathbf{body}.h \;=\; (\mathtt{i} := 0\,;\, h \,[\!]\, ?(\mathtt{i} \neq 0)\,;\, c)$$

for some command c to be chosen later. For every predicate p we have

$$wp.h.p \;=\; \mathit{false}\,,$$
$$wlp.h.p \;=\; (\mathtt{i} = 0 \vee wlp.c.p)\,.$$

We take $H = \{h\}$. We let $w \in MT^H$ be given by

$$w.h.p \;=\; (\mathtt{i} = 0) \quad \text{for every } p$$

and we have that function w is element of WT. One can verify that $wp.h \in Muc$ and $w.h \in Muc$. Since $Sx.Muc \subset \{h\}$, it follows with (3) that $w \in Wp.Muc$. We now choose

$$c \;=\; (\,[\!]\, n \in \mathbb{N} :: \mathtt{i} := n)\,.$$

Just as in the example of 8.1, we have

$$(23) \qquad w^0.(\mathbf{body}.h).p \;=\; \mathtt{i} = 0 \;\vee\; wp.c.p$$

and it remains to prove that $w^0.(\mathbf{body}.h) \notin Muc$. Now we consider the chain of predicates $(k \in \mathbb{N} :: \mathtt{i} < k)$ and observe

$$(\exists\, k :: w^0.(\mathbf{body}.h).(\mathtt{i} < k))$$
$$= \quad \{(23)\}$$
$$(\exists\, k :: \mathtt{i} = 0 \vee wp.c.(\mathtt{i} < k))$$
$$= \quad \{\text{definition } c\}$$
$$(\exists\, k :: \mathtt{i} = 0 \vee (\forall n \in \mathbb{N} :: wp.(\mathtt{i} := n).(\mathtt{i} < k)))$$
$$= \quad \{\text{assignment}\}$$
$$(\exists\, k :: \mathtt{i} = 0 \vee (\forall n \in \mathbb{N} :: n < k))$$
$$= \quad \{\text{calculus}\}$$
$$\mathtt{i} = 0\,,$$

whereas

$$w^0.(\mathbf{body}.h).(\exists\, k :: (\mathtt{i} < k))$$
$$= \quad \{(23)\}$$
$$\mathtt{i} = 0 \vee wp.c.(\exists\, k :: (\mathtt{i} < k))$$
$$= \quad \{\text{calculus}\}$$
$$\mathtt{i} = 0 \vee wp.c.\mathit{true}$$
$$= \quad \{\text{definition } c;\ \text{calculus}\}$$
$$\mathit{true}\,.$$

This proves that $w^0.(\mathbf{body}.h) \notin Muc$, and hence that $h \notin Sy.Muc$.

Of course, it is well possible that $h \cong q$ for some lower–level command $q \in S^{\odot}$. In that case, we have $q \in Sy.Muc$ by Theorem (9)(e). This shows that $Sy.Muc$ need not be closed under semantic equality. (End of example)

8.5 Exercises

Exercises of Section 8.1.

Exercise 0. Prove that $Sx.R = H \cap Sy.R$.

Exercises of Section 8.2.

Exercise 0. ♡ Let e and $g \in MT$ be such that $g \leq e$. Let R be the subset of MT given by

$$f \in R \quad \equiv \quad f \circ e \leq g \circ f \; .$$

Prove the following assertions.

(a) R is sup–closed in MT and $wp.q \in R$ for all $q \in Sy.R$.

(b) $Sy.R$ is closed under sequential composition.

(c) If g is finitely conjunctive, then $Sy.R$ is closed under finite choice.

Exercise 1. Let e and $g \in MT$ be such that $g \leq e$, and assume that e is universally disjunctive. Let R be given by

$$f \in R \quad \equiv \quad e \circ f \leq f \circ g \; .$$

Prove

(a) R is closed in MT and $wp.q \in R$ for all $q \in Sy.R$,

(b) $Sy.R$ is closed under sequential composition and unbounded choice.

CHAPTER 9

OPERATIONAL SEMANTICS OF RECURSION

9.0. In this chapter, we reconcile the definition of the semantics of recursive procedures, cf. Chapter 4, with the relational semantics of Chapter 6. The idea is that the two semantical paradigms meet halfway. Therefore, the chapter consists of two parts.

The first part is based on predicate–transformation semantics, cf. Chapter 4. In Section 9.1, we describe the stack implementation of recursive procedures. This implementation can be regarded as an interpreter: the whole recursive declaration is interpreted by means of a tail–recursive procedure with a stack of continuations as a value parameter. The correctness of the interpreter is proved in Section 9.2.

In the second part of the chapter we treat the relational semantics of recursive procedures. This is done in two steps. In Section 9.3, we define the relational semantics of a tail–recursive declaration by means of a transitive closure in a graph of configurations. By Chapter 6, these relational semantics induce predicate transformers. We then show that the predicate transformers correspond to *wp* and *wlp* as defined for such a declaration in Chapter 4. In Section 9.4, the ideas and results of the preceding sections are combined. The stack implementation of 9.1 is combined with the relational semantics of tail recursion (cf. Section 9.3) to define the relational semantics of an arbitrary recursive declaration. The results of 9.2 and 9.3 imply that these relational semantics correspond to the predicate–transformation semantics of Chapter 4.

We have the following reason for giving the relational semantics of tail recursion first. In Section 9.3, we relate the extreme fixpoints of functions D_e to the transitive closure in the configuration graph. So, it is here that the two paradigms meet. Due to the restriction to tail recursion, this meeting is not hindered by the additional complexity of stack operations.

9.1 The interpreter

In Section 2.8, the repetition was defined in terms of recursion. Every compiler, however, interprets recursion by means of a repetition with a stack that contains the sequence of commands that remain to be executed. In this section, we describe this formally.

Given are a set of simple commands S, a set of procedure names H and a declaration **body** $\in H \to A^{\odot}$. The stack implementation of recursion consists of one repetition, i.e. a new tail–recursive procedure, not in H, such that all calls of procedures in H are replaced by stack operations.

The value of the stack is an element of A^*, i.e. a string of elements of $A = S \cup H$. It is not a component of the state space. We could model it by extending the state space. It is more convenient, however, to model the stack as an input parameter of the new tail–recursive procedure. So we introduce a new set K of procedure names $k.q$ with $q \in A^*$. Function $k \in A^* \to K$ is bijective, i.e., ono to one and onto K. It can therefore be used as an identification of A^* and K. We shall not do so, however. The family of procedures $k.q$ is declared by

(0) $$\begin{aligned} \mathbf{body}.(k.\varepsilon) &= \varepsilon\ , \\ \mathbf{body}.(k.(c;q)) &= c; k.q\ , \\ \mathbf{body}.(k.(h;q)) &= (\,[\![\, s \in \mathbf{body}.h :: k.(s;q))\ , \end{aligned}$$

for all simple commands $c \in S$, procedure names $h \in H$, strings $q \in A^*$. In the third clause **body**.h is treated as a set of strings, cf. Section 4.3. Notice that formula (0) is a tail–recursive declaration that does not contain calls of procedures $h \in H$.

We claim that procedure k is a faithful interpreter, in the sense that $k.q \cong q$ for all strings $q \in A^*$. By 1(7), this is equivalent to

(1) $$(\forall q \in A^* :: wp.(k.q) = wp.q \quad \wedge \quad wlp.(k.q) = wlp.q)\ .$$

9.2 The proof of the faithful interpreter

The proof of formula (1) has two parts, one for wp and one for wlp. We begin with an investigation of $wp.(k.q)$ for all $q \in A^*$. The restriction $wp|K$ is the smallest (least) solution of the equation $D_0.v = v$ for $v \in K \to MT$. By declaration (0) and 4(21), this equation expands to

$$\begin{aligned} &v.(k.\varepsilon) = identity\ , \\ &v.(k.(c;q)) = ws_0.c \circ v.(k.q)\ , \\ &v.(k.(h;q)) = (\inf s \in \mathbf{body}.h :: v.(k.(s;q))) \end{aligned}$$

for all $c \in S$, $h \in H$, $q \in A^*$. If we write $wk = wp \circ k$, it follows that wk is the smallest solution $u \in A^* \to MT$ of the system of equations

(2) $$u.\varepsilon = identity\ ,$$
$$u.(c;q) = ws_0.c \circ u.q\ ,$$
$$u.(h;q) = (\inf s \in \mathbf{body}.h :: u.(s;q))\ .$$

The function $wp \in A^{\odot} \to MT$ restricts to a function $wp \in A^* \to MT$ that satisfies system (2). Since wk is the smallest solution, this proves that

(3) $$wp \circ k = wk \leq (wp|A^*)$$

with respect to the induced order of $A^* \to MT$. It requires more delicate arguments to obtain an equality in formula (3).

In fact, we first give the proof under an additional assumption. We assume that wk is 'submultiplicative' in the sense that

(4) $$(\forall q, r \in A^* :: wk.q \circ wk.r \leq wk.(q;r))\ .$$

By induction on the length of the strings, formula (4) implies that the extension $(wk|A)^*$, cf. 4(15), of the restriction $wk|A$ satisfies

(5) $$(wk|A)^* \leq wk \qquad \text{in } A^* \to MT.$$

For any $h \in H$, we observe

$$
\begin{array}{ll}
 & D_0.(wk|H).h \\
= & \{4(26)\} \\
 & (ws_0 \cup (wk|H))^{\odot}.(\mathbf{body}.h) \\
= & \{wk \text{ satisfies (2) with } q := \varepsilon\} \\
 & (wk|A)^{\odot}.(\mathbf{body}.h) \\
= & \{4(15)\} \\
 & (\inf s \in \mathbf{body}.h :: (wk|A)^*.s) \\
\leq & \{(5)\} \\
 & (\inf s \in \mathbf{body}.h :: wk.s) \\
= & \{wk \text{ satisfies (2) with } q := \varepsilon\} \\
 & wk.h\ .
\end{array}
$$

This proves $D_0.(wk|H) \leq wk|H$. Since wa_0 is the least fixpoint of D_0, it now follows from exercise 4.2.0 that $wa_0 \leq wk|H$. This implies $wp|A \leq wk|A$. Combining this inequality with (3) and (5), we obtain

$$wk \leq (wp|A^*) = (wp|A)^* \leq (wk|A)^* \leq wk\ .$$

This proves the first conjuncts in formula (1):

(6) $$wp \circ k = wp|A^*\ .$$

Therefore, with respect to wp, it remains to prove formula (4).

To this end, we investigate system (2) with strings $(q; r)$ as argument of u. For a fixed string $r \in A^*$, let $wr \in A^* \to MT$ be given by

$$wr.q = wk.(q; r) \quad \text{for all } q \in A^* .$$

Let function $F \in (A^* \to MT) \to (A^* \to MT)$ be defined by

(7) $\quad F.v.q = v.q \circ wk.r$, or equivalently

$$F.v.q.p = v.q.(wk.r.p) .$$

In order to prove formula (4), it suffices to prove

(8) $\quad F.wk \leq wr \quad$ in $A^* \to MT$.

Since wk is the smallest solution of equation (2) in u, it follows from the definition of wr that wr is a solution of the system of equations in u

(9) $\quad u.\varepsilon = wk.r$,

$$u.(c; q) = wp.c \circ u.q ,$$

$$u.(h; q) = (\inf s \in \mathbf{body}.h :: u.(s; q)) .$$

So it suffices to prove that $F.wk$ is the smallest solution of (9). Here we need the following auxiliary result:

(10) **Lemma.** Let W and Z be complete lattices. Let $D \in W \to W$ and $E \in Z \to Z$ be monotone functions. Let $x0$ be the least fixpoint of D. Let $F \in W \to Z$ be a function that commutes with suprema and satisfies $F \circ D = E \circ F$. Then $F.x0$ is the least fixpoint of E.

Proof. $F.x0$ is a fixpoint of E since

$$E.(F.x0) = F.(D.x0) = F.x0 .$$

Let $z \in Z$ be any fixpoint of E. In order to prove that $F.x0 \leq z$, we introduce the subset V of W given by

$$w \in V \quad \equiv \quad F.w \leq z .$$

The set V is sup–closed in W since for any subset U of W

$(\sup U) \in V$

$\equiv$ {definition V}

$F.(\sup U) \leq z$

$\equiv$ {F commutes with suprema}

$(\sup u \in U :: F.u) \leq z$

$\equiv$ {definition supremum}

$(\forall u \in U :: F.u \leq z)$

$\equiv$ {definition V}

$U \subset V$.

The set V is D–invariant since for any $w \in W$

$D.w \in V$
$\equiv$ {definition V}
$F.(D.w) \leq z$
$\equiv$ $\{F \circ D = E \circ F$; z fixpoint of $E\}$
$E.(F.w) \leq E.z$
$\Leftarrow$ {E is monotone; definition V}
$w \in V$.

By Theorem 4(8)(a), this implies that $x0 \in V$, that is, $F.x0 \leq z$. Therefore, $F.x0$ is the least fixpoint of E in Z. (End of proof)

Lemma (10) is applied with $x0 = wk$ and $W = Z = (A^* \rightarrow MT)$. The function F defined in (7) commutes with suprema, since, for every subset U of $A^* \rightarrow MT$ and every string $q \in A^*$ and every predicate $p \in \mathbb{P}$, we have

$F.(\sup U).q.p$
$=$ {(7)}
$(\sup U).q.(wk.r.p)$
$=$ {4(3) twice: $Y := A^*$ and $Y := \mathbb{P}$}
$(\sup u \in U :: u.q.(wk.r.p))$
$=$ {(7)}
$(\sup u \in U :: F.u.q.p)$
$=$ {4(3) twice: $Y := A^*$ and $Y := \mathbb{P}$}
$(\sup u \in U :: F.u).q.p$.

Let D be the fixpoint operator of (2) and let E be the fixpoint operator of (9). Unifying the operators D and E, we see that $D = \Delta.identity$ and $E = \Delta.(wk.r)$ where

$$\Delta.f.u.\varepsilon = f \ ,$$
$$\Delta.f.u.(c;q) = ws_0.c \circ u.q \ ,$$
$$\Delta.f.u.(h;q) = (\inf s \in \mathbf{body}.h :: u.(s;q)) \ ,$$

for all $f \in MT$, $u \in A^* \rightarrow MT$, $q \in A^*$, $c \in S$ and $h \in H$.

Function wk is the least fixpoint of D and we still have to prove that $F.wk$ is the least fixpoint of E. Therefore, by Lemma (10), it remains to prove that

$$F \circ D = E \circ F \ ,$$

or equivalently, that, for all $u \in A^* \rightarrow MT$ and $q \in A^*$,

(11) $\quad F.(D.u).q = E.(F.u).q$.

This is proved by case distiction on q. For $q := \varepsilon$, we observe

$F.(D.u).\varepsilon = E.(F.u).\varepsilon$
$\equiv$ {definitions of F and E}

$$D.u.\varepsilon \circ wk.r = wk.r$$
$$\equiv \quad \{\text{definition of } D\}$$
$$\text{true} \ .$$

For $q := c; q$, we observe

$$F.(D.u).(c;q) = E.(F.u).(c;q)$$
$$\equiv \quad \{\text{definitions of } F \text{ and } E\}$$
$$D.u.(c;q) \circ wk.r = ws_0.c \circ F.u.q$$
$$\equiv \quad \{\text{definitions of } D \text{ and } F\}$$
$$(ws_0.c \circ u.q) \circ wk.r = ws_0.c \circ (u.q \circ wk.r)$$
$$\equiv \quad \{\text{associativity}\}$$
$$\text{true} \ .$$

For $q := h; q$, we observe

$$F.(D.u).(h;q) = E.(F.u).(h;q)$$
$$\equiv \quad \{\text{definitions of } F, D \text{ and } E; \text{ let } s \text{ range over } \mathbf{body}.h\}$$
$$(\inf s :: u.(s;q)) \circ wk.r = (\inf s :: u.(s;q) \circ wk.r)$$
$$\equiv \quad \{\text{equality of functions; let } p \text{ range over } \mathbb{P}\}$$
$$(\forall p :: (\inf s :: u.(s;q)).(wk.r.p) = (\inf s :: u.(s;q) \circ wk.r).p)$$
$$\equiv \quad \{\text{Theorem 4(3)}\}$$
$$\text{true} \ .$$

This concludes the proof of (11), and hence of (8), and hence of (4) and (6), that is the *wp*–part of (1).

The *wlp*–part of (1) is proved by completely analogous arguments, but D_0 is replaced by D_1, least fixpoints are replaced by greatest fixpoints and sup–closedness is replaced by inf–closedness. In this way we obtain $wlp \circ k = wlp|A^*$. This concludes the proof of formula (1).

9.3 The operational interpretation of tail recursion

In this section, we give the operational justification of defining *wp* and *wlp* of tail–recursive procedures by means of extreme fixpoints of D_e (cf. Section 4.4). We first formalize the concept of tail–recursion. Then the operational meaning of a tail–recursive procedure h is defined in formula (15) below. Finally we show that, via formula 6(1), this operational meaning induces the formal meaning defined in 4(24).

So, we work in the setting of Section 4.4, and assume that only tail recursion occurs. Specifically, we assume that there is one procedure name *skip* $\in H$ with

(12) $\quad \mathbf{body}.skip \;=\; \varepsilon$

and that all other procedure names h satisfy

(13) $\quad \mathbf{body}.h \subset (S^*;H)$.

Here, $(S^*;H)$ is regarded as a subset of A^* by means of definition 4(40), so that indeed all nonempty subsets of $(S^*;H)$ are elements of $A^{\odot}$.

Remark. If we call the elements of H labels instead of procedure names, the program we get can be regarded as a nondeterminate go–to program! (End of remark)

The operational semantics of the elements of H is defined by means of the so–called configuration graph. This is the cartesian product of the state space X with the set H of procedure names, extended with a point ∞ to represent nontermination. So it is $(X \times H) \cup \{\infty\}$. It is made into a directed graph by means of the transition relation '$\to$' defined by

(14) $\quad \langle x,h\rangle \to \langle y,k\rangle \;\equiv\; (\exists s \in S^* :: (s;k) \in \mathbf{body}.h : [\![s]\!].y.x)$,
$\quad\quad \langle x,h\rangle \to \infty \;\equiv\; (\exists (s;k) \in \mathbf{body}.h :: [\![s]\!].\infty.x)$.

Informally speaking, a configuration $\langle x,h\rangle$ is interpreted as a state x in which procedure h is to be performed. A step $\langle x,h\rangle \to \langle y,k\rangle$ with $(s;k) \in \mathbf{body}.h$ and $[\![s]\!].y.x$ corresponds to an execution of string s that terminates in state y where procedure k is still to be performed. A step $\langle x,h\rangle \to \infty$ corresponds to a nonterminating execution of s for some string $(s;k) \in \mathbf{body}.h$.

We define relation '$\overset{*}{\to}$' on $X \times H$ as the reflexive transitive closure of the restriction of '$\to$'. We define $\langle x,h\rangle \overset{*}{\to} \infty$ to mean the existence of a finite sequence of transitions from $\langle x,h\rangle$ to ∞ or the existence of an infinite sequence of transitions starting in $\langle x,h\rangle$. Informally speaking, a finite sequence from $\langle x,h\rangle$ to ∞ means that after finitely many commands a simple command is encountered that need not terminate. An infinite path from $\langle x,h\rangle$ means that the execution contains infinitely many procedure calls.

The *operational meaning* of procedure $h \in H$ is defined as relation $M.h$ in the sense of Chapter 6, given by

(15) $\quad M.h.y.x \;\equiv\; \langle x,h\rangle \overset{*}{\to} \langle y, skip\rangle$,
$\quad\quad M.h.\infty.x \;\equiv\; \langle x,h\rangle \overset{*}{\to} \infty$.

In fact, the only way to reach termination is that the procedure still to be performed is *skip*.

We claim that the operational meaning defined in (15) induces via formula 6(1) the same meaning as the predicate–transformation semantics defined in Chapter 4. More specifically, we claim that $M.h \cong h$ for all $h \in H$, or equivalently, that

(16) $\quad w0.h = wp.h \quad \wedge \quad w1.h = wlp.h$

where

$$w0.h = wp.(M.h) \quad , \quad w1.h = wlp.(M.h) \; .$$

So, we want to prove formula (16). Since $wp|H = wa_0$ is the least fixpoint of D_0 and $wlp|H = wb_1$ is the greatest fixpoint of D_1, it suffices to prove that $w0$ and $w1$ are the least fixpoint of D_0 and the greatest fixpoint of D_1, respectively.

We begin by calculating $w0$ and $w1$. For $h \in H$ and $p \in \mathbb{P}$ and $x \in X$ we have

$$\begin{array}{l} w0.h.p.x \\ \equiv \quad \{\text{definition}\} \\ wp.(M.h).p.x \\ \equiv \quad \{6(1)\} \\ \neg M.h.\infty.x \quad \wedge \quad wlp.(M.h).p.x \\ \equiv \quad \{(15)\} \\ \neg(\langle x, h\rangle \overset{*}{\rightarrow} \infty) \quad \wedge \quad w1.h.p.x \end{array}$$

and

$$\begin{array}{l} w1.h.p.x \\ \equiv \quad \{\text{definition}\} \\ wlp.(M.h).p.x \\ \equiv \quad \{6(1)\} \\ (\forall y : M.h.y.x : p.y) \\ \equiv \quad \{(15)\} \\ (\forall y : \langle x, h\rangle \overset{*}{\rightarrow} \langle y, skip\rangle : p.y) \; . \end{array}$$

This proves

(17) $$\begin{array}{lll} w0.h.p.x & \equiv & \neg(\langle x, h\rangle \overset{*}{\rightarrow} \infty) \quad \wedge \quad w1.h.p.x \; , \\ w1.h.p.x & \equiv & (\forall y : \langle x, h\rangle \overset{*}{\rightarrow} \langle y, skip\rangle : p.y) \; . \end{array}$$

In order to show that $w0$ and $w1$ are the extreme fixpoints of the functions D_e for $e \in \{0, 1\}$, we need an analysis of these functions. It turns out that they can be expressed elegantly in terms of the configuration graph.

(18) **Lemma.** For $v \in MT^H$, we have

(a) $D_e.v.skip \; = \; identity \in MT \quad$ for $e \in \{0, 1\}$.

(b) For every $h \in H \setminus \{skip\}$ and $p \in \mathbb{P}$ and $x \in X$:

$$\begin{array}{lll} D_1.v.h.p.x & \equiv & (\forall y, k :: \langle x, h\rangle \rightarrow \langle y, k\rangle : v.k.p.y) \; , \\ D_0.v.h.p.x & \equiv & \neg(\langle x, h\rangle \rightarrow \infty) \quad \wedge \quad (\forall y, k :: \langle x, h\rangle \rightarrow \langle y, k\rangle : v.k.p.y) \; . \end{array}$$

Proof. Part (a) is proved in

$$D_e.v.skip$$

$= \quad \{4(21) \text{ and } (12)\} \quad (ws_e \cup v)^{\odot}.\varepsilon$
$= \quad \{4(15)\} \quad \mathit{identity}$.

(b) For D_1, we observe that

$D_1.v.h.p.x$
$\equiv \quad \{4(21) \text{ and } (13)\}$
$(\forall\, s \in S^*, k \in H : (s;k) \in \mathbf{body}.h : (ws_1 \cup v)^{\odot}.(s;k).p).x$
$\equiv \quad \{4(15) \text{ and } 1(1)\}$
$(\forall\, s \in S^*, k \in H : (s;k) \in \mathbf{body}.h : ws_1^*.s.(v.k.p).x)$
$\equiv \quad \{ws_1^* = wlp|S^* \text{ and } 6(15)\}$
$(\forall\, s \in S^*, k \in H : (s;k) \in \mathbf{body}.h : wlp.[\![s]\!].(v.k.p).x)$
$\equiv \quad \{6(1)\}$
$(\forall\, s \in S^*, k \in H : (s;k) \in \mathbf{body}.h : (\forall\, y : [\![s]\!].y.x : v.k.p.y))$
$\equiv \quad$ {calculus, compare exercise 1.1.4(b)}
$(\forall\, y \in X, k \in H : (\exists\, s \in S^* :: (s;k) \in \mathbf{body}.h \wedge [\![s]\!].y.x) : v.k.p.y)$
$\equiv \quad$ {definition (14)}
$(\forall\, y, k :: \langle x, h\rangle \rightarrow \langle y, k\rangle : v.k.p.y)$.

The proof for D_0 is analogous. Since it is not illuminating it is omitted.
(End of proof)

We now prove that $w0$ and $w1$ are fixpoints of function D_0 and D_1, respectively. As for $w0$, it suffices to show that for every procedure name $h \in H$, every predicate $p \in \mathbb{P}$, and every state $x \in X$

(19) $\quad w0.h.p.x \;\equiv\; D_0.w0.h.p.x$.

In view of Lemma (18), this requires a case distinction. For $h = \mathit{skip}$, it suffices to observe

$w0.\mathit{skip}.p.x$
$\equiv \quad \{(17)\}$
$\neg(\langle x, \mathit{skip}\rangle \overset{*}{\rightarrow} \infty) \;\wedge\; (\forall\, y : \langle x, \mathit{skip}\rangle \overset{*}{\rightarrow} \langle y, \mathit{skip}\rangle : p.y)$
$\equiv \quad \{\langle x, \mathit{skip}\rangle$ has no transitions, by (12) and (14)$\}$
$p.x$
$\equiv \quad$ {Lemma (18)(a)}
$D_0.w0.\mathit{skip}.p.x$.

For $h \neq \mathit{skip}$, we have

$w0.h.p.x$
$\equiv \quad \{(17)\}$
$\neg(\langle x, h\rangle \overset{*}{\rightarrow} \infty) \;\wedge\; (\forall\, y : \langle x, h\rangle \overset{*}{\rightarrow} \langle y, \mathit{skip}\rangle : p.y)$
$\equiv \quad$ {definition '$\overset{*}{\rightarrow}$' and $h \neq \mathit{skip}$}

$$\begin{array}{l} \quad \neg(\langle x,h\rangle \to \infty) \quad \wedge \\ \qquad (\forall z,k : \langle x,h\rangle \to \langle z,k\rangle : \\ \qquad \neg(\langle z,k\rangle \stackrel{*}{\to} \infty) \quad \wedge \quad (\forall y : \langle z,k\rangle \stackrel{*}{\to} \langle y, skip\rangle : p.y)) \\ \equiv \quad \{(17)\} \\ \quad \neg(\langle x,h\rangle \to \infty) \quad \wedge \quad (\forall z,k : \langle x,h\rangle \to \langle z,k\rangle : w0.k.p.z) \\ \equiv \quad \{\text{Lemma (18)(b)}\} \\ \quad D_0.w0.h.p.x \ . \end{array}$$

This proves formula (19), and hence $D_0.w0 = w0$. The proof of $D_1.w1 = w1$ can be obtained from the proof for $w0$ by deletion of the lefthand conjuncts.

It remains to prove that $w0$ and $w1$ are the extreme fixpoints. So we have to prove that for every $v \in MT^H$

$$\begin{array}{lll} D_1.v = v & \Rightarrow & v \leq w1 \ , \\ D_0.v = v & \Rightarrow & w0 \leq v \ . \end{array}$$

This means that for all procedure names $h \in H$ and all predicates $p \in \mathbb{P}$:

(20) $\quad D_1.v = v \quad \Rightarrow \quad [\, v.h.p \quad \Rightarrow \quad w1.h.p]$ and

(21) $\quad D_0.v = v \quad \Rightarrow \quad [\, w0.h.p \quad \Rightarrow \quad v.h.p] \ .$

We begin with the proof of (20). We prove the righthand side of (20) under assumption of the lefthand side. It suffices to observe that for every state $x \in X$

$$\begin{array}{l} \quad w1.h.p.x \\ \equiv \quad \{(17)\} \\ \quad (\forall y \in X : \langle x,h\rangle \stackrel{*}{\to} \langle y, skip\rangle : p.y) \\ \equiv \quad \{v = D_1.v \text{ yields } v.skip = D_1.v.skip = identity \text{ by (18)(a)}\} \\ \quad (\forall y \in X : \langle x,h\rangle \stackrel{*}{\to} \langle y, skip\rangle : v.skip.p.y) \\ \Leftarrow \quad \{\text{generalization}\} \\ \quad (\forall y \in X, k \in H : \langle x,h\rangle \stackrel{*}{\to} \langle y,k\rangle : v.k.p.y) \\ \Leftarrow \quad \{\text{induction with Lemma (18)(b), using } D_1.v = v\} \\ \quad v.h.p.x \ . \end{array}$$

The proof of (21) is more difficult. Again we prove the righthand side under assumption of the lefthand side, which is $D_0.v = v$. We begin with massaging the goal:

(22)
$$\begin{array}{l} \quad [\, w0.h.p \Rightarrow v.h.p] \\ \equiv \quad \{(17)\} \\ \quad (\forall x :: \neg(\langle x,h\rangle \stackrel{*}{\to} \infty) \wedge w1.h.p.x \quad \Rightarrow \quad v.h.p.x) \\ \equiv \quad \{\text{predicate calculus}\} \\ \quad (\forall x :: \neg v.h.p.x \wedge w1.h.p.x \quad \Rightarrow \quad \langle x,h\rangle \stackrel{*}{\to} \infty) \end{array}$$

$$\begin{array}{ll} \equiv & \{(17)\} \\ & (\forall x :: R.\langle x, h\rangle \;\Rightarrow\; \langle x, h\rangle \overset{*}{\rightarrow} \infty) \end{array}$$

where predicate $R.\langle x, h\rangle$ is defined by

$$R.\langle x, h\rangle \;\equiv\; \neg v.h.p.x \;\wedge\; (\forall y : \langle x, h\rangle \overset{*}{\rightarrow} \langle y, skip\rangle : p.y) \; .$$

The last formula of calculation (22) now suggests an inductive construction of a diverging execution sequence. The first step is to show that termination has not yet been reached:

(23) $\quad R.\langle x, h\rangle \;\Rightarrow\; h \neq skip$,

as is proved in

$$\begin{array}{ll} & R.\langle x, skip\rangle \\ \Rightarrow & \{\overset{*}{\rightarrow} \text{ is reflexive}\} \\ & \neg v.skip.p.x \;\wedge\; p.x \\ \Rightarrow & \{\text{calculus}\} \\ & v.skip \neq identity \\ \equiv & \{D_0.v = v \text{ and Lemma (18)(a)}\} \\ & \text{false} \; . \end{array}$$

We now show that predicate R leads to immediate nontermination or can be kept valid in the first execution step, that is,

(24) $\quad R.\langle x, h\rangle \;\Rightarrow\; \langle x, h\rangle \rightarrow \infty \;\vee\; (\exists z, k : \langle x, h\rangle \rightarrow \langle z, k\rangle : R.\langle z, k\rangle)$.

This is proved in

$$\begin{array}{ll} & R.\langle x, h\rangle \;\wedge\; \neg(\langle x, h\rangle \rightarrow \infty) \\ \Rightarrow & \{\text{definition } R,\ D_0.v = v \text{ and (23)}\} \\ & h \neq skip \;\wedge\; \neg(\langle x, h\rangle \rightarrow \infty) \\ & \wedge\; \neg D_0.v.h.p.x \;\wedge\; (\forall y : \langle x, h\rangle \rightarrow \langle y, skip\rangle : p.y) \\ \Rightarrow & \{\text{Lemma (18)(b) and calculus}\} \\ & (\exists z, k : \langle x, h\rangle \rightarrow \langle z, k\rangle : \neg v.k.p.z) \\ & \wedge\; (\forall y : \langle x, h\rangle \overset{*}{\rightarrow} \langle y, skip\rangle : p.y) \\ \Rightarrow & \{\text{if } \alpha \rightarrow \beta \text{ and } \beta \overset{*}{\rightarrow} \gamma \text{ then } \alpha \overset{*}{\rightarrow} \gamma\} \\ & (\exists z, k : \langle x, h\rangle \rightarrow \langle z, k\rangle : \\ & \quad \neg v.k.p.z \;\wedge\; (\forall y : \langle z, k\rangle \overset{*}{\rightarrow} \langle y, skip\rangle : p.y)) \\ \equiv & \{\text{definition } R\} \\ & (\exists z, k : \langle x, h\rangle \rightarrow \langle z, k\rangle : R.\langle z, k\rangle) \; . \end{array}$$

By mathematical induction, it follows from (24) that

$$R.\langle x, h\rangle \;\Rightarrow\; \langle x, h\rangle \overset{*}{\rightarrow} \infty \; .$$

By calculation (22), this concludes the proof of (21), and hence of (16).

9.4 General operational semantics

We now combine the construction of Section 9.3 with the ideas of Sections 9.1 and 9.2, to define the operational semantics of an arbitrary declaration $\mathbf{body} \in H \to A^{\odot}$.

In Section 9.2, the declaration is shown to be equivalent to a tail–recursive declaration of a set K of procedure names $k.q$ with $q \in A^*$ given by

(25) $$\begin{aligned} \mathbf{body}.(k.\varepsilon) &= \varepsilon \ , \\ \mathbf{body}.(k.(c;q)) &= c; k.q \ , \\ \mathbf{body}.(k.(h;q)) &= (\, [\!] \, s \in \mathbf{body}.h :: k.(s;q)) \ , \end{aligned}$$

for all simple commands $c \in S$, procedure names $h \in H$, and strings $q \in A^*$.

If we compare this with Section 9.3, we see that $k.\varepsilon \in K$ plays the rôle of *skip*, cf. formula (12). Since $\varepsilon \in S^*$ satisfies $(\varepsilon; r) = r$ for all commands r, we have $\mathbf{body}.(k.q) \subset (S^*; K)$ for all $q \in A^* \setminus \{\varepsilon\}$. This shows that the conditions of Section 9.3 are met. Therefore, we can define the operational semantics by means of a configuration graph $(X \times K) \cup \{\infty\}$. Since $k \in A^* \to K$ is a bijective function, we can replace $X \times K$ by $X \times A^*$. It follows from the formulae (14) and (25), together with

$$[\![\varepsilon]\!].y.x \ \equiv \ (x = y) \ ,$$

that transition relation '$\to$', when transferred to $X \times A^*$, satisfies

$$\begin{aligned} &\langle x, q\rangle \to \langle y, r\rangle \ \equiv \\ &(\exists\, c \in S :: q = c; r \wedge [\![c]\!].y.x) \\ &\vee \ \ (\exists\, h \in H, s \in \mathbf{body}.h, t \in A^* :: q = h; t \wedge r = s; t \wedge x = y) \ . \end{aligned}$$

The set $(X \times A^*) \cup \{\infty\}$ with relation '$\to$' is called the *configuration graph of general recursion.*

We define '$\stackrel{*}{\to}$' and '$\stackrel{*}{\to} \infty$' in same way as after formula (14). The operational meaning of $q \in A^*$ is defined as relation $M.q$ given by

$$\begin{aligned} M.q.y.x &\equiv \ \langle x, q\rangle \stackrel{*}{\to} \langle y, \varepsilon\rangle \ , \\ M.q.\infty.x &\equiv \ \langle x, q\rangle \stackrel{*}{\to} \infty \ . \end{aligned}$$

For every $q \in A^*$, we now obtain

$$\begin{aligned} &M.q \\ \cong \ &\{(16)\} \quad k.q \\ \cong \ &\{(1)\} \quad q \ . \end{aligned}$$

So, indeed, the operational semantics is in agreement with predicate–transformation semantics as defined in Chapter 4.

9.5 Exercises

Exercises of Section 9.3.

Exercise 0. Prove the equivalence for D_0 in Lemma (18)(b).

CHAPTER 10

PROCEDURE SUBSTITUTIONS

10.0. In this chapter, we develop the concept of substitution in command expressions. In spite of the presence of unbounded choice, substitution is an easy concept and it has the usual properties. Substitution is used to describe and justify a program transformation that consists of the introduction of mediating procedures. In later chapters, we are mainly interested in two special cases: substitutions in which procedure names are replaced by their bodies, and substitutions in which procedure names are replaced by *abort*.

10.1 Substitutions

In this section we introduce substitution of procedure names. The simple commands $s \in S$ are always unchanged. For the sake of flexibility, we allow substitution of symbols from other sets than H.

Let $f \in K \to A^{\odot}$ be a given function, where K is a set disjoint from S. Put $U = S \cup K$. For a 'command' $c \in U^{\odot}$, the *substitution* $f^{\odot}.c$ is constructed from c by replacing every symbol $k \in K$ in expression c by $f.k$.

The formal definition is that $f^{\odot} \in U^{\odot} \to A^{\odot}$ is the unique function that satisfies

(0)
$$\begin{aligned} &(\forall c \in S :: f^{\odot}.c = c) \ \wedge \ (\forall k \in K :: f^{\odot}.k = f.k) \\ \wedge \ &(\forall c, d \in U^{\odot} :: f^{\odot}.(c; d) = f^{\odot}.c; f^{\odot}.d) \\ \wedge \ &(\forall C : \emptyset \neq C \subset U^{\odot} :: f^{\odot}.(\,[\!]\, C) = (\,[\!]\, c \in C :: f^{\odot}.c)) \ . \end{aligned}$$

The construction of $f^{\odot}$ is analogous to the construction of function $w^{\odot}$ in Section 4.3. A formal proof that formula (0) has precisely one solution, $f^{\odot}$, is left to the reader.

It is convenient to have a special notation for concrete substitutions in the case $K = H$. For example, if h, k are different elements of H, and q, $r \in A^{\odot}$, the double substitution $[q/h, r/k]$ is defined by $[q/h, r/k] = f^{\odot} \in A^{\odot} \to A^{\odot}$, where $f \in H \to A^{\odot}$ is given by

$$f.h = q \quad , \quad f.k = r \ ,$$
$$f.x = x \quad \text{for all } x \in H \setminus \{h, k\} \ .$$

We use analogous notations for single substitutions and for other multiple substitutions.

10.2 Substitution commutes with extension

Recall from definition 4(25) that for $v \in MT^H$

$$v^e = (ws_e \cup v)^{\odot} \in A^{\odot} \to MT \ .$$

Similarly, for $v \in K \to MT$, we define $v^e = (ws_e \cup v)^{\odot} \in U^{\odot} \to MT$. Let $f \in K \to A^{\odot}$ be a given function and let $f^{\odot} \in U^{\odot} \to A^{\odot}$ be the associated substitution function, cf. formula (0).

We claim that for a function from H to the set of the *positively conjunctive* predicate transformers, substitution commutes with extension. More specifically, we claim that, for every function $v \in H \to MP$, we have

(1) $\qquad v^e \circ f^{\odot} = (v^e \circ f)^e \in U^{\odot} \to MP \ .$

This is proved by structural induction over $U^{\odot}$. Function $(ws_e \cup v)$ is an element of $A \to MP$. By Theorem 4(42), it follows that function $v^e = (ws_e \cup v)^{\odot}$ is a homomorphism in $A^{\odot} \to MP$. It follows with (0) that $v^e \circ f^{\odot}$ is a homomorphism in $U^{\odot} \to MP$. Similarly, $(v^e \circ f)^e$ is a homomorphism in $U^{\odot} \to MP$. A homomorphism in $U^{\odot} \to MP$ is completely determined by its restriction to U. Therefore, it suffices to prove that

$$v^e \circ f^{\odot}|U = (v^e \circ f)^e|U \ .$$

Now $U = S \cup K$ and both functions restrict to ws_e on the set S and restrict to $v^e \circ f$ on the set K. Therefore, they are equal.

10.3 Procedure abstraction is allowed

In the remainder of this chapter we develop a theorem concerning the declaration of intermediate procedures. This result is subsequently used in a classical example of program transformation. The result is not used in later chapters.

If some procedure body contains a complicated command expression q, one may replace that expression by a new procedure name $k1$ with body q. This means that the old declaration looks like

$$\mathbf{body}.h0 \;=\; [q/k1].r \;,$$

where command r may contain the symbols $k1$ and $h0$, and q may contain $h0$. In the new declaration, we use $k0$ as the new name of $h0$ and obtain

$$\begin{aligned}\mathbf{body}.k0 &= [k0/h0].r \;,\\ \mathbf{body}.k1 &= [k0/h0].q \;.\end{aligned}$$

Intuitively, it is obvious that such a transformation should be correct in the sense that $h0 \cong k0$. This is proved, formalized and generalized, as follows. In the formalization, we use a function i to generalize the renaming $h0 \mapsto k0$, and a function f to generalize $k0 \mapsto h0$ and $k1 \mapsto q$.

Let K be disjoint from S and let $U = S \cup K$. Let the symbols in H and K be regarded as procedure names declared by

$$\mathbf{body}_H \in H \to A^{\odot} \quad \text{and} \quad \mathbf{body}_K \in K \to U^{\odot} \;.$$

(2) **Theorem.** Let $i \in H \to K$ and $f \in K \to A^{\odot}$ be such that

(a) $\quad f \circ i = \mathit{identity\ of\ } H \;,$

(b) $\quad \mathbf{body}_H = f^{\odot} \circ \mathbf{body}_K \circ i \;,$

(c) $\quad \mathbf{body}_K|L = i^{\odot} \circ f|L$ where $L = K \setminus \mathit{Image}(i)$.

Then $i.h \cong h$ for all $h \in H$ and $f.k \cong k$ for all $k \in K$.

Proof. The set L is the complement of the image of function i. It follows that, for functions $w0$ and $w1$ on K, we have

(3) $\quad w0 = w1 \;\equiv\; w0 \circ i = w1 \circ i \;\wedge\; w0|L = w1|L \;.$

For any function $v \in H \to MP$, we can define $w = v^e \circ f \in K \to MP$. Conversely, for any function $w \in K \to MP$, we can define $v = w \circ i \in H \to MP$. Both correspondences are monotone. Moreover, for functions $v \in H \to MP$ and $w \in K \to MP$, we have

$$\begin{aligned}
& v = v^e \circ \mathbf{body}_H \;\wedge\; w = v^e \circ f\\
\equiv\;& \{(b)\}\\
& v = v^e \circ f^{\odot} \circ \mathbf{body}_K \circ i \;\wedge\; w = v^e \circ f\\
\equiv\;& \{(1) \text{ and } (3)\}\\
& v = w^e \circ \mathbf{body}_K \circ i \;\wedge\; w|L = v^e \circ f|L \;\wedge\; w \circ i = v^e \circ f \circ i\\
\equiv\;& \{(a)\}\\
& v = w^e \circ \mathbf{body}_K \circ i \;\wedge\; w|L = v^e \circ f|L \;\wedge\; w \circ i = v\\
\equiv\;& \{\text{third conjunct and } (1)\}\\
& w \circ i = w^e \circ \mathbf{body}_K \circ i \;\wedge\; w|L = w^e \circ i^{\odot} \circ f|L \;\wedge\; w \circ i = v\\
\equiv\;& \{(c) \text{ and } (3)\}\\
& w = w^e \circ \mathbf{body}_K \;\wedge\; w \circ i = v \;.
\end{aligned}$$

For $e = 0$, this calculation shows that the smallest solution of the fixpoint equation $v = v^0 \circ \mathbf{body}_H$ is $w \circ i$, where w is the smallest solution of the fixpoint equation $w = w^0 \circ \mathbf{body}_K$, which happens to satisfy $w = v^0 \circ f$. By definition 4(24), it follows that $wp.h = wp.(i.h)$ for all $h \in H$ and $wp.k = wp.(f.k)$ for all $k \in K$. If we use biggest solutions, the same calculation yields that $wlp.h = wlp.(i.h)$ for all $h \in H$ and $wlp.k = wlp.(f.k)$ for all $k \in K$. (End of proof)

Remark. Theorem (2) has a flavour of symmetry, but we could not find a useful symmetric generalization. (End of remark)

Example. Let procedures g and h be declared by

$$\begin{array}{lcl} \mathbf{body}.g & = & (c \parallel q; r; g) \\ \mathbf{body}.h & = & r; (c \parallel q; h) \end{array}$$

where $c, q, r \in S^{\odot}$. We use two applications of Theorem (2) to prove that $(r; g) \cong h$. In both cases, we use the set $K = \{k0, k1\}$ with the declaration

$$\begin{array}{lcl} \mathbf{body}.k0 & = & (c \parallel q; k1) \\ \mathbf{body}.k1 & = & r; k0 \ . \end{array}$$

One can use one application of Theorem (2) with $H = \{g\}$ and $i.g = k0$ and $f.k1 = (r; g)$ to prove that $(r; g) \cong k1$. Another application of Theorem (2) with $H = \{h\}$ and $i.h = k1$ and $f.k0 = (c \parallel q; h)$ can be used to prove that $k1 \cong h$. This proves $(r; g) \cong h$. The remaining instantiations and verifications are left to the reader. (End of example)

10.4 A classical example

In [de Bakker-de Roever 1973] p. 183, a tree traversal problem is described, as an application of the so–called mu–calculus. The task is to perform an action A in the nodes of the trees of a forest. Let, for any node, $s(x)$ be interpreted as 'has x a son?' and $b(x)$ as 'has x a brother?'. Let $S(x)$ be: 'visit the first son of x', and $B(x)$: 'visit the first brother of x', and $F(x)$: 'visit the father of x'. Let procedures $h0$, $h1$, $h2 \in H$ be declared by

$$\text{(4)} \qquad \begin{array}{lcl} \mathbf{body}.h0 & = & A; (?\neg s \parallel ?s; S; h0; F); (?\neg b \parallel ?b; B; h0) \ , \\ \mathbf{body}.h1 & = & A; (?\neg s \parallel ?s; S; h1; h2; F) \ , \\ \mathbf{body}.h2 & = & (?\neg b \parallel ?b; B; h1; h2) \ . \end{array}$$

The problem is to prove that $h0 \cong (h1; h2)$.

This can be done by means of two applications of Theorem (2). In fact, let $k0$, $k1$, $k2$ be declared by

$$(13)\qquad \begin{aligned} \mathbf{body}.k0 &= k1; k2\ , \\ \mathbf{body}.k1 &= A; (?\neg s \;[\!]\; ?s; S; k0; F)\ , \\ \mathbf{body}.k2 &= (?\neg b \;[\!]\; ?b; B; k0)\ . \end{aligned}$$

Put $K = \{k0, k1, k2\}$. We use Theorem (2) to show that $h0 \cong k0$. To this end we define $i \in \{h0\} \to K$ by $i.h0 = k0$ and $f \in K \to A^{\odot}$ by

$$\begin{aligned} f.k0 &= h0\ , \\ f.k1 &= A; (?\neg s \;[\!]\; ?s; S; h0; F)\ , \\ f.k2 &= (?\neg b \;[\!]\; ?b; B; h0)\ . \end{aligned}$$

The verification of the conditions of Theorem (2) is immediate. This shows that $h0 \cong k0$. By another instantiation of Theorem (2) with $i \in \{h1, h2\} \to K$ and $f.k0 = (h1; h2)$, we get $h1 \cong k1$ and $h2 \cong k2$. By declaration (13), we have $k0 \cong k1; k2$. This proves that $h0 \cong h1; h2$.

Remark. In the mu–calculus of [de Bakker-de Roever 1973], mutual recursion is expressed in terms of simple recursion and procedure parameters. Therefore, our treatment of this example cannot be completely faithful to the original problem. On the other hand, semantic equivalence in loc.cit. is only equivalence for *wlp*. So, our assertion of semantic equality is stronger. (End of remark)

10.5 Exercises

Exercises of Section 10.3.

Exercise 0. Complete the proof of the example.

Exercise 1. Let G be a subset of H such that $\mathbf{body}.g \in (S \cup G)^{\odot}$ for all $g \in G$.
(a) Prove that $wp|G$ is the smallest solution of the equation in $v \in MT^G$

$$v = (ws_0 \cup v)^{\odot} \circ (\mathbf{body}|G)$$

and that $wlp|G$ is the biggest solution of the equation in $v \in MT^G$

$$v = (ws_1 \cup v)^{\odot} \circ (\mathbf{body}|G)\ .$$

Hint: use Theorem (2).
(b) Let $K = H \setminus G$. Prove that $wp|K$ is the smallest solution of the equation in $v \in MT^K$

$$v = (ws_0 \cup (wp|G) \cup v)^{\odot} \circ (\mathbf{body}|K)$$

and that $wlp|K$ is the biggest solution of

$$v = (ws_1 \cup (wlp|G) \cup v)^{\odot} \circ (\mathbf{body}|K)\ .$$

Remark. The set G can be regarded as a layer of lower level procedures used as a foundation for the upper level procedures in K. Part (a) asserts that the interpretation of the elements of G is independent of the existence of the upper level K. Part (b) asserts that the interpretation of the upper level K does not change if the lower level procedures (in G) are treated as simple commands. This justifies the assertion in Section 2.6 that lower level procedures may be treated as simple commands. (End of remark)

CHAPTER 11

INDUCTION AND SEMANTIC EQUALITY

11.0. In this chapter we announce a version of the induction rule of De Bakker and Scott, cf. [Manna 1974] 5.5 and [de Bakker 1980] 7.11. The rule is stated here in a form that differs considerably from the forms in these books. In our opinion, the formalism to be described is more convenient for applications to program transformation. The present version is somewhat more general than our previous versions in [Hesselink 1989a] Theorem (40) and [Hesselink 1990] Section 5.

The semantics of the simple commands $s \in S$ are given by the functions $ws_0 = (wp|S)$ and $ws_1 = (wlp|S)$, regarded as known. It is convenient to postulate the existence of a simple command *abort* $\in S$ as defined in 1(9). We define $\mathbf{abort} \in H \to A^{\odot}$ by

(0) $\qquad \mathbf{abort}.h = abort \qquad$ for all $h \in H$.

By Section 10.1, there are induced substitution functions $\mathbf{body}^{\odot}, \mathbf{abort}^{\odot} \in A^{\odot} \to A^{\odot}$. It is easy to see that $\mathbf{body}^{\odot}$ and $\mathbf{abort}^{\odot}$ restrict on the set $S^{\odot}$ to the identity function, and that $\mathbf{abort}^{\odot}.q \in S^{\odot}$ for all $q \in A^{\odot}$.

The idea of the induction rule is to give sufficient conditions on a set E of pairs of commands such that $q \cong r$ for all pairs $\langle q, r\rangle \in E$. The principal condition will be that E is somehow stable under unfolding, where the unfolding of $q \in A^{\odot}$ is the command $\mathbf{body}^{\odot}.q$ which consists of expression q with all procedures replaced by their bodies. The base case of the induction will consist of semantic equalities of the form:

$$\mathbf{abort}^{\odot}.q \;\cong\; \mathbf{abort}^{\odot}.r \qquad \text{for all pairs } \langle q, r\rangle \in E\,.$$

After some further technical preparations, the main result is postulated in Section 11.3. The remainder of the chapter consists of examples and comments. The constructions and proofs are postponed to Chapters 12 and 13.

11.1 Congruences

In order to prove semantic equalities $q \cong r$, we need other relations '$\sim$' that share the main algebraic properties of '$\cong$'. Therefore, we define a *congruence* on $A^{\odot}$ to be an equivalence relation '$\sim$' such that

(1) for all q, r, s, t we have $q \sim r \quad \wedge \quad s \sim t \quad \Rightarrow \quad q;s \sim r;t$,

(2) for every pair of nonempty families $(i \in I :: c.i)$ and $(i \in I :: d.i)$ in $A^{\odot}$:

$$(\forall i \in i :: c.i \sim d.i) \quad \Rightarrow \quad (\,[\!]\, i :: c.i) \sim (\,[\!]\, i :: d.i)\ .$$

By convention, we let a binary relation '$\lhd$' be identified with the set of pairs $(\lhd)$ given by

$$\langle q, r\rangle \in (\lhd) \quad \equiv \quad q \lhd r\ .$$

For a function $w \in A^{\odot} \to MT$, the *equalizer* $Eq.w$ is defined as the binary relation on $A^{\odot}$ given by

(3) $\langle q, r\rangle \in Eq.w \quad \equiv \quad w.q = w.r\ .$

A straightforward calculation shows that, if w is a homomorphism, then $Eq.w$ is a congruence on $A^{\odot}$. It is easy to see that any intersection of congruences is a congruence. Since $(\cong)$ is the intersection of the congruences $Eq.wp$ and $Eq.wlp$, it follows that $(\cong)$ is a congruence. So, indeed, the concept of congruence is a generalisation of semantic equality.

11.2 The set *Lia*

We need a subset *Lia* of $A^{\odot}$ that occurs in a condition in a proof rule. Its name refers to 'linear approximation'. The definition of *Lia* is very technical and therefore postponed to Section 13.6. In order to show that *Lia* has enough elements, we give some sufficient conditions, the validity of which is proved below in Sections 13.7 and 13.8. In part (d), we use the subset *Sy.Muc* of $A^{\odot}$ defined and investigated in Section 8.4. Knowledge of *Sy.Muc* is not necessary for understanding the theory of this chapter. In the applications where *Sy.Muc* is needed, we shall only use Theorem 8(20).

(4) **Theorem.** (a) $H \cup S^{\odot} \subset Lia$.

(b) If q, $r \in Lia$ then $q \,[\!]\, r \in Lia$.

(c) If $f \in I^X$ and $q.t \in Lia$ for all $t \in I$, then $q.f \in Lia$.

(d) Let q, $r \in Lia$. If $q \in Sy.Muc$ or $r \in S^{\odot}$ then $q;r \in Lia$.

By (a), *Lia* contains $S^\odot$ and all procedure names. It is stable under finite choice (cf. (b)) and deterministic infinite choice (cf. (c)). We must be careful with the composition, cf. (d).

Remark. The antecedent of the implication in part (d) is nasty. In 11.7, we give an example to show that it cannot be replaced by true. On the other hand, each of the two disjuncts of the antecedent is useful, as is shown in 11.5 and the example of 11.3. It is not known whether *Sy.Muc* is contained in *Lia*. The sets *Sy.Muc* and *Lia* are not closed under semantic equality. See the concluding example in Section 8.4.

11.3 The strong congruence

We now present the induction rule to prove semantic equalities $q \cong r$ for commands q and r that may contain recursive procedures. The underlying definitions and justifications are postponed.

In Section 12.3, we construct a congruence '$\approx$' on $A^\odot$, which is called the *strong congruence* and has the following two properties:

(5) **Semantic Rule.** $(\forall q, r \in A^\odot : q \approx r : q \cong r)$.

(6) **Accumulation Rule.** Let E be a binary relation on $A^\odot$ such that
$$(\forall \langle q,r\rangle \in E :: \mathbf{abort}^\odot.q \cong \mathbf{abort}^\odot.r \quad \wedge \quad q,r \in Lia)$$
and that, for every congruence $\sim$ on $A^\odot$ with $E \cup (\approx) \subset (\sim)$, we have
$$(\forall \langle q,r\rangle \in E :: \mathbf{body}^\odot.q \sim \mathbf{body}^\odot.r) .$$
Then $q \approx r$ for all pairs $\langle q,r\rangle \in E$.

Remark. The classical induction rules mentioned in 11.0 are closer to the following version.

Induction Rule. Let E be a binary relation on $A^\odot$ such that
$$(\forall \langle q,r\rangle \in E :: \mathbf{abort}^\odot.q \cong \mathbf{abort}^\odot.r \quad \wedge \quad q,r \in Lia)$$
and that, for every congruence $\sim$ on $A^\odot$ with $E \subset (\sim)$, we have
$$(\forall \langle q,r\rangle \in E :: \mathbf{body}^\odot.q \sim \mathbf{body}^\odot.r) .$$
Then $q \cong r$ for all pairs $\langle q,r\rangle \in E$.

It is easy to see that the Induction Rule follows from the combination of (5) and (6). The combination of (5) and (6) is methodologically more convenient than the Induction Rule, for it allows us to accumulate knowledge concerning '$\approx$' that can be used in subsequent investigations. On the other hand, the accumulation rule becomes invalid if relation ($\approx$) is replaced by ($\cong$), see exercise 11.3.3. (End of remark)

Example. Let c, q, $r \in S^{\odot}$ be commands. Let procedures g and $h \in H$ be declared by

$$\begin{array}{lcl} \mathbf{body}.g & = & (q; g \parallel c; r) \ , \\ \mathbf{body}.h & = & (q; h \parallel c) \ . \end{array}$$

Then we have $g \approx h; r$. This is proved by means of rule (6) with $E = \{\langle g \, , \, h; r \rangle\}$. In fact, by Theorem (4)(a,d), commands g and $(h; r)$ are elements of *Lia*. Moreover,

$$\begin{array}{ll} & \mathbf{abort}^{\odot}.g \ \cong \ \mathbf{abort}^{\odot}.(h; r) \\ \equiv & \{\text{definition of } \mathbf{abort}\} \\ & abort \ \cong \ abort; r \\ \equiv & \{1(14)\} \\ & \text{true.} \end{array}$$

Finally, let $\sim$ be a congruence such that $E \subset (\sim)$, that is $g \sim h; r$. Then

$$\begin{array}{ll} & \mathbf{body}^{\odot}.(h; r) \\ = & \{\text{declaration } h\} \\ & (q; h \parallel c); r \\ = & \{\text{distributivity}\} \\ & q; h; r \parallel c; r \\ \sim & \{\text{assumption; } \sim \text{ is a congruence}\} \\ & q; g \parallel c; r \\ = & \{\text{declaration } g\} \\ & \mathbf{body}^{\odot}.g \ . \end{array}$$

Therefore, accumulation rule (6) implies that $E \subset (\approx)$, that is $g \approx h; r$. By rule (5), it follows that $g \cong h; r$.

This example goes back to [de Bakker-de Roever 1973] Lemma 4.4, where equivalence for *wlp* is proved in the case $c = \varepsilon$. We do not know whether, alternatively, Theorem 10(2) is strong enough to prove that $g \cong h; r$. (End of example)

The theory of this section is usually described as computational induction. With respect to classical forms of computational induction, cf. [de Bakker 1980] 7.11 and [Manna 1974] 5.5, the main difference is the condition in rule (6) that $q, r \in$ *Lia*. Classical forms of computational induction have the condition that all commands involved are deterministic or at most finitely nondeterminate. Our condition $q, r \in Lia$ is much weaker. If conjunct $q, r \in Lia$ is omitted from rule (6), the rule is no longer valid. This is shown in Section 11.7 below.

11.4 Semantic default rules

Rules (5) and (6) can be used to prove some important additional rules. For example, we have

(7) $$(\forall q, r \in S^{\odot} :: q \approx r \quad \equiv \quad q \cong r) .$$

This equivalence is proved by mutual implication. Formula (5) yields '$\Rightarrow$'. For the other implication, we use rule (6) with for E the set of the pairs $\langle q, r\rangle$ with $q, r \in S^{\odot}$ and $q \cong r$. By (4) and 10(0), every $q \in S^{\odot}$ satisfies $\mathbf{body}^{\odot}.q = q$ and $\mathbf{abort}^{\odot}.q = q$ and $q \in Lia$. Now the condition of rule (6) is easily verified, so that $E \subset (\approx)$. This concludes the proof of (7). By a similar verification one can prove

(8) **Corollary**. For every $q \in A^{\odot}$:

$$miracle; q \approx miracle \quad , \quad abort; q \approx abort \quad ,$$
$$skip; q \approx q \quad , \quad q; skip \approx q \quad , \quad q \,[\!]\, miracle \approx q \, .$$

11.5 An application: the storage of a parameter

We now have enough material for an application. Some other applications are given in [Hesselink 1989a] and [Hesselink 1990] Sections 6 and 7. The present application was suggested by the result of Section 9.2. There, general recursion was implemented by means of one tail–recursive procedure with an input parameter. The next step is to implement an input parameter of a tail–recursive procedure by means of a memory location.

A procedure with an input parameter is formalized as a family of procedures indexed by the parameter. So, we let $(i \in I :: h.i)$ be a nonempty family of procedures in H declared by

$$\mathbf{body}.(h.i) \quad = \quad q.i \,[\!]\, (\,[\!]\, j \in I :: r.i.j; h.j) \, ,$$

where $q.i$ and $r.i.j$ are element of $S^{\odot}$. Our purpose is to replace the parameter i by a memory location. Therefore, we assume that there is a program variable $\mathtt{y}$ of type I which is independent of the commands $q.i$ and $r.i.j$. Family $(i :: h.i)$ is now replaced by the family $(i :: h1.i)$ declared by

(9) $$\mathbf{body}.(h1.i) \quad = \quad (\mathtt{y} := i); (q.i \,[\!]\, (\,[\!]\, j \in I :: r.i.j; h1.j)) \, .$$

Here the only change is that program variable y holds the parameter value of the latest call of $h1$. The formalisation of this statement is left to the reader. We want to implement $h1$ by means of the parameterless tail–recursive procedure $g \in H$ declared by

(10) $\quad \mathbf{body}.g \;=\; (\,[\!]\, i \in I :: ?(\mathrm{y} = i); (q.i \,[\!]\, (\,[\!]\, j \in I :: r.i.j; \mathrm{y} := j; g)))\,.$

We claim that for all $i \in I$:

(11) $\quad h1.i \;\cong\; (\mathrm{y} := i; g)\,.$

This can be proved as follows. We apply the accumulation rule (6) to the set E of the pairs $\langle h1.i, (\mathrm{y} := i; g)\rangle$ with $i \in I$. For every $i \in I$ we have

$$\begin{array}{ll} & \mathbf{abort}^{\odot}.(h1.i) \;\cong\; \mathbf{abort}^{\odot}.(\mathrm{y} := i; g) \\ \equiv & \{(0)\} \\ & abort \;\cong\; \mathrm{y} := i; abort \\ \equiv & \{\mathrm{y} := i \text{ is total}\} \\ & \text{true.} \end{array}$$

It follows from Theorem (4) that the three commands $h1.i$ and $\mathrm{y} := i$ and g are elements of *Lia*. Since $\mathrm{y} := i$ is a deterministic simple command, it is element of *Sy.Muc*. Therefore, $(\mathrm{y} := i; g) \in Lia$ by Theorem (4)(d). Let $\sim$ be a congruence on $A^{\odot}$ with $E \cup (\approx) \subset (\sim)$. For any i, we have

$$\begin{array}{ll} & \mathbf{body}^{\odot}.(\mathrm{y} := i; g) \\ = & \{10(0), (10)\} \\ & \mathrm{y} := i; (\,[\!]\, k \in I :: ?(\mathrm{y} = k); (q.k \,[\!]\, (\,[\!]\, j \in I :: r.k.j; \mathrm{y} := j; g))) \\ \sim & \{E \subset (\sim) \text{ and } \sim \text{ is a congruence}\} \\ & \mathrm{y} := i; (\,[\!]\, k \in I :: ?(\mathrm{y} = k); (q.k \,[\!]\, (\,[\!]\, j \in I :: r.k.j; h1.j))) \\ = & \{\text{distributivity}\} \\ & (\,[\!]\, k \in I :: \mathrm{y} := i;\ ?(\mathrm{y} = k); (q.k \,[\!]\, (\,[\!]\, j \in I :: r.k.j; h1.j))) \\ \sim & \{\text{ in } S^{\odot} \text{ we have } \mathrm{y} := i;\ ?(\mathrm{y} = i) \cong \mathrm{y} := i \text{ and} \\ & \quad \mathrm{y} := i;\ ?(\mathrm{y} = k) \cong \mathit{miracle} \text{ if } i \neq k;\text{ use (7) and } (\approx) \subset (\sim)\} \\ & \mathrm{y} := i; (q.i \,[\!]\, (\,[\!]\, j \in I :: r.i.j; h1.j)) \\ & [\!]\, (\,[\!]\, k : k \neq i : \mathit{miracle}; (q.k \,[\!]\, (\,[\!]\, j \in I :: r.k.j; h1.j))) \\ \sim & \{(\approx) \subset (\sim), \text{(8) and (9)}\} \\ & \mathbf{body}^{\odot}.(h1.i)\,. \end{array}$$

This concludes the verification of the condition in rule (6). So the rule implies that $E \subset (\approx)$. By formula (5), this proves that $E \subset (\cong)$, thus proving formula (11).

Remark. The theory of 11.3 is not necessary for proving formula (11). An alternative proof can be given along the following lines. First, one shows that $wp.(\mathrm{y} := i; g)$

satisfies the defining equation for $wp.(h1.i)$. Since $wp.(h1.i)$ is the smallest solution of that equation, this implies $wp.(h1.i) \leq wp.(y := i; g)$. Then one shows that

$$wp.g \leq wp.(\, [\!]\, j :: ?(y = j); h1.j)$$

by proving that the righthand side satisfies the defining equation for the lefthand side. As a third step, one verifies that

$$wp.(y := i; (\, [\!]\, j :: ?(y = j); h1.j)) \;\leq\; wp.(h1.i) \;.$$

An inclusion argument then yields

$$wp.(h1.i) \quad = \quad wp.(y := i; g) \;.$$

The proof for *wlp* is analogous. This proves (11). If the theory of Section 11.3 is available, the above proof of (11) is definitely shorter. (End of remark)

11.6 Compositionality of the strong congruence

Compositionality of '$\approx$' with respect to recursive declarations is the following property. Let $H0$ and $H1$ be disjoint sets of procedure names, which are coupled by means of a function $f \in H1 \rightarrow H0$. Write $A0 = S \cup H0$ and $A1 = S \cup H1$. Let $f^{\odot}$ be the induced function $A1^{\odot} \rightarrow A0^{\odot}$. Let the declaration function $\mathbf{body} \in H0 \rightarrow A0^{\odot}$ and $\mathbf{body} \in H1 \rightarrow A1^{\odot}$ be such that $f^{\odot}.(\mathbf{body}.h) \approx \mathbf{body}.(f.h)$ for all $h \in H1$. Compositionality is the property that $h \approx f.h$ for all $h \in H1$. This is proved as follows. We form $H = H0 \cup H1$ and extend f to a function $H \rightarrow H$ by taking $f.h = h$ for all $h \in H0$. Now we use the following result:

(12) **Theorem.** Let $f \in H \rightarrow H$ be a function such that

(13) $\quad (\forall h \in H :: f^{\odot}.(\mathbf{body}.h) \approx \mathbf{body}.(f.h))$.

Then $h \approx f.h$ for all $h \in H$.

Proof. We apply the accumulation rule, (6), with for E the set of the pairs $\langle h, f.h \rangle$ with $h \in H$. By (0) and (4), the first condition of (6) is satisfied. If $\sim$ is a congruence on $A^{\odot}$ with $E \cup (\approx) \subset (\sim)$, then

$$
\begin{array}{ll}
 & (\forall h \in H :: \mathbf{body}^{\odot}.h \sim \mathbf{body}^{\odot}.(f.h)) \\
\equiv & \{10(0)\} \\
 & (\forall h \in H :: \mathbf{body}.h \sim \mathbf{body}.(f.h)) \\
\equiv & \{(13) \text{ and } (\approx) \subset (\sim)\} \\
 & (\forall h \in H :: \mathbf{body}.h \sim f^{\odot}.(\mathbf{body}.h)) \\
\Leftarrow & \{\text{generalisation}\} \\
 & (\forall q \in A^{\odot} :: q \sim f^{\odot}.q) \\
\equiv & \{\text{structural induction on } q\text{, using (1), (2), 10(0)}\}
\end{array}
$$

$$
\begin{array}{ll}
& (\forall h \in H :: h \sim f.h) \\
\equiv & \{E \subset (\sim)\} \\
& \text{true} .
\end{array}
$$

This proves the second condition of rule (6). Therefore $E \subset (\approx)$. (End of proof)

Remark. Theorem (12) looks very innocent, but the analogous statement with the strong congruence '$\approx$' replaced by semantic equality '$\cong$' is false. The simplest example is as follows. Let $H = \{h0, h1\}$ with the declaration

$$
\begin{array}{l}
\mathbf{body}.h0 = \mathit{skip} , \\
\mathbf{body}.h1 = h1 .
\end{array}
$$

Let $f \in H \to H$ be given by $f.h1 = h0$ and $f.h0 = h0$. Clearly, $h1 \cong \mathit{abort}$ and $h0 \cong \mathit{skip}$, so that $h1 \not\cong f.h1$. Nevertheless, formula (13) with '$\approx$' replaced by '$\cong$' is satisfied, as is shown by

$$
\begin{array}{ll}
& f^{\odot}.(\mathbf{body}.h1) \;\cong\; \mathbf{body}.(f.h1) \\
\equiv & \{\text{declaration } h1\} \\
& f^{\odot}.h1 \;\cong\; \mathbf{body}.(f.h1) \\
\equiv & \{\text{definition } f \text{ and definition } 10(0)\} \\
& h0 \;\cong\; \mathbf{body}.h0 \\
\equiv & \{\text{standard property: } 4(19)\} \\
& \text{true} ,
\end{array}
$$

and an even simpler calculation for $h0$. (End of remark)

11.7 The necessity of *Lia*

In this section we give an example to show that the condition $q, r \in \mathit{Lia}$ in rule (6) cannot be omitted. The example also shows the existence of elements $q, r \in \mathit{Lia}$ such that $q;r \notin \mathit{Lia}$. Since we have the disposal of unbounded choice, the example is somewhat easier than the analogous example in [Hesselink 1990] Section 5.6.

Let there be an integer program variable $\mathtt{i}$. Let command c be defined by

(14) $\qquad c \;=\; ([\!] \, n \in \mathbb{N} :: \mathtt{i} := n); h$

where procedure $h \in H$ is declared by

$$\mathbf{body}.h \;=\; ?(\mathtt{i} \le 0) \; [\!] \; ?(\mathtt{i} > 0); \mathtt{i} := \mathtt{i} - 1; h \; .$$

It is easy to show that command c necessarily terminates. Therefore, c is not semantically equivalent to $c \; [\!] \; \mathit{abort}$. In order to use rule (6), we observe that

(15) $\qquad \mathbf{body}^{\odot}.c$

$$= \quad \{(14)\}$$

$$
\begin{array}{cl}
& (\,\| n \in \mathbb{N} :: \mathtt{i} := n; ?(\mathtt{i} \le 0) \,\|\, \mathtt{i} := n; ?(\mathtt{i} > 0); \mathtt{i} := \mathtt{i} - 1; h) \\
\approx & \{(8),\ \text{split off } n = 0\} \\
& (\mathtt{i} := 0 \,\|\, \mathit{miracle}; \mathtt{i} := \mathtt{i} - 1; h) \,\|\, (\,\| n : n > 0 : \mathit{miracle} \,\|\, \mathtt{i} := n - 1; h) \\
\approx & \{(8),\ \text{renaming}\} \\
& \mathtt{i} := 0 \,\|\, (\,\| n \in \mathbb{N} :: \mathtt{i} := n; h) \\
= & \{(14),\ \text{distributivity}\} \\
& \mathtt{i} := 0 \,\|\, c\ .
\end{array}
$$

We now apply rule (6) to the set E that consists of the pair $\langle c, c \,\|\, \mathit{abort}\rangle$. For every congruence $\sim$ on $A^{\odot}$ with $E \cup (\approx) \subset (\sim)$, we have

$$
\begin{array}{cl}
& \mathbf{body}^{\odot}.c \quad \sim \quad \mathbf{body}^{\odot}.(c \,\|\, \mathit{abort}) \\
\equiv & \{(15),\ (\approx) \subset (\sim)\} \\
& (\mathtt{i} := 0 \,\|\, c) \quad \sim \quad (\mathtt{i} := 0 \,\|\, c \,\|\, \mathit{abort}) \\
\equiv & \{E \subset (\sim)\} \\
& \text{true.}
\end{array}
$$

On the other hand, it is easy to verify that

$$\mathbf{abort}^{\odot}.c \quad \cong \quad \mathbf{abort}^{\odot}.(c \,\|\, \mathit{abort})\ .$$

Since c is not semantically equivalent to $c \,\|\, \mathit{abort}$, rule (5) implies that $E \not\subset (\approx)$. Therefore, it follows from rule (6), that $c \notin \mathit{Lia}$ or $(c \,\|\, \mathit{abort}) \notin \mathit{Lia}$. By Theorem (4), we have $\mathit{abort} \in \mathit{Lia}$, and hence $c \notin \mathit{Lia}$. Notice that $c = c0; h$ where $c0 = (\,\| n \in \mathbb{N} :: \mathtt{i} := n)$. By Theorem (4), both $c0$ and h are elements of Lia.

11.8 Exercises

Exercises of Section 11.1.

Exercise 0. Prove that the equalizer $Eq.w$ of a homomorphism $w \in A^{\odot} \to MT$ is a congruence.

Exercises of Section 11.3.

Exercise 0. Let commands s, $c \in S^{\odot}$ and predicate $b \in \mathbb{P}$ be such that (cf. formulae 5(5) and 5(6)):

$$
\begin{array}{l}
s; c \quad \cong \quad c; s\ , \\
s; ?b \quad \cong \quad ?b; s \quad \wedge \quad s; ?\neg b \quad \cong \quad ?\neg b; s\ .
\end{array}
$$

Assume that command s is total and finitely nondeterminate. Let $L \in H$ be declared by

$$\mathbf{body}.L \quad = \quad (?\neg b \,\|\, ?b; c; L)\ .$$

Prove that $s; L \cong L; s$, cf. formula 5(7).

Exercise 1. ♡ Let I be a monoid, i.e. a set with an associative binary operator '$*$' with a neutral element 1. Let v be a program variable of type I. Let c and $d.i$, $i \in I$, be commands in $S^{\odot}$ such that for all i, $k \in I$

$$c; \mathtt{v} := k \;\cong\; \mathtt{v} := k; c \;,$$
$$d.i; \mathtt{v} := k \;\cong\; \mathtt{v} := k; d.i \;.$$

Let procedures g, $h \in H$ be declared by

$$\mathbf{body}.g \;=\; c; \mathtt{v} := 1 \;[\!]\; (\;[\!]\; i \in I :: d.i; g; \mathtt{v} := i * \mathtt{v}) \;,$$
$$\mathbf{body}.h \;=\; c \;[\!]\; (\;[\!]\; i \in I :: d.i; \mathtt{v} := \mathtt{v} * i; h) \;.$$

Prove that for all $k \in I$

$$g; \mathtt{v} := k * \mathtt{v} \;\cong\; \mathtt{v} := k; h \;.$$

Exercise 2. Let q be a rational program variable and let **s** be a program variable for sequences of integers. In exercise 2.5.4, procedure g was declared by

$$\mathbf{body}.g \;=\;$$
$$(\;?(\mathtt{q} = 0)\;;\; \mathtt{s} := \varepsilon$$
$$[\!]\; ?(\mathtt{q} \neq 0)\;;\; (\,[\!]\, j :: ?(\tfrac{1}{j+1} < \mathtt{q} \le \tfrac{1}{j})\;;\; \mathtt{q} := \tfrac{1}{j} - \mathtt{q}\;;\; g\;;\; \mathtt{s} := (j; \mathtt{s})))\;,$$

where j ranges over the positive integers. Use the previous exercise to obtain a repetition L with $g \cong (\mathtt{s} := \varepsilon\;;\; L)$.

Exercise 3. In the accumulation rule (6), the conjunct $\mathbf{abort}^{\odot}.q \cong \mathbf{abort}^{\odot}.r$ cannot be omitted. Prove this by taking $E = \{\langle h, skip\rangle\}$ where $h \in H$ is declared by $\mathbf{body}.h = h$.

Exercise 4. ♡ Consider the following variation of the Induction Rule:

Invalid Rule. Let E is a binary relation on $A^{\odot}$ such that

$$(\forall \langle q, r\rangle \in E :: \mathbf{abort}^{\odot}.q \cong \mathbf{abort}^{\odot}.r \quad\wedge\quad q, r \in Lia)$$

and that, for every congruence $\sim$ on $A^{\odot}$ with $E \cup (\cong) \subset (\sim)$, we have

$$(\forall \langle q, r\rangle \in E :: \mathbf{body}^{\odot}.q \sim \mathbf{body}^{\odot}.r) \;.$$

Then $q \cong r$ for all pairs $\langle q, r\rangle \in E$.

Show that this rule is not valid, by considering $E = \{\langle L, M\rangle\}$ with L and M declared by

$$\mathbf{body}.L \;=\; ?\neg b \;[\!]\; ?b\;;\; c\;;\; L\;,$$
$$\mathbf{body}.M \;=\; ?\neg b \;[\!]\; ?b\;;\; M\;,$$

say with $b = (\mathtt{i} \neq 0)$ and $c = (\mathtt{i} := \mathtt{i} - 1)$ for an integer program variable i.

Exercises of Section 11.4.

Exercise 0. Prove corollary (8).

Exercise 1. Let a predicate b and commands s, $t \in S^{\odot}$ be given such that

$$?b; s \cong s; ?b \quad \wedge \quad ?\neg b; s \cong s; ?\neg b \,.$$

Let repetitions $L0$ and $L1$ in H be given by

$L0$: **while** b **do** $s; t$ **od**

$L1$: **while** b **do** $t; s$ **od** .

Prove that $s; L1 \cong L0; s$. (One can apply the results of the examples in 10.3 and 11.3, but there may be easier solutions.)

CHAPTER 12

INDUCTION AND REFINEMENT

12.0. Refinement is defined by regarding a command q as being refined by a command r if r satisfies all Hoare–triple specifications of q, see Section 5.1. In practice, we are often more interested in refinement than in semantic equality, but the theory presented in Section 11.3 is not convenient for proving refinement relations. Therefore, we develop a slightly stronger theory, which is adequate for both refinements and semantic equalities. In this theory the rôle of congruences is taken over by 'admissible preorders'.

The most important admissible preorder will be the refinement relation introduced in Section 5.1. Recall from definition 5(0) that a command d is a refinement of c (notation $c \sqsubseteq d$) if and only if it satisfies every Hoare–triple specification of c:

$$\begin{aligned} & c \sqsubseteq d \;\; \equiv \\ & \quad (\forall p, q :: (\{p\}\ c\ \{q\} \;\Rightarrow\; \{p\}\ d\ \{q\}\ ) \\ & \quad \wedge \;\; (p\ \{c\}\ q \Rightarrow p\ \{d\}\ q)) \ , \end{aligned}$$

or equivalently (by 5(1))

(0) $\qquad c \sqsubseteq d \;\equiv\; (wp.c \leq wp.d) \wedge (wlp.c \leq wlp.d)$.

Here, relation '$\leq$' is the induced order on MT, cf. Section 4.1.

12.1 Admissible preorders

Recall that a *preorder* is a reflexive and transitive binary relation. We define a preorder '$\triangleleft$' on the set $A^{\odot}$ of commands to be *admissible* if and only if

(1) for all q, r, s, t we have: $q \triangleleft r \wedge s \triangleleft t \;\Rightarrow\; q;s \triangleleft r;t$,

(2) for every nonempty set I and every pair of families $(i \in I :: c.i)$ and $(i \in I :: d.i)$ in $A^{\odot}$:

$$(\forall i \in i :: c.i \triangleleft d.i) \;\Rightarrow\; (\,[\!]\, i :: c.i) \triangleleft (\,[\!]\, i :: d.i)\ .$$

If $w \in A^{\odot} \rightarrow MT$ is a homomorphism, the 'less–than–equalizer' $Leq.w$ is defined as the binary relation on $A^{\odot}$ given by

(3) $\langle q, r\rangle \in Leq.w \quad \equiv \quad w.q \leq w.r$.

Since '$\leq$' is a partial order on MT, relation $Leq.w$ is a preorder on $A^{\odot}$. Actually, it is an admissible preorder. This is proved as follows. Condition (1) is verified in

$$\begin{array}{l} \langle q; s\,,\, r; t\rangle \in Leq.w \\ \equiv \quad \{(3) \text{ and } w \text{ is a homomorphism}\} \\ w.q \circ w.s \leq w.r \circ w.t \\ \Leftarrow \quad \{\text{Theorem 4(7)(c) and (3)}\} \\ \langle q, r\rangle \in Leq.w \quad \wedge \quad \langle s, t\rangle \in Leq.w \ . \end{array}$$

The verification of condition (2) is straightforward.

The intersection of a family of admissible preorders is an admissible preorder. In particular, the intersection of $Leq.wp$ and $Leq.wlp$ is an admissible preorder. This preorder is the refinement preorder '$\sqsubseteq$' of formula (0).

12.2 The strong preorder

In this section we announce the existence and properties of a particular preorder '$\ll$', which is called the *strong preorder*. The strong preorder is constructed in Section 13.3 below. Its main properties are analogous to the properties of the strong congruence, cf. Section 11.3, and are proved in Sections 13.3 up to 13.6. They are as follows.

(4) **Semantic Rule.** $(\forall q, r \in A^{\odot} : q \ll r : q \sqsubseteq r)$.

(5) **Accumulation Rule.** Let E be a binary relation on $A^{\odot}$ such that

$$(\forall \langle q, r\rangle \in E :: \mathbf{abort}^{\odot}.q \sqsubseteq \mathbf{abort}^{\odot}.r \quad \wedge \quad q \in Lia)$$

and that for every admissible preorder $\lhd$ on $A^{\odot}$ with $E \cup (\ll) \subset (\lhd)$ we have

$$(\forall \langle q, r\rangle \in E :: \mathbf{body}^{\odot}.q \lhd \mathbf{body}^{\odot}.r) \ .$$

Then $q \ll r$ for all pairs $\langle q, r\rangle \in E$.

By the same arguments as used to prove formula 11(7), one can easily prove that relation '$\ll$' coincides with '$\sqsubseteq$' on the set $S^{\odot}$ of lower-level commands, that is

(6) $(\forall q, r \in S^{\odot} :: \ q \ll r \equiv q \sqsubseteq r)$.

12.3 Construction of the strong congruence

In this section we use the strong preorder postulated above to construct the strong congruence of Section 11.3. We first observe that a straightforward verification shows

(7) **Lemma.** Let '$\triangleleft$' be an admissible preorder. Let relation '$\sim$' be given by

$$q \sim r \quad \equiv \quad q \triangleleft r \land r \triangleleft q \qquad \text{for all } q, r \ .$$

Then '$\sim$' is a congruence.

Using Lemma (7), we define the *strong congruence* as the congruence given by

(8) $$q \approx r \quad \equiv \quad q \ll r \land r \ll q \quad \text{for all } q, r \ .$$

Formula 11(5) is an immediate consequence of the formulae (4) and (0). The accumulation rule 11(6) is proved in

(9) **Theorem.** Let E be a binary relation on $A^{\odot}$ such that

(10) $$(\forall \langle q, r\rangle \in E :: \mathbf{abort}^{\odot}.q \cong \mathbf{abort}^{\odot}.r \quad \land \quad q, r \in \mathit{Lia})$$

and that for every congruence $\sim$ on $A^{\odot}$ with $E \cup (\approx) \subset (\sim)$ we have

(11) $$(\forall \langle q, r\rangle \in E :: \mathbf{body}^{\odot}.q \sim \mathbf{body}^{\odot}.r) \ .$$

Then $E \subset (\approx)$.

Proof. Let $E1$ be the smallest symmetric relation that contains E, so that

$$\langle q, r\rangle \in E1 \quad \equiv \quad \langle q, r\rangle \in E \lor \langle r, q\rangle \in E \ .$$

By an easy calculation it follows from formula (8) that

(12) $$E \subset (\approx) \quad \equiv \quad E1 \subset (\ll) \ .$$

Therefore, we apply the accumulation rule (5) to relation $E1$. The first condition of (5) on $E1$ follows from condition (10). In order to verify the second condition of (5), let '$\triangleleft$' be an admissible preorder on $A^{\odot}$ with

(13) $$E1 \cup (\ll) \subset (\triangleleft) \ .$$

Let '$\sim$' be the congruence (cf. Lemma (7)) given by

$$q \sim r \quad \equiv \quad q \triangleleft r \land r \triangleleft q \quad \text{for all } q, r \ .$$

Then we have

$$\begin{aligned}
& E1 \cup (\approx) \subset (\sim) \\
\equiv \quad & \{\text{calculus}\} \\
& E1 \subset (\sim) \quad \land \quad (\approx) \subset (\sim) \\
\Leftarrow \quad & \{E1 \text{ is symmetric, definitions} \approx \text{and} \sim\} \\
& E1 \subset (\triangleleft) \quad \land \quad (\ll) \subset (\triangleleft) \\
\equiv \quad & \{(13)\} \\
& \text{true.}
\end{aligned}$$

By assumption this implies condition (11):

$$(\forall \langle q, r\rangle \in E1 :: \mathbf{body}^{\odot}.q \sim \mathbf{body}^{\odot}.r) \ ,$$

and hence, by the definition of '$\sim$',

$$(\forall \langle q, r\rangle \in E1 :: \mathbf{body}^{\odot}.q \triangleleft \mathbf{body}^{\odot}.r) \ .$$

By the accumulation rule (5), this proves $E1 \subset (\ll)$. Now we conclude with formula (12). (End of proof)

12.4 Commutation up to refinement

Commutation is the phenomenon that the sequential composition of two commands is semantically independent of the order of the commands. So, for a command s, we are interested in the set of commands q with $q;s \cong s;q$. Sometimes this requirement is too strong. Then the question can be separated into two questions: $q;s \sqsubseteq s;q$ and $s;q \sqsubseteq q;s$. Condition $q;s \sqsubseteq s;q$ means that in every program $s;q$ can be replaced by $q;s$. Similarly, $s;q \sqsubseteq q;s$ means that $q;s$ can be replaced by $s;q$. By rule (5), the questions $q;s \sqsubseteq s;q$ and $s;q \sqsubseteq q;s$ can be replaced by $q;s \ll s;q$ and $s;q \ll q;s$. In order to deal with these questions, we need the following definitions.

Let a subset U of $A^{\odot}$ be called a *subalgebra* if and only if

- if $q, r \in U$ then $(q;r) \in U$,
- if V is a nonempty subset of U then $(\,[\!]\, q \in V :: q) \in U$.

It is easy to see that every intersection of subalgebras is a subalgebra. Therefore, if T is a subset of $A^{\odot}$, the intersection of all subalgebras that contain T is a subalgebra and hence the smallest subalgebra that contains T. This allows us to define the subalgebra generated by T (notation $gen.T$) to be the smallest subalgebra that contains T.

If s is a given command and '$\triangleleft$' is an admissible preorder, the set of commands q with $q;s \triangleleft s;q$ is easily seen to be a subalgebra. It follows that for any set U of commands

(14) $\quad (\forall q \in U :: q;s \triangleleft s;q)$
$\quad\quad \equiv \quad (\forall q \in gen.U :: q;s \triangleleft s;q)\ .$

Now the first part of the above question is dealt with in

(15) **Theorem.** Let $s \in S^{\odot}$. Define T to be the subset of $A^{\odot}$ given by

(16) $\quad q \in T \quad \equiv \quad q \in S^{\odot} \quad \wedge \quad q;s \sqsubseteq s;q\ .$

Let K be a subset of H such that

(17) $\quad (\forall h \in K :: \mathbf{body}.h \in gen.(T \cup K))\ .$

Then $q;s \ll s;q$ for all $q \in gen.(T \cup K)$.

Proof. By formula (14), it suffices to prove that $q;s \ll s;q$ for all $q \in T \cup K$. By (16) and (6), we have $q;s \ll s;q$ for all $q \in T$. So it remains to prove $q;s \ll s;q$

for all $q \in K$. Therefore, we use the accumulation rule (5) with for E the set of the pairs

$$\langle h; s\ ,\ s; h\rangle \qquad \text{with } h \in K\ .$$

We first observe that $(h; s) \in \mathit{Lia}$ for all $h \in K$, by Theorem 11(4). Now, the rest of the first condition of rule (5) is verified in

$$\begin{array}{ll} & \mathbf{abort}^{\odot}.(h; s) \sqsubseteq \mathbf{abort}^{\odot}.(s; h) \\ \equiv & \{\text{definition } \mathbf{abort}^{\odot}\} \\ & \mathit{abort}; s \sqsubseteq s; \mathit{abort} \\ \equiv & \{\text{definitions in Chapter 1}\} \\ & (\forall p \in \mathbb{P} :: [\mathit{false} \Rightarrow \mathit{wp}.s.\mathit{false}] \wedge [\mathit{true} \Rightarrow \mathit{wlp}.s.\mathit{true}]) \\ \equiv & \{\text{calculus and 3(5)}\} \\ & \text{true}\ . \end{array}$$

For the second condition of rule (5), it suffices to verify that for every admissible preorder $\triangleleft$ with $E \cup (\ll) \subset (\triangleleft)$ and any $h \in K$ we have

$$\begin{array}{ll} & \mathbf{body}^{\odot}.(h; s) \triangleleft \mathbf{body}^{\odot}.(s; h) \\ \equiv & \{\text{definition}\} \\ & \mathbf{body}.h; s \triangleleft s; \mathbf{body}.h \\ \Leftarrow & \{(17)\} \\ & (\forall q \in \mathit{gen}.(T \cup K) :: q; s \triangleleft s; q) \\ \Leftarrow & \{(14)\} \\ & (\forall q \in T \cup K :: q; s \triangleleft s; q) \\ \equiv & \{(6), (16) \text{ and assumption on } \triangleleft\} \\ & \text{true}\ . \end{array}$$

(End of proof)

Example. Let commands s, q, r, $t \in S^{\odot}$ be such that

$$q; s \sqsubseteq s; q \quad \wedge \quad r; s \sqsubseteq s; r \quad \wedge \quad t; s \sqsubseteq s; t\ .$$

Let procedure $h \in H$ be declared by

$$\mathbf{body}.h \quad = \quad (q \,\|\, r; h; t)\ .$$

Then $h; s \sqsubseteq s; h$. In fact, we clearly have q, r, $t \in T$ and hence

$$\mathbf{body}.h \in \mathit{gen}.(T \cup \{h\})\ .$$

(End of example)

In the other case, the result is less satisfactory, for we have to impose extra conditions on command s.

(18) **Theorem.** Let $s \in S^{\odot}$ be total and finitely nondeterminate. Define U to be the subset of $A^{\odot}$ given by

(19) $\quad q \in U \;\equiv\; q \in S^{\odot} \;\wedge\; s;q \sqsubseteq q;s\,.$

Let K be a subset of H such that $\mathbf{body}.h \in gen.(U \cup K))$ for all $h \in K$. Then $s;q \ll q;s$ for all $q \in gen.(U \cup K)$.

Proof. We use the same method as in the previous proof. Again, it suffices to prove that $s;q \ll q;s$ for all $q \in K$. Let E be the set of the pairs

$$\langle s;h\,,\ h;s\rangle \qquad \text{with } h \in K\,.$$

Since s is finitely nondeterminate and element of $S^{\odot}$, we have $(s;h) \in Lia$ for all $h \in K$, by Theorem 11(4). The rest of the first condition of rule (5) is verified in

$$\begin{array}{ll} & \mathbf{abort}^{\odot}.(s;h) \sqsubseteq \mathbf{abort}^{\odot}.(h;s) \\ \equiv & \{\text{definition } \mathbf{abort}^{\odot}\} \\ & s;abort \sqsubseteq abort;s \\ \equiv & \{1(10)\} \\ & (\forall p \in \mathbb{P} :: [\,wp.s.false \Rightarrow false] \wedge [\,wlp.s.true \Rightarrow true]) \\ \equiv & \{s \text{ is total and calculus}\} \\ & \text{true}\,. \end{array}$$

The second condition of rule (5) is verified in the same way as in the previous proof. Now the assertion follows from rule (5). (End of proof)

Remark. In Theorem (18), the extra conditions on s are essential. It is easy to see that totality of s cannot be omitted, see the exercises. The next example shows that finite nondeterminacy of s cannot be omitted. (End of remark)

Example. Let v be an integer program variable. Let command s be given as in the example of 5.4, so that

$$s \;=\; (?(\mathrm{v} \geq 0) \;[\!]\; ?(\mathrm{v} < 0); (\;[\!]\; m : m > 0 : \mathrm{v} := m))\,.$$

Clearly, command s is total but not finitely nondeterminate. We may assume that $s \in S^{\odot}$. Let T and U be given by formulae (16) and (19). We consider predicate $b = (\mathrm{v} \neq 0)$ and commands $?b$, $?\neg b$, and

$$c \;=\; (?(\mathrm{v} < 0) \;[\!]\; ?(\mathrm{v} \leq 0); \mathrm{v} := 0 \;[\!]\; ?(\mathrm{v} > 0); \mathrm{v} := \mathrm{v} - 1)\,.$$

As verified in the example of Section 5.4, the commands c, $?b$ and $?\neg b$ are element of $T \cap U$. Let repetition L be declared by

$$\mathbf{body}.L \;=\; (?\neg b \;[\!]\; ?b; c; L)\,.$$

Then we have

$$\mathbf{body}.L \in gen.((T \cap U) \cup \{L\})\,.$$

By Theorem (15), it follows that $L; s \sqsubseteq s; L$. In Section 5.4, we proved that $\neg(s; L \sqsubseteq L; s)$. Therefore, in Theorem (18), we cannot omit the assumption that s be finitely nondeterminate. (End of example)

12.5 Exercises

Exercises of Section 12.4.

Exercise 0. Let $b \in \mathbb{P}$ and $c,\ s \in S^{\odot}$ be such that $c; s \sqsubseteq s; c$ and that

$$[b \Rightarrow wp.s.b] \ \wedge \ [\neg b \Rightarrow wp.s.(\neg b)] \ .$$

Prove that $L =$ **while** b **do** c **od** satisfies $L; s \sqsubseteq s; L$. Compare Section 5.4 and the exercises 5.1.4 and 11.3.0.

Exercise 1. Show that in Theorem (18) totality of s cannot be omitted, in the following way. Put $s = ?\mathit{false}$.

(a) Prove that $s; q \sqsubseteq q; s$ if and only if q is always terminating.

(b) Let U be given by formula (19). Give a declaration of a procedure h such that **body**.$h \in gen.(U \cup \{h\})$ and that $\neg(s; q \sqsubseteq q; s)$, and hence $\neg(s; q \ll q; s)$.

CHAPTER 13

THE STRONG PREORDER

13.0. In this chapter we fulfil the remaining proof obligations of Chapter 12. Section 13.1 contains a strengthened version of Theorem 4(8), our version of the theorem of Knaster–Tarski. In Section 13.2, we provide the basic set–up, in which we need not yet distinguish between *wp* and *wlp*. Section 13.3 contains the construction of the strong preorder and the proofs of rule 12(4) and a variation of rule 12(5). In this way, the proof of the accumulation rule 12(5) is reduced to the verification of two technical conditions: sup–safety (for *wp*) and inf–safety (for *wlp*). These conditions comprise the base case of the induction and a continuity property.

In Section 13.4, the base case is reduced to a condition on function $\mathbf{abort}^{\odot}$. Section 13.5 contains the proof for inf–safety. Section 13.6 contains the definition of the set *Lia* and the proof for sup–safety. In Sections 13.7 and 13.8 we justify the rules for *Lia* stated in Section 11.2.

It may seem unsatisfactory that, in the presence of unbounded nondeterminacy, computational induction needs such a complicated theory. The examples in Sections 11.7 and 12.4, however, show that the accumulation rules 11(6) and 12(5) need their complicated conditions. Therefore, corresponding complications must occur in the construction or in the proofs.

13.1 Intermezzo: an extension of the theorem of Knaster–Tarski

Recall from Section 7.2, that a subset L of a complete lattice W is called a *chain* if and only if

$$(\forall x, y \in L :: x \leq y \vee y \leq x) .$$

A subset V of W is called *sup–decked* if and only if $(\sup L) \in V$ for every chain L in V. Similarly, V is called *inf–decked* if and only if $(\inf L) \in V$ for every chain L in V. Notice that every sup–closed subset of W is sup–decked, but not vice versa, and similarly for inf–closed and inf–decked.

Example of decked and closed sets. Let W be the set of the subsets of the plane $\mathbb{R}^2$, ordered by inclusion. Now, suprema are unions and infima are intersections. An element $w \in W$, i.e. a subset w of $\mathbb{R}^2$, is called *convex* if and only if, for every two points $x, y \in w$, the line segment from x to y is contained in w. Let V be the subset of W that consists of the convex elements of W. Now, V is inf–closed in W and sup–decked, but not sup–closed: in fact, any intersection of convex sets is convex, any union of a chain of convex sets is convex, but an arbitrary union of (say two) convex sets need not be convex. (End of example)

We need the following version of the theorem of Knaster–Tarski, which extends Theorem 4(8).

(0) **Theorem.** Let W be a complete lattice and let $D : W \to W$ be a monotone function. Let V be a subset of W that is D–invariant, i.e. $(\forall v \in V :: D.v \in V)$.
(a) If V is sup–decked then V contains the least fixpoint of D.
(b) If V is inf–decked then V contains the greatest fixpoint of D.

Proof. A self–contained proof falls outside the scope of this book. In [Hesselink 1990] Theorem 2(10), we gave a complete and elementary proof. Prompted by Jaap van der Woude, we here only provide a short proof for readers acquainted with Zorn's Lemma. In general, Zorn's Lemma (see e.g. [Gallier 1987] p. 9) implies that every sup–decked subset U of an ordered set contains a maximal element, i.e. an element $u \in U$ with $(\forall x \in U : u \le x : u = x)$. By symmetry, every inf–decked subset contains a minimal element.

By symmetry, it suffices to treat case (a). So let V be sup–decked and D–invariant. Let P and Q be the subsets of W given by

$$x \in P \ \equiv\ x \le D.x \ ,$$
$$x \in Q \ \equiv\ (\forall y \in W : D.y = y : x \le y) \ .$$

It is easy to see that the sets P and Q, and hence $V \cap P \cap Q$, are sup–decked. Now Zorn's Lemma implies that $V \cap P \cap Q$ contains a maximal element, say wa. The intersection $V \cap P \cap Q$ is D–invariant, since for every $x \in W$

$$
\begin{array}{ll}
 & D.x \in V \cap P \cap Q \\
\equiv & \{\text{definitions}\} \\
 & D.x \in V \ \wedge\ D.x \le D.(D.x) \ \wedge\ (\forall y \in W : D.y = y : D.x \le y) \\
\Leftarrow & \{V \text{ is } D\text{–invariant; } D.y = y\} \\
 & x \in V \ \wedge\ D.x \le D.(D.x) \ \wedge\ (\forall y \in W : D.y = y : D.x \le D.y) \\
\Leftarrow & \{D \text{ is monotone}\}
\end{array}
$$

$$x \in V \quad \wedge \quad x \leq D.x \quad \wedge \quad (\forall y \in W : D.y = y : x \leq y)$$
$$\equiv \quad \{\text{definitions}\}$$
$$x \in V \cap P \cap Q \,.$$

This implies that $D.\mathrm{wa} \in V \cap P \cap Q$. Since $\mathrm{wa} \in P$ we have $\mathrm{wa} \leq D.\mathrm{wa}$. By maximality of wa, it follows that $\mathrm{wa} = D.\mathrm{wa}$, so that wa is a fixpoint of D. Since $\mathrm{wa} \in Q$, it is the least fixpoint. Since $\mathrm{wa} \in V$, this proves that V contains the least fixpoint of D. (End of proof)

13.2 Unfolding

Recall from Section 4.4, that the restriction $wp|H$ is the least fixpoint of D_0 in MT^H, and $wlp|H$ is the greatest fixpoint of D_1 in MT^H, where, for $e = 0$ or 1, the unfold operations $D_e \in MT^H \to MT^H$ are given by

(1) $\qquad D_e = w^e \circ \mathbf{body} \in H \to MT \,,$

with $w^e \in A^{\odot} \to MT$ given by $w^e = (ws_e \cup w)^{\odot}$.

We aim at fixpoint induction for the functions D_e, so we need various subsets of MT^H. It turns out that some arguments can be given uniformly for $e = 0$ and 1, whereas other arguments need a case distinction.

For $e = 0$ and 1, we define the subsets WG_e of MT^H by

(2) $\qquad WG_1 = MU^H \,,$

$\qquad WG_0 = Wp.R \,,$

where we refer to 8(3) for the definition of $Wp.R$, and where R is a sup–closed subset of MT yet to be determined.

In the choice of WG_0 we keep some freedom for tuning the result. The choice of R is postponed to Section 13.8. It will serve to ensure property 11(4)(d). Apart from the tuning of WG_0 in 13.8, all relevant properties of WG_0 and WG_1 are contained in the next lemma.

(3) **Lemma.** (a) For both $e = 0$ and 1, WG_e is a subset of MP^H. For every $w \in WG_e$, function w^e is a homomorphism $A^{\odot} \to MP$.
(b) WG_0 is D_0–invariant and sup–closed in MT^H.
(c) WG_1 is D_1–invariant and inf–closed in MT^H.

Proof. Since $MU \subset MP$ (cf. Section 4.1), we have $WG_1 \subset MP^H$. It follows from 8(3) and 4(43)(b) that $WG_0 \subset MP^H$. The second assertion of part (a) follows from Theorem 4(42). Part (b) is Theorem 8(4)(b). Part (c) is 4(28) and 4(29). (End of proof)

In order to define the strong preorder announced in Section 12.2, we investigate binary relations E on $A^{\odot}$ as considered in accumulation rule 12(5). For a binary relation E, we define the subsets $Wg_0.E$ and $Wg_1.E$ of MT^H by

(4) $\quad v \in Wg_e.E \;\equiv\; v \in WG_e \;\wedge\; E \subset Leq.v^e \quad$ where $e \in \{0,1\}$.

This definition is justified by

(5) **Lemma.** (a) If $Wg_0.E$ is sup–decked and D_0–invariant, then $wp.q \leq wp.r$ for all pairs $\langle q,r\rangle \in E$.
(b) If $Wg_1.E$ is inf–decked and D_1–invariant, then $wlp.q \leq wlp.r$ for all pairs $\langle q,r\rangle \in E$.

Proof. (a) It follows from Theorem (0) that $Wg_0.E$ contains the least fixpoint of D_0. By Section 4.4, this least fixpoint is wa_0, the restriction $wp|H$. Since $wp = \mathsf{wa}_0^0$, it follows from definition (4) that $E \subset Leq.wp$, in other words that $wp.q \leq wp.r$ for all pairs $\langle q,r\rangle \in E$.

(b) This case is proved analogously. (End of proof)

The binary relation E on $A^{\odot}$ is said to be *stable under unfolding* if and only if for every admissible preorder '$\triangleleft$' on $A^{\odot}$ we have

(6) $\quad (\forall \langle q,r\rangle \in E :: q \triangleleft r) \;\Rightarrow\; (\forall \langle q,r\rangle \in E :: \mathbf{body}^{\odot}.q \triangleleft \mathbf{body}^{\odot}.r)$.

The relevance of this condition is shown in the next lemma.

(7) **Lemma.** Let E be stable under unfolding, and $e = 0$ or 1. Then $Wg_e.E$ is D_e–invariant.

Proof. We first claim that unfolding commutes with extending in the sense that for every $w \in WG_e$

(8) $\quad (D_e.w)^e = w^e \circ \mathbf{body}^{\odot}$.

This is proved by

$$
\begin{array}{ll}
 & (D_e.w)^e \\
= & \{(1)\} \\
 & (w^e \circ \mathbf{body})^e \\
= & \{(3)(\text{a}) \text{ and } 10(1)\} \\
 & w^e \circ \mathbf{body}^{\odot} \;.
\end{array}
$$

Now it suffices to verify that for $v \in MT^H$

$$
\begin{array}{ll}
 & D_e.v \in Wg_e.E \\
\equiv & \{(4)\} \\
 & D_e.v \in WG_e \;\wedge\; E \subset Leq.(D_e.v)^e
\end{array}
$$

$\Leftarrow \quad \{(3), (8)\}$
$v \in WG_e \quad \wedge \quad E \subset Leq.(v^e \circ \mathbf{body}^{\odot})$
$\Leftarrow \quad \{E$ is stable under unfolding: (6) with $(\triangleleft) = Leq.v^e\}$
$v \in WG_e \quad \wedge \quad E \subset Leq.v^e$
$\equiv \quad \{(4)\}$
$v \in Wg_e.E$.

(End of proof)

In view of Lemmas (5) and (7), we introduce the following definitions. A relation E on commands is defined to be *sup–safe* if and only if $Wg_0.E$ is sup–decked in MT^H. It is defined to be *inf–safe* if and only if $Wg_1.E$ is inf–decked in MT^H. It is defined to be *safe* if and only if it is sup–safe and inf–safe and stable under unfolding. The above results are summarised in:

(9) **Summary.** (a) If relation E is sup–safe and stable under unfolding, we have $wp.q \leq wp.r$ for all pairs $\langle q, r\rangle \in E$.
(b) If relation E is inf–safe and stable under unfolding, then $wlp.q \leq wlp.r$ for all pairs $\langle q, r\rangle \in E$.
(c) If E is safe, then $q \sqsubseteq r$ for all pairs $\langle q, r\rangle \in E$.

13.3 The construction of the strong preorder

In this section we construct the strong preorder, postulated in Section 12.2, as the union of all safe relations.

(10) **Lemma.** Let $(i \in I :: E.i)$ be a nonempty family of relations on $A^{\odot}$.
(a) If $E.i$ is stable under unfolding for every $i \in I$, then the union $(\bigcup i :: E.i)$ is stable under unfolding.
(b) $Wg_e.(\bigcup i :: E.i) \quad = \quad (\bigcap i :: Wg_e.(E.i))$.
(c) If $E.i$ is sup–safe (inf–safe) for every $i \in I$, then $(\bigcup i :: E.i)$ is sup–safe (inf–safe).

Proof. Parts (a) and (b) are proved by direct appeal to the definitions. Part (c) follows from (b) and the observation that any intersection of sup–decked sets is sup–decked, and similarly for inf–decked sets. The details are left to the reader. (End of proof)

(11) **Lemma.** Let relation E on commands be stable under unfolding. There is a unique smallest admissible preorder that contains E. This preorder, to be called $sap.E$, is stable under unfolding and satisfies $Wg_e.(sap.E) = Wg_e.E$ for both $e = 0$ and $e = 1$.

Proof. Since an intersection of admissible preorders is an admissible preorder (see Section 12.1), the intersection of all admissible preorders that contain E is $sap.E$. In order to prove that $sap.E$ is stable under unfolding, we let $\langle q, r\rangle \in sap.E$. We have to prove $\langle \mathbf{body}^{\odot}.q, \mathbf{body}^{\odot}.r\rangle \in sap.E$. Since $sap.E$ is the intersection of all admissible preorders '$\lhd$' with $E \subset (\lhd)$, it suffices to observe, for every admissible preorder '$\lhd$':

$$\begin{array}{ll} & \mathbf{body}^{\odot}.q \lhd \mathbf{body}^{\odot}.r \\ \Leftarrow & \{\text{define } F \text{ by } \langle s,t\rangle \in F \;\equiv\; \mathbf{body}^{\odot}.s \lhd \mathbf{body}^{\odot}.t\} \\ & sap.E \subset F \\ \Leftarrow & \{\text{definition } sap.E, \text{ and } F \text{ is an admissible preorder by } 10(0)\} \\ & E \subset F \\ \equiv & \{\text{definition of } F\} \\ & (\forall \langle s,t\rangle \in E :: \mathbf{body}^{\odot}.s \lhd \mathbf{body}^{\odot}.t) \\ \Leftarrow & \{E \text{ is stable under unfolding: } (6)\} \\ & E \subset (\lhd)\ . \end{array}$$

This proves that $sap.E$ is stable under unfolding. The equality is proved by observing that for any $v \in WG_e$

$$\begin{array}{ll} & v \in Wg_e.(sap.E) \;\equiv\; v \in Wg_e.E \\ \equiv & \{(4)\} \\ & sap.E \subset Leq.v^e \;\equiv\; E \subset Leq.v^e \\ \equiv & \{Leq.v^e \text{ is an admissible preorder; definition } sap.E\} \\ & \text{true}\ . \end{array}$$

(End of proof).

The *strong preorder* $\ll$ is defined as the union of all safe relations on $A^{\odot}$. This definition is justified by

(12) **Theorem.** (a) Relation $\ll$ is safe and it is an admissible preorder.
(b) If $q \ll r$ in $A^{\odot}$ then $q \sqsubseteq r$.

Proof. (a) It follows from the definition of $\ll$ and Lemma (10)(a, c) that relation $\ll$ is safe. It follows from Lemma (11) that relation $sap.(\ll)$ is also safe, and hence equal to $(\ll)$. This proves that relation $\ll$ is an admissible preorder.

(b) This follows from part (a) and (9)(c). (End of proof)

This result proves rule 12(4). As a first step towards rule 12(5), we claim

(13) **Theorem.** Let relation E be sup–safe and inf–safe. Assume that for every admissible preorder '$\triangleleft$' on $A^{\odot}$ with $E \cup (\ll) \subset (\triangleleft)$:

$$(\forall \langle q, r\rangle \in E :: \mathbf{body}^{\odot}.q \triangleleft \mathbf{body}^{\odot}.r) .$$

Then $E \subset (\ll)$.

Proof. It follows from the assumptions, Lemma (10)(c) and Theorem (12)(a), that the union $E \cup (\ll)$ is sup–safe and inf–safe. It is easy to verify that $E \cup (\ll)$ is stable under unfolding. Therefore, $E \cup (\ll)$ is safe, and hence contained in the strong preorder $(\ll)$. (End of proof)

13.4 The abortive interpretations

Comparison of Theorem (13) with accumulation rule 12(5) tells us that it remains to prove that relation E is sup–safe and inf–safe if it satisfies

(14) $$(\forall \langle q, r\rangle \in E :: \mathbf{abort}^{\odot}.q \sqsubseteq \mathbf{abort}^{\odot}.r \quad \land \quad q \in Lia) .$$

We first concentrate on the lefthand conjuncts of condition (14). We observe

$$\begin{aligned} & (\forall \langle q, r\rangle \in E :: \mathbf{abort}^{\odot}.q \sqsubseteq \mathbf{abort}^{\odot}.r) \\ \equiv \quad & \{12(0)\} \\ & E \subset Leq.(wp \circ \mathbf{abort}^{\odot}) \quad \land \quad E \subset Leq.(wlp \circ \mathbf{abort}^{\odot}) . \end{aligned}$$

By the definitions of $\mathbf{abort}^{\odot}$ and *abort* in 10(0), 11(0) and 1(10), we have

$$\begin{aligned} wp \circ \mathbf{abort}^{\odot} &= (ws_0 \cup \bot)^{\odot} = \bot^0 , \\ wlp \circ \mathbf{abort}^{\odot} &= (ws_1 \cup \top)^{\odot} = \top^1 , \end{aligned}$$

where $\top$ and $\bot$ in MT^H are given by

$$\top.h.p = true \quad \land \quad \bot.h.p = false \qquad \text{for all } h \in H,\ p \in \mathbb{P} .$$

One verifies that $\bot = (\sup \emptyset)$ and $\top = (\inf \emptyset)$, so that $\bot \in WG_0$ and $\top \in WG_1$ by Lemma (3)(b,c). Therefore we have

(15) $$\begin{aligned} & (\forall \langle q, r\rangle \in E :: \mathbf{abort}^{\odot}.q \sqsubseteq \mathbf{abort}^{\odot}.r) \\ \equiv \quad & \{\text{above}\} \\ & E \subset Leq.(\bot^0) \quad \land \quad E \subset Leq.(\top^1) \\ \equiv \quad & \{(4)\} \\ & (\sup \emptyset) \in Wg_0.E \quad \land \quad (\inf \emptyset) \in Wg_1.E . \end{aligned}$$

In the next section we shall use this equivalence.

13.5 Inf–safety

We now attack the inf–safety of relation E. Relation E is inf–safe if and only if $Wg_0.E$ is inf–decked, i.e. $(\inf L) \in Wg_1.E$ for every chain L in $Wg_1.E$. By calculation (15), condition (14) suffices to treat the empty chain. Therefore, we may restrict our attention to nonempty chains L in $Wg_1.E$.

(16) **Lemma.** For every nonempty chain L of WG_1 and every $q \in A^{\odot}$, we have

(17) $$(\inf L)^1.q = (\inf v \in L :: v^1.q) \ .$$

Proof. We use structural induction on q. For $q \in S$, we have

$$\begin{array}{ll} & (\inf L)^1.q = (\inf v \in L :: v^1.q) \\ \equiv & \{4(25)\} \\ & wlp.q = (\inf v \in L :: wlp.q) \\ \equiv & \{L \text{ is nonempty}\} \\ & \text{true.} \end{array}$$

For $q \in H$, we have

$$\begin{array}{ll} & (\inf L)^1.q = (\inf v \in L :: v^1.q) \\ \equiv & \{4(25)\} \\ & (\inf L).q = (\inf v \in L :: v.q) \\ \equiv & \{\text{Theorem } 4(3)\} \\ & \text{true.} \end{array}$$

Since $A = S \cup H$, this proves formula (17) for $q \in A$. For $q = \varepsilon$ in A^*, we have

$$\begin{array}{ll} & (\inf L)^1.\varepsilon = (\inf v \in L :: v^1.\varepsilon) \\ \equiv & \{4(15)\} \\ & identity = (\inf v \in L :: identity) \\ \equiv & \{L \text{ is nonempty}\} \\ & \text{true.} \end{array}$$

The delicate case is the induction step in A^*. This step is taken by observing for any $a \in A$, any $s \in A^*$ and any predicate $p \in \mathbb{P}$ that

$$\begin{array}{ll} & (\inf L)^1.(a;s).p \\ = & \{\text{Lemma } (3)\} \\ & ((\inf L)^1.a \circ (\inf L)^1.s).p \\ = & \{(17) \text{ for } a \in A, \text{ induction hypothesis } (17) \text{ for } s \in A^*\} \\ & (\inf v \in L :: v^1.a).((\inf w \in L :: w^1.s).p) \\ = & \{4(6) \text{ twice}\} \\ & (\forall v \in L :: v^1.a.(\forall w \in L :: w^1.s.p)) \end{array}$$

$=$ {$v^1.a \in MP$ by Lemma (3), and 3(1)}
$(\forall v, w \in L :: v^1.a.(w^1.s.p))$
$=$ {L is a chain, diagonalisation cf. Lemma 8(17)}
$(\forall v \in L :: v^1.a.(v^1.s.p))$
$=$ {same steps as above, using (3) and 4(6)}
$(\inf v \in L :: v^1.(a; s)).p$.

This proves formula (17) for $q \in A^*$. Finally, we prove formula (17) for $q \in A^{\odot}$ in

$(\inf L)^1.q = (\inf v \in L :: v^1.q)$
$\equiv$ {4(15)}
$(\inf s \in q :: (\inf L)^1.s) = (\inf v \in L :: (\inf s \in q :: v^1.s))$
$\equiv$ {(17) for $s \in A^*$, and interchange of quantifications}
true.

(End of proof)

Now we can prove

(18) **Lemma.** Relation E is inf–safe if it satisfies condition (14).

Proof. By calculation (15), it suffices to observe that for any nonempty chain L in $Wg_1.E$ we have

$(\inf L) \in Wg_1.E$
$\equiv$ {(4); WG_1 is inf–closed by Lemma (3)}
$E \subset Leq.(\inf L)^1$
$\equiv$ {definition 12(3)}
$(\forall \langle q, r\rangle \in E :: (\inf L)^1.q \le (\inf L)^1.r)$
$\equiv$ {L nonempty, Lemma (16)}
$(\forall \langle q, r\rangle \in E :: (\inf v \in L :: v^1.q) \le (\inf v \in L :: v^1.r))$
$\Leftarrow$ {calculus}
$(\forall \langle q, r\rangle \in E :: (\forall v \in L :: v^1.q \le v^1.r))$
$\equiv$ {12(3)}
$(\forall v \in L :: E \subset Leq.v^1)$
$\Leftarrow$ {(4)}
$L \subset Wg_1.E$.

(End of proof)

13.6 Sup–safety

For the treatment of sup–safety, we need the introduction of the set *Lia*. So, here we finally give the definition announced in Section 11.2. A command $q \in A^{\odot}$ is said to be ***linearly approximating*** if and only if for every nonempty chain L in WG_0

(19) $\quad (\sup L)^0.q \;=\; (\sup v \in L :: v^0.q)$.

We write *Lia* to denote the set of the linearly approximating elements of $A^{\odot}$.

(20) **Lemma.** Relation E is sup–safe if it satisfies condition (14).

Proof. The proof is similar to the proof of Lemma (18). By calculation (15), it remains to observe that for any nonempty chain L in WG_0 we have

$$\begin{aligned}
& (\sup L) \in Wg_0.E \\
\equiv\; & \{(4);\ WG_0 \text{ is sup–closed in } MT^H \text{ by Lemma (3)}\} \\
& (\forall \langle q,r\rangle \in E :: (\sup L)^0.q \le (\sup L)^0.r) \\
\Leftarrow\; & \{E \subset Lia \times A^{\odot} \text{ so that } q \in Lia;\ (19)\} \\
& (\forall \langle q,r\rangle \in E :: (\sup v \in L :: v^0.q) \le (\sup L)^0.r) \\
\equiv\; & \{4(0)\} \\
& (\forall \langle q,r\rangle \in E, v \in L :: v^0.q \le (\sup L)^0.r) \\
\Leftarrow\; & \{\text{structural induction, monotony: } v^0.r \le (\sup L)^0.r \text{ for all } v \in L\} \\
& (\forall \langle q,r\rangle \in E, v \in L :: v^0.q \le v^0.r) \\
\Leftarrow\; & \{\text{definitions (4) and 12(3)}\} \\
& L \subset Wg_0.E \ .
\end{aligned}$$

(End of proof)

By Lemmas (18) and (20), condition (14) implies that E is inf–safe and sup–safe. By Theorem (13), this proves the accumulation rule 12(5).

13.7 Linear approximation

It remains to justify the rules of Theorem 11(4), which imply that $A^{\odot}$ contains sufficiently many linearly approximating commands. In this section we treat the parts (a), (b) and (c) of that Theorem.

We begin with the claim of part (a) of Theorem 11(4) that $H \cup S^{\odot} \subset Lia$. For any $h \in H$ and any nonempty chain L in WG_0 we observe

$$\begin{aligned}
& (\sup L)^0.h = (\sup v \in L :: v^0.h) \\
\equiv\; & \{4(25) \text{ and } h \in H\}
\end{aligned}$$

$$
\begin{array}{ll}
& (\sup L).h = (\sup v \in L :: v.h) \\
\equiv & \{4(3) \text{ applied to } L \subset MT^H\} \\
& \text{true} .
\end{array}
$$

By definition (19), this proves that $H \subset Lia$. Similarly, for any $q \in S^{\odot}$ and any nonempty chain L in WG_0 we observe

$$
\begin{array}{ll}
& (\sup L)^0.q = (\sup v \in L :: v^0.q) \\
\equiv & \{4(25) \text{ and } q \in S^{\odot}\} \\
& (wp|S)^{\odot}.q = (\sup v \in L :: (wp|S)^{\odot}.q) \\
\equiv & \{L \text{ is nonempty}\} \\
& \text{true} .
\end{array}
$$

This proves that $S^{\odot} \subset Lia$. Together with the previous inclusion this concludes the proof of Theorem 11(4)(a).

Let q, $r \in Lia$. In order to prove that $q \,[\!]\, r \in Lia$, it suffices to observe that for any nonempty chain L in WG_0 and any predicate p

$$
\begin{array}{ll}
& (\sup L)^0.(q \,[\!]\, r).p \\
= & \{(3)(a)\} \\
& (\sup L)^0.q.p \wedge (\sup L)^0.r.p \\
= & \{q,\ r \in Lia,\ (19)\} \\
& (\sup v \in L :: v^0.q).p \wedge (\sup w \in L :: w^0.r).p \\
= & \{4(6)\} \\
& (\exists\, v \in L :: v^0.q.p) \wedge (\exists\, w \in L :: w^0.r.p) \\
= & \{\text{distributivity}\} \\
& (\exists\, v, w \in L :: v^0.q.p \wedge w^0.r.p) \\
= & \{L \text{ is a chain; diagonalisation } 8(17)\} \\
& (\exists\, v \in L :: v^0.q.p \wedge v^0.r.p) \\
= & \{(3) \text{ and } 4(6)\} \\
& (\sup v \in L :: v^0.(q \,[\!]\, r)).p .
\end{array}
$$

This proves part (b) of Theorem 11(4).

We now turn to part (c), which asserts that the set Lia is closed under deterministic choice. Let $(i \in I :: q.i)$ be a family of linearly approximating commands and let f be a state function in I^X. We have to prove that $q.f$ is linearly approximating. By definition (19), it suffices to observe that for any nonempty chain L in WG_0 and every predicate $p \in \mathbb{P}$

$$
\begin{array}{ll}
& (\sup L)^0.(q.f).p \\
= & \{8(14)\} \\
& (\exists\, i :: (f = i) \wedge (\sup L)^0.(q.i).p)
\end{array}
$$

$$= \quad \{q.i \in Lia,\ (19),\ 4(6)\}$$
$$(\exists i :: (f = i) \wedge (\exists v \in L :: v^0.(q.i).p))$$
$$= \quad \{\text{predicate calculus and } 8(14) \text{ again}\}$$
$$(\exists v \in L :: v^0.(q.f).p)$$
$$= \quad \{4(6)\}$$
$$(\sup v \in L :: v^0.(q.f)).p \ .$$

This concludes the proof of part (c) of Theorem 11(4).

13.8 The set *Lia* and sequential composition

We now investigate the composition of linearly approximating commands q and r, in order to obtain Theorem 11(4)(d). We follow the calculation of [Hesselink 1990] Section 5.5. Let L be a nonempty chain in WG_0 and let $p \in \mathbb{P}$. We observe

$$(\sup L)^0.(q;r).p$$
$$= \quad \{\text{Lemma } (3)(a)\}$$
$$(\sup L)^0.q.((\sup L)^0.r.p)$$
$$= \quad \{q, r \in Lia;\ (19);\ \text{let } v,\ w \text{ range over } L\}$$
$$(\sup v :: v^0.q).((\sup w :: w^0.r).p)$$
$$= \quad \{4(6), \text{ twice}\}$$
$$(\exists v :: v^0.q.(\exists w :: w^0.r.p))$$
(*) $$= \quad \{\text{provided } v^0.q \in Muc \text{ (cf. } 8(15)), \text{ or } w^0.r.p \text{ constant}\}$$
$$(\exists v, w :: v^0.q.(w^0.r.p))$$
$$= \quad \{L \text{ is a chain; diagonalisation by Lemma } 8(17)\}$$
$$(\exists v :: v^0.q.(v^0.r.p))$$
$$= \quad \{v \in WT \text{ and } 4(43)(b)\}$$
$$(\exists v :: v^0.(q;r).p) \ .$$

The critical step is indicated by (*). If $r \in S^{\odot}$ then $w^0.r = wp.r$ and, therefore, $w^0.r$ is independent of w.

We now choose $R = Muc$ in definition (2). By definition (2) and formula 8(5), it follows that $v^0.q \in Muc$ for all $v \in WG_0$ and $q \in Sy.Muc$. Therefore, the above calculation implies

$$(\forall q, r \in Lia : q \in Sy.Muc \vee r \in S^{\odot} : q;r \in Lia) \ .$$

This concludes the proof of Theorem 11(4)(d).

13.9 Exercises

Exercises of Section 13.1.

Exercise 0. In [Hesselink 1990] Theorem 2(9), it is proved that *MC* is sup–decked in *PT*. The purpose of this exercise is to show that *MP* is not sup–decked in *MT*. Let there be precisely one program variable v, which is of type integer. A state x is characterised by the value of v. We may therefore regard state x as an integer.
(a) For integer i, let $q.i$ be the nondeterminate choice of an integer bigger than i:

$$q.i \quad = \quad (\,[\!]\, y : y > i : \mathrm{v} := y)\ .$$

Prove that the predicate transformer $f.i = wp.(q.i)$ satisfies

$$f.i.p.x \quad = \quad (\forall\, y : y > i : p.y)\ .$$

(b) Prove that the family $(i :: f.i)$ forms a chain in *MP*.
(c) Prove that $f1 = (\sup i :: f.i)$ satisfies

$$f1.p.x \quad = \quad (\exists\, i :: (\forall\, y : y > i : p.y))\ .$$

(d) Prove that $f1 \notin MP$ by showing that

$$f1.(\forall\, j :: u.j) \ \neq\ (\forall\, j :: f1.(u.j))$$

where $u.j \in \mathbb{P}$ is given by $u.j.x \equiv (j \leq x)$.
(e) Prove that *MP* is not sup–decked in *MT*.

Exercises of Section 13.3.

Exercise 0. Prove the assertions of Lemma (10).

Exercise 1. Let a relation E on $A^{\odot}$ be called *wlp–safe* if and only if it is inf–safe and stable under unfolding. Let R be the union of all *wlp*–safe relations. Prove the following facts:
(a) R is *wlp*–safe and an admissible preorder,
(b) $wlp.q \leq wlp.r$ for every pair $\langle q, r\rangle \in R$,
(c) if E is a binary relation on $A^{\odot}$ such that

$$(\forall\, \langle q,r\rangle \in E :: wlp.(\mathbf{abort}^{\odot}.q) \leq wlp.(\mathbf{abort}^{\odot}.r))$$

and that for every admissible preorder $\triangleleft$ on $A^{\odot}$ with $E \cup R \subset (\triangleleft)$ we have

$$(\forall\, \langle q,r\rangle \in E :: \mathbf{body}^{\odot}.q \triangleleft \mathbf{body}^{\odot}.r)\ ,$$

then $E \subset R$.

Exercises of Section 13.4.

Exercise 0. ♡ Prove that for all q, $r \in A^{\odot}$

$$q \ll r \quad \Rightarrow \quad \mathbf{abort}^{\odot}.q \sqsubseteq \mathbf{abort}^{\odot}.r\ .$$

Show that $q \ll r$ does not imply $q \in Lia$.

CHAPTER 14

TEMPORAL OPERATORS

14.0. Up to this point, the semantics of the commands is determined by the relation between precondition and postcondition. This point of view is too restricted for the treatment of concurrent programs and reactive systems. The usual example is that of an operating system which is supposed to perform useful tasks without ever reaching a postcondition.

For this purpose, the semantics of commands must be extended by consideration of conditions at certain moments during execution. We do not want to be forced to consider all intermediate states or to formalize sequences of intermediate states. We have chosen the following level of abstraction. To every procedure name h, a predicate $z.h$ is associated. The temporal semantic properties of a command q depend on the values of $z.h.x$ for the procedure calls, say of procedure h in state x, induced by execution of command q. The main properties are 'always' and 'eventually', which are distinguished by the question whether $z.h.x$ should hold for all induced calls or for at least one induced call. The concept of 'always' is related to stability and safety. The concept of 'eventually' is related to progress and liveness.

In this chapter, we regard nontermination of simple commands as malfunctioning and nontermination of procedures as potentially useful infinite behaviour. We therefore use *wp* for the interpretation of simple commands and *wlp* for procedure calls.

The definitions we propose are generalizations of the definitions in [Morris 1990] for the case of simple tail recursion. The framework of Chapter 4 is well suited for such a generalization: mutual recursion and unbounded choice are smoothly incorporated.

We expect that temporal predicate transformers will turn out to be useful in the treatment of concurrent programs and reactive systems. Most applications in these areas, however, have many other important but distracting aspects and fall therefore outside the scope of this monograph. As a single application, we give in the next chapter a treatment of predicative fairness.

14.1 Stability and the function 'always'

The main temporal property of a condition is *stability*. Operationally speaking, it means that the validity of the condition at a certain procedure call implies its validity at all induced recursive calls. The condition may depend on the procedure name and the state. So it is a function in $\mathbb{P}^H$.

We associate to such a function $z \in \mathbb{P}^H$ a function $wl.z \in MT^H$, which is a variation of *wlp* that could have been inspired by termination law 4(38). It is defined by

(0) $\quad wl.z.h.p \;=\; z.h \wedge wlp.h.p \quad$ for all $h \in H$, $p \in \mathbb{P}$.

Since $wlp.h.true = true$, it follows that $wl.z.h.true = z.h$, so that $wl.z \in WT$, cf. definition 4(33). By formula 4(34), it follows that the induced function $(wl.z)^0 \in A^{\odot} \to MT$, cf. definition 4(25), satisfies

(1) $\quad (wl.z)^0.r.p \;=\; (wl.z)^0.r.true \wedge wlp.r.p \quad$ for all $r \in A^{\odot}$, $p \in \mathbb{P}$.

Henceforward, we write $wl.z$ also to denote $(wl.z)^0 \in A^{\odot} \to MT$. It follows from corollary 4(43) that $wl.z$ is a homomorphism $A^{\odot} \to MP$.

Intuitively, $wl.z.r.true$ is the weakest precondition such that every simple command invoked terminates and $z.h$ holds whenever execution of r directly calls a procedure h. There is not yet any heredity: $z.k$ need not hold when procedure h in turn calls a procedure k. The claim made just now is formalized by means of the relational semantics of Chapter 6 in the following way:

(2) **Theorem.** Let $r \in A^*$, $x \in X$ and $z \in \mathbb{P}^H$. Then $wl.z.r.true.x$ holds if and only if, for all u, $v \in A^*$ and $a \in A$ such that $r = (u;a;v)$ and all $y \in X$ with $[\![u]\!].y.x$, we have $\neg[\![a]\!].\infty.y$ if $a \in S$ and $z.a.y$ if $a \in H$.

Proof. We use induction on the length of string r. For empty r the assertion holds since $wl.z.\varepsilon.true = true$ and ε has no decompositions of the form $(u;a;v)$. For a string $(b;r)$ with $b \in A$ we observe

$$\begin{array}{ll} & wl.z.(b;r).true.x \\ \equiv & \{wl.z \text{ is a homomorphism}\} \\ & wl.z.b.(wl.z.r.true).x \\ \equiv & \{wl.z = (wl.z)^0;\ (0) \text{ and } 4(25)\} \end{array}$$

$$(b \in S \;\Rightarrow\; ws_0.b.(wl.z.r.true).x)$$
$$\wedge\;\; (b \in H \;\Rightarrow\; z.b.x \wedge wlp.(wl.z.r.true).x)$$
$$\equiv\;\; \{ws_0 = wp \text{ and } 6(1)\}$$
$$(b \in S \;\Rightarrow\; \neg[\![b]\!].\infty.x) \;\wedge\; (b \in H \;\Rightarrow\; z.b.x)$$
$$\wedge\;\; (\forall y \in X : [\![b]\!].y.x : wl.z.r.true.y) \,.$$

Now the assertion follows by induction. (End of proof)

We define function $z \in \mathbb{P}^H$ to be *stable* if and only if

(3) $\quad [\,z.h \;\Rightarrow\; wl.z.(\mathbf{body}.h).true\,] \qquad$ for all $h \in H$.

In terms of the configuration graph $(X \times A^*) \cup \{\infty\}$ of Section 9.4, the operational meaning of stability can be described as follows.

(4) **Theorem.** A function $z \in \mathbb{P}^H$ is stable if and only if, in the configuration graph, every pair $\langle x, h\rangle$ with $x \in X$, $h \in H$ and $z.h.x$ has no finite path to ∞ and is such that $z.k.y$ holds for every finite path to a pair $\langle y, k; t\rangle$ with $y \in X$, $k \in H$ and $t \in A^*$.

Proof. The proof is by mutual implication, with two applications of Theorem (2). Since it is not enlightening, the details are better left to the interested reader. (End of proof)

The next lemma is the technical basis for most properties of stability.

(5) **Lemma.** The supremum of a set of stable functions is stable.

Proof. We calculate a sufficient condition for the stability of the supremum of a subset Z of $\mathbb{P}^H$, by observing that for every $h \in H$

$$[\,(\sup Z).h \;\Rightarrow\; wl.(\sup Z).(\mathbf{body}.h).true\,]$$
$$\equiv\;\; \{\text{definition supremum}\}$$
$$(\forall z \in Z :: [\,z.h \;\Rightarrow\; wl.(\sup Z).(\mathbf{body}.h).true\,])$$
$$\Leftarrow\;\; \{\text{by exercise 4.4.3, function } z \mapsto (wl.z)^0 \text{ is monotone; notice that } Z \text{ empty is allowed}\}$$
$$(\forall z \in Z :: [\,z.h \;\Rightarrow\; wl.z.(\mathbf{body}.h).true\,])$$
$$\equiv\;\; \{(3)\}$$
$$\text{all } z \in Z \text{ are stable.}$$

(End of proof)

The temporal function $alw \in \mathbb{P}^H \to \mathbb{P}^H$ (pronounced 'always') is defined by

(6) $\quad alw.z \;=\; (\sup x \in \mathbb{P}^H : x \le z \;\wedge\; x \text{ stable } : x)$.

We now have

(7) **Theorem.** (a) $alw.z$ is stable for every $z \in \mathbb{P}^H$.
(b) $z \in \mathbb{P}^H$ is stable if and only if $alw.z = z$.
(c) Function $alw \in \mathbb{P}^H \to \mathbb{P}^H$ is idempotent.
(d) Function $alw \in \mathbb{P}^H \to \mathbb{P}^H$ is monotone.

Proof. (a) Follows from definition (6) and Lemma (5).

(b) If z is stable then definition (6) implies that $alw.z = z$. If $alw.z = z$ then part (a) implies that z is stable.

(c) Follows from (a) and (b).

(d) Follows from definition (6).

(End of proof)

Example. Let i be an integer program variable. Let $H = \{h\}$ with procedure h declared by

$$\mathbf{body}.h \quad = \quad (\mathtt{i} := \mathtt{i} + 1 \, ; \, h) \, .$$

Let $z \in \mathbb{P}^H$ be given by $z.h = p \in \mathbb{P}$. Then we have

$$\begin{array}{ll} & z \text{ is stable} \\ \equiv & \{(3)\} \\ & [p \;\Rightarrow\; wl.z.(\mathbf{body}.h).true] \\ \equiv & \{4(25) \text{ and declaration } h\} \\ & [p \;\Rightarrow\; wp.(\mathtt{i} := \mathtt{i}+1).(wl.z.h.true)] \\ \equiv & \{(0)\} \\ & [p \;\Rightarrow\; wp.(\mathtt{i} := \mathtt{i}+1).(z.h \wedge wlp.h.true)] \\ \equiv & \{z.h = p \text{ and } wlp.h.true = true\} \\ & [p \;\Rightarrow\; wp.(\mathtt{i} := \mathtt{i}+1).p] \, . \end{array}$$

Therefore, z is stable if $p = false$ or $p = true$ or $p = (\mathtt{i} \geq n)$ for some integer n. This is in agreement with the intuitive notion of stability.

This example can be used to show that function alw need not commute with suprema. If, for simplicity of notation, we identify z and p, we find

$$\begin{array}{lll} alw.(\mathtt{i} < n) & = & false \quad \text{and} \\ alw.true & = & true \, . \end{array}$$

Since $(\sup n \in \mathbb{Z} :: \mathtt{i} < n) = true$ in $\mathbb{P}^H$, this shows that function $alw \in \mathbb{P}^H \to \mathbb{P}^H$ does not commute with suprema. (End of example)

14.2 Termination and unfolding

The idea of functions in $\mathbb{P}^H$ and the associated function *wl*, cf. definition (0), suggest a new view on termination and total correctness. In fact, termination is determined by the function $term \in \mathbb{P}^H$ defined by

(8) $\quad term.h \;=\; wp.h.true$.

From definition (0) and the termination law, it follows that

(9) $\quad wp \;=\; wl.term$.

Definition (3) suggests to define the unfolding function $unf \in \mathbb{P}^H \to \mathbb{P}^H$ by

(10) $\quad unf.z.h \;=\; wl.z.(\mathbf{body}.h).true$.

We observe that by formula (3)

(11) $\quad z$ is stable $\;\equiv\; z \leq unf.z$.

Function $unf \in \mathbb{P}^H \to \mathbb{P}^H$ is easily seen to be monotone. Therefore, it follows from (11) that

(12) $\quad z$ is stable $\;\Rightarrow\; unf.z$ is stable .

The next result is an elegant characterization of termination. We did not notice it before, since function *wl* was not available.

(13) **Theorem.** (a) Function *term* is the least fixpoint of *unf*.
(b) Function *term* is also the least fixpoint of $alw \circ unf$.

Proof. Function *term* is a fixpoint, since for every $h \in H$

$$
\begin{array}{ll}
 & unf.term.h \\
= & \{(10)\} \\
 & wl.term.(\mathbf{body}.h).true \\
= & \{(9)\} \\
 & wp.(\mathbf{body}.h).true \\
= & \{\text{fixpoint equation of } wp \text{ and } (8)\} \\
 & term.h\ .
\end{array}
$$

It is the least one, since for every $z \in \mathbb{P}^H$

$$
\begin{array}{ll}
 & term \leq z \\
\Leftarrow & \{(8) \text{ and } (0)\} \\
 & wp|H \leq wl.z \quad \text{in } MT^H \\
\Leftarrow & \{wp|H \text{ is least fixpoint; let } h \text{ range over } H \text{ and } p \text{ over } \mathbb{P}\} \\
 & (\forall\, h,p :: \; wl.z.h.p = wl.z.(\mathbf{body}.h).p) \\
\equiv & \{(0) \text{ and } (1)\} \\
 & (\forall\, h,p :: \; z.h \wedge wlp.h.p = wl.z.(\mathbf{body}.h).true \wedge wlp.(\mathbf{body}.h).p)
\end{array}
$$

$\Leftarrow$ {fixpoint equation of *wlp* and (10)}
$z = unf.z$.

(b) It suffices to prove that *unf* and *alw* ∘ *unf* have the same fixpoints. This is proved by mutual implication. For any $z \in \mathbb{P}^H$ we observe

$z = alw.(unf.z)$
$\equiv$ {(7)(a)}
$z = alw.(unf.z) \quad \wedge \quad z$ is stable
$\Rightarrow$ {(12)}
$z = alw.(unf.z) \quad \wedge \quad unf.z$ is stable
$\Rightarrow$ {(7)(b)}
$z = unf.z$.

The other implication is proved in

$z = unf.z$
$\equiv$ {(11)}
$z = unf.z \quad \wedge \quad z$ is stable
$\Rightarrow$ {(7)(b)}
$z = alw.(unf.z)$.

(End of proof)

Remark. Theorem (13) could be used as a definition of *term* independent of *wp*. Then formula (9) could be used as a definition of *wp*. We found Theorem (13) inspired by a remark in [Morris 1990] that suggested part (b). The easiest proof of part (b) turned out to yield part (a) as well. (End of remark)

14.3 The temporal predicate transformer for always

We now construct for $z \in \mathbb{P}^H$ a homomorphism $Alw.z \in A^{\odot} \to MP$. Predicate $Alw.z.r.p$ is the weakest precondition such that during execution of command r every simple command terminates and every procedure call h occurs in a state where $z.h$ holds and that r does not terminate or terminates in a state where p holds. Function *Alw* is defined by

(14) $\quad Alw.z \quad = \quad wl.(alw.z) \in A^{\odot} \to MT$.

The next theorem provides a nice characterization of function *Alw*. It is based on the following fact (compare exercise 4.2.0):

(15) **Greatest–fixpoint property.** For a complete lattice W, let $D \in W \to W$ be a monotone function. Then $(\sup w \in W : w \leq D.w : w)$ is the greatest element w with $w \leq D.w$; it satisfies $w = D.w$ and hence is the greatest fixpoint of D.

(16) **Theorem.** The restriction $(Alw.z|H)$ is the greatest solution of the equation in $v \in MT$

(17) $\quad v.h.p \;=\; z.h \wedge v^0.(\mathbf{body}.h).p \qquad$ for all $h \in H$, $p \in \mathbb{P}$.

Proof. By property (15), it suffices to prove that $(Alw.z|H)$ is the greatest solution of the equation in $v \in MT$

(18) $\quad [\,v.h.p \;\Rightarrow\; z.h \wedge v^0.(\mathbf{body}.h).p\,] \qquad$ for all $h \in H$, $p \in \mathbb{P}$.

We first verify that, indeed, $(Alw.z|H)$ solves equation (18). For every $h \in H$ and $p \in \mathbb{P}$, we have

$[\,Alw.z.h.p \;\Rightarrow\; z.h \wedge Alw.z.(\mathbf{body}.h).p\,]$

$\equiv\quad$ {left (14) and (0); right (14) and (1)}

$[\,alw.z.h \wedge wlp.h.p$

$\quad\Rightarrow\; z.h \wedge Alw.z.(\mathbf{body}.h).true \wedge wlp.(\mathbf{body}.h).p\,]$

$\Leftarrow\quad$ {fixpoint equation of wlp}

$[\,alw.z.h \;\Rightarrow\; z.h \wedge Alw.z.(\mathbf{body}.h).true\,]$

$\equiv\quad$ {$alw.z \leq z$ from (6); use (14)}

$[\,alw.z.h \;\Rightarrow\; wl.(alw.z).(\mathbf{body}.h).true\,]$

$\equiv\quad$ {$alw.z$ is stable by (7)(a); then use (3)}

true .

Now let $v \in MT^H$ be an arbitrary solution of equation (18). Then $v \leq v^0 \circ \mathbf{body}$. By property (15) and the definition of wlp, the restriction $(wlp|H)$ is the greatest solution of the latter equation. This implies that

(19) $\quad v \leq (wlp|H)$.

We now compare v with $(Alw.z|H)$:

$v \leq (Alw.z|H)$

$\equiv\quad$ {(14), (0); let h range over H and p over $\mathbb{P}$}

$(\forall\, h, p :: [\,v.h.p \;\Rightarrow\; alw.z.h \wedge wlp.h.p\,])$

$\equiv\quad$ {(19)}

$(\forall\, h, p :: [\,v.h.p \;\Rightarrow\; alw.z.h\,])$

$\equiv\quad$ {monotony of $v.h$}

$(\forall\, h :: [\,v.h.true \;\Rightarrow\; alw.z.h\,])$

$\Leftarrow\quad$ {(6); let $z1.h = v.h.true$}

$(z1 \leq z) \;\wedge\; z1$ is stable

$\equiv$ {(18) implies $z1 \le z$; use (3)}
$(\forall h :: [\, z1.h \;\Rightarrow\; wl.z1.(\mathbf{body}.h).true\,])$
$\equiv$ {definition $z1$}
$(\forall h :: [\, v.h.true \;\Rightarrow\; wl.z1.(\mathbf{body}.h).true\,])$
$\Leftarrow$ {(18) with $p := true$}
$(\forall h :: [\, v^0.(\mathbf{body}.h).true \;\Rightarrow\; wl.z1.(\mathbf{body}.h).true\,])$
$\Leftarrow$ {exercise 4.4.3}
$v \le wl.z1$
$\equiv$ {(0) and definition of $z1$}
$(\forall h, p :: [\, v.h.p \;\Rightarrow\; v.h.true \wedge wlp.h.p\,])$
$\equiv$ {monotony of $v.h$ and (19)}
true .

This proves that $(Alw.z|H)$ is the greatest solution of (18) and hence also of (17). (End of proof)

Remark. In [Morris 1990], function $\mathcal{A}$ is defined as the greatest solution of the analogue of equation (17). Therefore, it is the analogue of our function *Alw*. Our approach seems to be simpler, but it does not work for the function 'eventually' to be treated next. (End of remark)

14.4 Temporal functions for eventually

We now construct a function *Evt* (pronounced 'eventually'). It is the analogue of function $\mathcal{E}$ of [Morris 1990]. For $z \in \mathbb{P}^H$, $r \in A^{\odot}$ and $p \in \mathbb{P}$, predicate $Evt.z.r.p$ is the weakest precondition such that command r terminates in a state where p holds or $z.h$ holds at some induced procedure call h.

The description of *Evt* implies that $Evt.z.c = ws_0.c$ for every simple command c. It also implies that $Evt.z$ should be a homomorphism. Therefore, function $Evt.z$ is determined by its restriction to the set H, and we expect $Evt.z = v^0$ for some function $v \in MT^H$. The description of $Evt.z$ implies that for all $h \in H$ and $p \in \mathbb{P}$ we expect

(20) $\quad Evt.z.h.p \;=\; z.h \vee Evt.z.(\mathbf{body}.h).p$.

If $z.h = false$ for all h, then $Evt.z$ should coincide with *wp*. In this way, we arrive at the following definition.

We define function $Evt \in \mathbb{P}^H \to (A^{\odot} \to MT)$ by $Evt.z = v^0$, where v is the least (i.e. strongest) solution of equation

(21) $\quad v.h.p \;=\; z.h \vee v^0.(\mathbf{body}.h).p \qquad$ for all $h \in H$, $p \in \mathbb{P}$.

We use a little trick to avoid unnecessary proofs. Let **bov** be a modified procedure declaration given by

$$\mathbf{bov}.h \;=\; ?(\neg z.h)\;;\;\mathbf{body}.h\,.$$

Then equation (21) is equivalent to

$$v.h.p \;=\; v^0.(\mathbf{bov}.h).p \qquad \text{for all } h \in H,\, p \in \mathbb{P}.$$

The least solution of this equation is the function *wp* with respect to the modified declaration **bov**. Therefore, *Evt.z* is well–defined and satisfies formula (20). By corollary 4(43)(b), we even have

(22) **Theorem.** *Evt.z* is a homomorphism $A^{\odot} \to MP$.

Since *Evt.z* is nothing but function *wp* with respect to the modified declaration **bov**, Recursion Theorem 2(16) immediately extends to the following proof rule:

(23) **Theorem.** In order to prove that

$$(\forall i \in I :: [\,p.i \Rightarrow Evt.z.(h.i).(q.i)\,])\,,$$

it suffices to give a function $vf \in I \to \mathbb{Z}^X$ such that for every integer n

$$(\forall i \in I :: [\,p.i \wedge vf.i < n \wedge n \geq 0 \Rightarrow Evt.z.(h.i).(q.i)\,])$$
$$\Rightarrow \quad (\forall i \in I :: [\,p.i \wedge vf.i \leq n \Rightarrow z.(h.i) \vee Evt.z.(\mathbf{body}.(h.i)).(q.i)\,])\,.$$

A special case is captured in function $evt \in \mathbb{P}^H \to (A^{\odot} \to \mathbb{P})$, defined by

(24) $\quad evt.z.r \;=\; Evt.z.r.false\,.$

Predicate *evt.z.r* expresses that execution of r leads to some induced procedure call h where $z.h$ holds. It turns out that the restricted function $evt \in \mathbb{P}^H \to \mathbb{P}^H$ satisfies many properties analogous to function *alw*.

(25) **Theorem.** (a) $z \leq evt.z$ for every $z \in \mathbb{P}^H$.
(b) If $z \leq z1$ in $\mathbb{P}^H$ then $Evt.z \leq Evt.z1$ in $A^{\odot} \to MP$.
(c) $Evt.(evt.z) = Evt.z$ for every $z \in \mathbb{P}^H$.
(d) Function $evt \in \mathbb{P}^H \to \mathbb{P}^H$ is monotone and idempotent.

Proof. (a) For every $h \in H$ we observe

$$z.h$$
$$\Rightarrow \quad \{(20)\} \quad Evt.z.h.false$$
$$\equiv \quad \{(24)\} \quad evt.z.h\,.$$

(b) It suffices to observe

$$Evt.z \leq Evt.z1 \quad \text{in } A^{\odot} \to MP$$

$\Leftarrow$ {exercise 4.4.3}
$Evt.z|H \le Evt.z1|H \quad \text{in } H \to MP$
$\Leftarrow$ {definition of Evt in (21) and exercise 4.2.1(a)}
$(\forall v \in MT^H, h \in H, p \in \mathbb{P} ::$
$z.h \vee v^0.(\mathbf{body}.h).p \le z1.h \vee v^0.(\mathbf{body}.h).p)$
$\Leftarrow$ {calculus}
$z \le z1$.

(c) It follows from (a) and (b) that $Evt.z \le Evt.(evt.z)$. The other inequality is proved in

$Evt.(evt.z) \le Evt.z$
$\Leftarrow$ {as above}
$Evt.(evt.z)|H \le Evt.z|H$
$\Leftarrow$ {$Evt.(evt.z)$ is least solution of (21) with $z := evt.z$}
$(\forall h \in H, p \in \mathbb{P} :: Evt.z.h.p = evt.z.h \vee Evt.z.(\mathbf{body}.h).p)$
$\equiv$ {(24)}
$(\forall h \in H, p \in \mathbb{P} :: Evt.z.h.p = Evt.z.h.false \vee Evt.z.(\mathbf{body}.h).p)$
$\equiv$ {(20) twice}
$(\forall h \in H, p \in \mathbb{P} :: z.h \vee Evt.z.(\mathbf{body}.h).p =$
$z.h \vee Evt.z.(\mathbf{body}.h).false \vee Evt.z.(\mathbf{body}.h).p)$
$\equiv$ {monotony and $[false \Rightarrow p]$}
true .

(d) This follows from definition (24) and the parts (b) and (c).
(End of proof)

14.5 Possible termination

Let c be an arbitrary command. As argued in Section 3.2, predicate $\neg wlp.c.false$ characterizes the initial states where execution of c may terminate. This is sometimes expressed by saying that command c angelically terminates.

We now specialize to procedures. The function of angelic termination $aterm \in \mathbb{P}^H$ is defined by

(26) $\quad aterm.h \;=\; \neg wlp.h.false$.

In principle, the associated function $wl.aterm$ has some practical importance. It is the weakest precondition function for the abundant implementation which creates in each case of a nondeterminate choice in a procedure body sufficiently many identical processes, all with a separate state and charged with a different choice. When finally some processes terminate, one result is chosen nondeterministically.

Example. Let n be an integer program variable. Let $h0$ and $h1$ be declared by

$$\begin{array}{lcl} \mathbf{body}.h0 & = & ((\mathrm{n} := 0 \,[\!]\, \mathrm{n} := 1) \,;\, h1) \,, \\ \mathbf{body}.h1 & = & (\,?(\mathrm{n} = 0) \,[\!]\, ?(\mathrm{n} \neq 0) \,;\, h1) \,. \end{array}$$

Then $wl.aterm.h0 = wp.(\mathrm{n} := 0)$. Notice, however, that

$$wl.aterm.(\mathbf{body}.h0).p \;=\; false \quad \text{for all predicates } p.$$

(End of example)

Recall from 1(12) that a command c is total if and only if $[\,\neg wp.c.false\,]$. Let syntactic totality be defined by saying that command c is ***syntactically total*** if and only if

(27) $\quad [\,\neg wl.aterm.c.false\,]$.

The adverb 'syntactically' is not completely adequate, for the concept relies on a mixture of syntax and *wlp*–semantics. For every command $s \in S^{\odot}$, we have $wl.aterm.s = wp.s$. Therefore, $s \in S^{\odot}$ is syntactically total if and only if it is total.

(28) **Lemma.** Every procedure $h \in H$ is syntactically total.

Proof. It suffices to observe that

$$\begin{array}{ll} & wl.aterm.h.false \\ = & \{(0)\} \\ & aterm.h \;\wedge\; wlp.h.false \\ = & \{(26) \text{ and calculus}\} \\ & false\ . \end{array}$$

(End of proof)

(29) **Theorem.** The following conditions are equivalent:

(a) every procedure $h \in H$ is total,

(b) $term \leq aterm$,

(c) every syntactically total command $r \in A^{\odot}$ is total.

Proof. We prove the equivalence (a) $\equiv$ (b) and the two implications (b) $\Rightarrow$ (c) and (c) $\Rightarrow$ (a). The equivalence (a) $\equiv$ (b) is proved in

$$\begin{array}{ll} & term \leq aterm \\ \equiv & \{\text{induced order; definitions (8) and (26)}\} \\ & (\forall h \in H :: [\, wp.h.true \Rightarrow \neg wlp.h.false\,]) \end{array}$$

$\equiv$ {predicate calculus}
$(\forall h \in H :: [\, wp.h.true \wedge wlp.h.false \equiv false \,])$
$\equiv$ {termination law}
$(\forall h \in H :: [\, wp.h.false \equiv false \,])$
$\equiv$ {definition totality}
all $h \in H$ are total .

The implication (b) $\Rightarrow$ (c) is proved in

$term \leq aterm$
$\Rightarrow$ {monotony of wl}
$[\, wl.term.r.false \;\Rightarrow\; wl.aterm.r.false \,]$
$\equiv$ {(9) and calculus}
$[\, \neg wl.aterm.r.false \;\Rightarrow\; \neg wp.r.false \,]$
$\Rightarrow$ {(27)}
if r is syntactically total then r is total .

The implication (c) $\Rightarrow$ (a) follows from Lemma (28). (End of proof)

Example. We show that totality need not imply syntactic totality. Let b be a boolean program variable. Let procedure h be declared by

body.h = $(h \,[\!]\, \mathtt{b} := \text{false})$.

The composition $(h;\ ?\mathtt{b})$ is total because of

$wp.(h;\ ?\mathtt{b}).false$
$=$ {composition}
$wp.h.(wp.(?\mathtt{b}).false)$
$=$ {h need not terminate}
$false$.

The composition $(h;\ ?\mathtt{b})$ is not syntactically total because of

$wl.aterm.(h;\ ?\mathtt{b}).false$
$=$ {calculus}
$aterm.h \;\wedge\; wlp.h.(wl.aterm.(?\mathtt{b}).false)$
$=$ {declaration h; definition wl}
$true \;\wedge\; wlp.h.(\neg \mathtt{b})$
$=$ {declaration h and calculus}
$true$.

(End of example)

14.6 Exercises

Exercises of Section 14.1.

Exercise 0. We show that function wl commutes with nonempty infima in $\mathbb{P}^H$. Let Z be a nonempty subset of $\mathbb{P}^H$. Let K be the subset of $A^{\odot}$ of the commands r with

$$wl.(\inf Z).r \quad = \quad (\inf z \in Z :: wl.z.r) \; .$$

(a) Prove that $r \in K \;\Rightarrow\; a;r \in K$ for every $a \in A$.

(b) Prove that $K = A^{\odot}$.

Exercise 1. Use the previous exercise to prove that the infimum of a nonempty set of stable functions in $\mathbb{P}^H$ is stable.

Exercise 2. Use the previous exercise to prove that function $alw \in \mathbb{P}^H \to \mathbb{P}^H$ commutes with nonempty infima, i.e.

$$alw.(\inf Z) = (\inf z \in Z :: alw.z) \; .$$

Exercise 3. ♡ Let $\mathtt{v}$ be an integer program variable and let $H = \{h\}$. Let i be an integer value and let $z \in \mathbb{P}^H$ be given by $z.h = (\mathtt{v} > i)$.

(a) Prove that z is stable if

$$\mathbf{body}.h \quad = \quad \mathtt{v} := \mathtt{v}+1 \; ; \; h \; ; \; \mathtt{v} := \mathtt{v}-2 \; ; \; h \; .$$

(b) Prove that z is not stable if

$$\mathbf{body}.h \quad = \quad (skip \;[\!]\; \mathtt{v} := \mathtt{v}+1 \; ; \; h \; ; \; \mathtt{v} := \mathtt{v}-2 \; ; \; h) \; .$$

Exercises of Section 14.2.

Exercise 0. ♡ Prove that $z \in \mathbb{P}^H$ is a fixpoint of unf if and only if $wl.z \in MT^H$ is a fixpoint of function D_0, cf. definition 4(26).

Exercises of Section 14.4.

Exercise 0. In the example of 14.1, use Theorem (23) to prove that

$$[\, evt.(m \leq \mathtt{i}).h \,] \qquad \text{for every integer } m.$$

CHAPTER 15

PREDICATIVE FAIRNESS

15.0. The nondeterminacy considered thus far in this monograph was loose in the sense of [Park 1979]: any choice or sequence of choices allowed by the command is acceptable behaviour of the implementation, but the fact that a choice is allowed does not mean that it can ever occur.

While reasoning about concurrent computations, and in the design of communicating processes, we have to deal with unpredictable execution, which is yet not completely loose. We may want to assume that a computation delegated to another process eventually yields an answer or that, if a stream of messages is sent, eventually an acknowledgement comes back.

Such assumptions are called fairness assumptions. Fairness is a subject in itself with a highly operational flavour. There are many different kinds of fairness, cf. [Francez 1986] and [Lehmann e.a. 1981], but it seems that most definitions cannot elegantly be expressed in terms of predicate–transformation semantics. Therefore, we restrict ourselves to predicative fairness, a kind of fairness proposed in [Morris 1990] and [Queille-Sifakis 1983].

In the literature, fairness is usually treated only for repetitions. In [Morris 1990], fairness of tail–recursive procedures without mutual recursion is treated. We give a definition applicable to arbitrary procedures. Our formalization is in agreement with the treatment of loc.cit. in the case of tail recursion. Mutual recursion and 'calls before the tail' seem to be adequately treated. Our formalization leads to overly optimistic specifications if a procedure body contains sequentially ordered recursive calls. A more realistic version can be obtained by means of the standard reduction of recursion to tail recursion, cf. Section 9.1. The result of that reduction is far from elegant because of the stack administration involved. We prefer to give the elegant version in its full generality. We shall provide examples to show where the formalism works reasonably well and where it may be regarded as being too optimistic.

15.1 Starvation of predicates

Consider the not–necessarily terminating repetition

(0) **while** $x > 0$ **do** (*skip* $[\!]$ $x := x - 1$) **od** .

In this case, nontermination is generally regarded as unfair. Therefore, the repetition is said to be fairly terminating. In general, a command is said to be *fairly terminating* if and only if every infinite execution sequence is unfair. It remains to discuss the meaning of the word 'unfair'. In the case of the above repetition, every infinite execution sequence has a tail in which the second alternative of the body is never chosen. These sequences are regarded as unfair because of the existence of an alternative that eventually is always enabled and never taken. We could speak of starvation of branches.

Now consider the repetition

(1) **while** x **mod** $3 \neq 0$ **do** ($x := x + 1$ $[\!]$ $x := x - 1$) **od** .

Given an initial state with x **mod** $3 \neq 0$, there is precisely one infinite execution sequence. In this sequence the alternatives are taken alternately. So, we cannot speak of starvation of branches. Nevertheless, one may want to regard the sequence as unfair. For, at every moment of choice, there is an alternative that establishes x **mod** $3 = 0$. Therefore, the unfairness can be justified here by the existence of a predicate P that is false along the execution sequence even though at every choice there is an alternative that establishes P. One might say that the sequence is unfair because of the starvation of a predicate. If unfairness is defined by means of starvation of predicates, we speak of *predicative fairness*.

Traditionally, one distinguishes between weak fairness and strong fairness, cf. [Francez 1986]. As above, these concepts are defined in terms of the unfairness of the execution sequences. An execution sequence is said to be *not weakly fair* if there is an alternative that eventually is always enabled and never taken. The sequence is said to be *not strongly fair* if there is an alternative that is enabled infinitely often and never taken.

For predicative fairness, one might want to use the obvious analogues: let a sequence be called *not weakly pp–fair* if there is a predicate, eventually false along the sequence, that eventually can be established at every choice; let the sequence be called *not strongly pp–fair* if there is a predicate, eventually false along the sequence, that can be established at infinitely many choices.

This definition is suggested in [Morris 1990], but it does not correspond to his formalization. The crucial example is a variation of repetition (1). Consider, for an integer constant $m > 3$, the repetition

(2) **while** x **mod** $m \neq 0$ **do** (x := x + 1 $\|$ x := x − 1) **od** .

We claim that every infinite execution sequence of (2) is not strongly pp–fair. This is shown as follows. For a given infinite execution sequence, there is an integer i such that x **mod** $m = i + 1$ occurs infinitely often and x **mod** $m = i$ occurs at most finitely often. Therefore, the predicate x **mod** $m = i$ is eventually false along the sequence, but it can be established at infinitely many choices. This shows that repetition (2) is fairly terminating with respect to strong pp–fairness. It can be shown that, if $m \geq 5$, repetition (2) does not fairly terminate with respect to the strong fairness of [Morris 1990].

We do not adopt pp–fairness as defined above, for it seems to be overly optimistic. We feel that starvation of an arbitrary predicate is not sufficient for calling a sequence unfair. The reason is that it may be easy to make the predicate true and then false again. Therefore, instead of using starvation of arbitrary predicates, we shall use starvation of stable predicates. Here, stability is the same concept as in Section 14.1. For a repetition **while** b **do** c **od**, a predicate p is stable if and only if $[\, p \wedge b \;\Rightarrow\; wp.c.p\,]$.

We thus define a sequence to be *not weakly p–fair* if there is a stable predicate, false along the sequence, that eventually can be established at every choice. The sequence is called *not strongly p–fair* if there is a stable predicate, false along the sequence, that can be established at infinitely many choices. The corresponding concepts of weak p–fairness and strong p–fairness seem to be very close to Morris's formalizations of fairness. We do not claim equality, since the above description is not yet a strict definition.

As an example, consider repetition (2) with $m = 4$. In this case, every infinite execution sequence is infinitely often in a position where it can choose to establish x **mod** $4 = 0$. Therefore, repetition (2) with $m = 4$ terminates fairly with respect to strong p–fairness.

For $m \geq 5$, however, an execution sequence with (eventually) x alternating between 2 and 3 has no stable predicate, false along the sequence, that can be established infinitely often. Therefore, if $m \geq 5$ and initially x **mod** $m \neq 0$, repetition (2) does not fairly terminate with respect to strong p–fairness.

15.2 An abstract syntax and weak fairness

In the remainder of the chapter we describe a formalization of predicative fairness, which is inspired by [Morris 1990], but applicable to an arbitrary recursive declaration.

Our first concern is that we need syntactic means to indicate which choices are supposed to be fair, and when such a choice is enabled. We do not want to change the main syntax. So we retain the set $A^{\odot}$, the declaration **body** and the induced functions *wp* and *wlp*. In particular, we retain the operator '$[\!]$' for nondeterminate choice.

We restrict our fairness considerations to the choices made when execution opens a procedure body. The fairness constraints of these choices are specified by extending the declaration **body** in the following way. We assume that for every procedure $h \in H$ a nonempty set $\mathbf{fc}.h$ is given consisting of pairs $\langle c, t\rangle \in \mathbb{P} \times A^{\odot}$ such that

(3) $\quad \mathbf{body}.h \;=\; ([\!] \langle c,t\rangle \in \mathbf{fc}.h :: ?c; t)$.

Symbol **fc** stands for 'fair choice'. Predicate c is the enabling condition of branch t. We postulate that, for every procedure h and every state, at least one branch is enabled, that is

(4) $\quad [(\exists \langle c,t\rangle \in \mathbf{fc}.h :: c)] \qquad$ for all $h \in H$.

In the concrete syntax for the extended declaration, we shall use a fair choice operator '$[\!]_f$' and the notation

$$\mathbf{body}.h \;=\; ([\!]_f\, i \in I :: c.i \rightarrow t.i)$$

when $\mathbf{fc}.h$ is the set of the pairs $\langle c.i, t.i\rangle$ with $i \in I$. If the set I is finite, we often use '$[\!]_f$' as an infix operator. If $c.i = true$, we may prefer to omit '$c.i \rightarrow$'.

The semantics given by *wp* and *wlp* is unchanged, but the extended declaration **fc** is used to construct a weakest fair precondition function *wfp*. Since the only effect of a fairness assumption is to neglect certain infinite execution sequences, we expect *wfp* to satisfy the termination law

(5) $\quad wfp.r.p \;=\; wfp.r.true \wedge wlp.r.p \qquad$ for all $r \in A^{\odot}$, $p \in \mathbb{P}$.

Fair termination of a command should only depend on the fair termination of its induced procedure calls. Therefore, we postulate that

(6) $\quad wfp = wl.fter$,

cf. formula 14(0), where $fter \in \mathbb{P}^H$ is the function such that $fter.h$ is the precondition that h fairly terminates.

We come back to the extended declaration. It is important to know whether a call h has an enabled branch that fairly terminates. This condition is expressed by

$(\exists \langle c,t\rangle \in \mathbf{fc}.h :: c \wedge wfp.t.true)$.

By formula (6) this condition is equivalent to *weak.fter.h* where, for every $z \in \mathbb{P}^H$, we define

(7) $weak.z.h \quad = \quad (\exists \langle c,t\rangle \in \mathbf{fc}.h :: c \wedge wl.z.t.true)$.

Notice that function $weak \in \mathbb{P}^H \to \mathbb{P}^H$ is monotone.

Weak fairness means that a procedure call h fairly terminates whenever all its induced procedure calls have an enabled branch that fairly terminates. This is formalized in

$$[\, alw.(weak.fter).h \quad \Rightarrow \quad fter.h \,] \qquad \text{for all } h \in H,$$

and hence

(8) $alw.(weak.fter) \le fter$.

In this way we come to the following definition, cf. [Morris 1990]. Function $fter \in \mathbb{P}^H$ is defined as the smallest solution of inequality (8), or rather

(9) $fter = (\inf z \in \mathbb{P}^H : alw.(weak.z) \le z : z)$.

15.3 A general fairness definition

We generalize definition (9) as follows. For every monotone function $\psi \in \mathbb{P}^H \to \mathbb{P}^H$, we define $fair.\psi$ by

(10) $fair.\psi \quad = \quad (\inf z \in \mathbb{P}^H :: alw.(\psi.z) \le z : z)$.

Now definition (9) becomes

(11) $fter \quad = \quad fair.weak$,

so that, henceforth, the function *fair.weak* can be used to characterize weakly fair termination.

By a version of the theorem of Knaster–Tarski (cf. exercise 4.2.0), the element $fair.\psi$ is the smallest fixpoint of $alw \circ \psi$, i.e. the smallest solution z of

(12) $alw.(\psi.z) = z$.

Now, it follows from Theorem 14(13), that

(13) $term \quad = \quad fair.unf$.

By an exercise of Section 4.2, the expression $fair.\psi$ is monotone in ψ. This implies that

(14) $unf \le \psi \quad \Rightarrow \quad term \le fair.\psi$.

This implication is used to prove that termination implies weakly fair termination:

(15) $term \le fair.weak$.

In fact, by (13) and (14), it suffices to prove $unf \le weak$. This is verified by observing that for every $z \in \mathbb{P}^H$ and $h \in H$

$$\begin{array}{ll}
& unf.z.h \\
= & \{\text{definition 14(10)}\} \\
& wl.z.(\mathbf{body}.h).true \\
= & \{(3);\ \text{let } \langle c,t\rangle \text{ range over } \mathbf{fc}.h\} \\
& (\forall \langle c,t\rangle :: wl.z.(?c;t).true) \\
= & \{\text{calculus}\} \\
& (\forall \langle c,t\rangle :: c \Rightarrow wl.z.t.true) \\
= & \{\text{postulate (4)}\} \\
& (\exists \langle c,t\rangle :: c) \quad \wedge \quad (\forall \langle c,t\rangle :: c \Rightarrow wl.z.t.true) \\
\Rightarrow & \{\text{calculus}\} \\
& (\exists \langle c,t\rangle ::\ c \wedge (c \Rightarrow wl.z.t.true)) \\
= & \{\text{calculus and (7)}\} \\
& weak.z.h\ .
\end{array}$$

Surprisingly, the general fairness definition (10) suffices to prove a correctness rule and a necessity rule. We begin with the correctness rule for general fair termination.

(16) **Theorem.** Let N be a well–founded set (cf. Section 5.6). Let $(n \in N :: v.n)$ be a family of stable functions in $\mathbb{P}^H$ such that for all $n \in N$

$$v.n \leq (\sup i \in N : i < n : \psi.(v.i))\ .$$

Then $v.n \leq fair.\psi$ for all $n \in N$.

Proof. By induction over the well–founded set N, it suffices to prove that for every $n \in N$

$$(\forall i \in N : i < n : v.i \leq fair.\psi) \quad \Rightarrow \quad v.n \leq fair.\psi\ .$$

This is proved in

$$\begin{array}{ll}
& v.n \leq fair.\psi \\
\Leftarrow & \{\text{transitivity of } \leq\text{, and assumption}\} \\
& (\sup i \in N : i < n : \psi.(v.i)) \leq fair.\psi \\
\equiv & \{\text{definition supremum in 4(0)}\} \\
& (\forall i \in N : i < n : \psi.(v.i) \leq fair.\psi) \\
\equiv & \{(12)\} \\
& (\forall i \in N : i < n : \psi.(v.i) \leq alw.(\psi.(fair.\psi))) \\
\Leftarrow & \{alw.z \leq z \text{ and } \psi \text{ monotone}\} \\
& (\forall i \in N : i < n : v.i \leq fair.\psi)\ .
\end{array}$$

(End of proof)

General fairness also has a necessity rule (compare 2(26)):

(17) **Rule.** Let $z \in \mathbb{P}^H$ be a function with $\psi.z \leq z$. Then $fair.\psi \leq z$.

Proof. It suffices to observe that

$$\begin{array}{ll} & fair.\psi \leq z \\ \Leftarrow & \{(10)\} \\ & alw.(\psi.z) \leq z \\ \Leftarrow & \{\text{definition of } alw\} \\ & \psi.z \leq z \ . \end{array}$$

(End of proof)

It is reasonable to expect that fair termination implies the possibility of termination. We must be careful, however. In fact, even necessary termination only implies possible termination for total commands (cf. Section 3.2). We now show that weakly fair termination implies possible termination under a certain totality condition on the extended declaration.

(18) **Theorem**. Assume that, for every branch $\langle c, t\rangle \in \mathbf{fc}.h$, command t is syntactically total. Then $fair.weak \leq aterm$.

Proof.

$$\begin{array}{ll} & fair.weak \leq aterm \\ \Leftarrow & \{(17)\} \\ & weak.aterm \leq aterm \\ \equiv & \{(7);\ \text{let } h \text{ range over } H\text{, and } \langle c,t\rangle \text{ over } \mathbf{fc}.h\} \\ & (\forall\, h :: [(\exists\, c,t :: c \wedge wl.aterm.t.true) \Rightarrow aterm.h\,]) \\ \equiv & \{\text{predicate calculus: exercise 1.1.4(b)}\} \\ & (\forall\, h,c,t :: [\,c \wedge wl.aterm.t.true \Rightarrow aterm.h\,]) \\ \equiv & \{14(26)\} \\ & (\forall\, h,c,t :: [\,c \wedge wl.aterm.t.true \Rightarrow \neg wlp.h.false\,]) \\ \equiv & \{\text{declaration (3); fixpoint property of } wlp\} \\ & (\forall\, h,c,t :: [\,c \wedge wl.aterm.t.true \Rightarrow \neg(\forall\, c,t :: c \Rightarrow wlp.t.false)\,]) \\ \equiv & \{\text{predicate calculus}\} \\ & (\forall\, h,c,t :: [\,c \wedge wl.aterm.t.true \Rightarrow (\exists\, c,t :: c \wedge \neg wlp.t.false)\,]) \\ \Leftarrow & \{\text{one point rule; calculus}\} \\ & (\forall\, h,t :: [\,wl.aterm.t.true \Rightarrow \neg wlp.t.false\,]) \\ \equiv & \{\text{predicate calculus and 14(1)}\} \end{array}$$

$$(\forall h, t :: [\, wl.aterm.t.false \Rightarrow false \,])$$
$$\equiv \quad \{14(27)\}$$
all t are syntactically total.

(End of proof)

15.4 Examples

Example 1. In [Morris 1990] we find an example with an integer program variable i and two procedures $g1$ and $g4$ declared by

$$\mathbf{body}.g1 \;=\; (skip \,[\!]_f\, \mathtt{i} := \mathtt{i}+1 \,;\, g1) \,,$$
$$\mathbf{body}.g4 \;=\; (\,?(\mathtt{i}=10) \,[\!]\, ?(\mathtt{i} \neq 10) \,;\, \mathtt{i} := 0 \,;\, g1 \,;\, g4) \,.$$

Morris gives two systems of fairness (see loc. cit.). In his first system, a call of $g4$ terminates fairly. In his second system, however, it only terminates fairly under the precondition $\mathtt{i} = 10$. Our definition of fairness turns out to lead to the second conclusion. This is proved by means of rule (17), taking $H = \{g1, g4\}$ and $z \in \mathbb{P}^H$ given by

$$z.g1 = true \quad , \quad z.g4 = (\mathtt{i} = 10) \,.$$

Since $z.g1 = true$, we have

$$weak.z \leq z \quad \equiv \quad [\, weak.z.g4 \Rightarrow z.g4 \,] \,.$$

The righthand side holds, as is proved in

$$weak.z.g4$$
$$= \quad \{\text{definition (7); } \mathbf{body}.g4 \text{ contains no '}[\!]_f\text{'}\}$$
$$wl.z.(\mathbf{body}.g4).true$$
$$= \quad \{14(0) \text{ and declaration}\}$$
$$(\mathtt{i} = 10 \Rightarrow true) \quad \wedge \quad (\mathtt{i} \neq 10 \Rightarrow wlp.(\mathtt{i} := 0).(wl.z.g1.(wl.z.g4.true)))$$
$$= \quad \{\text{calculus; } 14(0);\ z.g1 = true \text{ and } wlp.g4.true = true\}$$
$$\mathtt{i} = 10 \quad \vee \quad wlp.(\mathtt{i} := 0).(wlp.g1.(z.g4))$$
$$= \quad \{\text{definition } z.g4 \text{ and declaration } g1\}$$
$$\mathtt{i} = 10 \quad \vee \quad wlp.(\mathtt{i} := 0).false$$
$$= \quad \{\text{calculus and definition } z.g4\}$$
$$z.g4 \,.$$

By rule (17) this shows that $fair.weak \leq z$ and hence

$$[\, fair.weak.g4 \quad \Rightarrow \quad \mathtt{i} = 10 \,] \,.$$

The converse implication is easy. (End of example)

Example 2. Let $H = \{h0\}$ be declared by

$$\mathbf{body}.h0 \quad = \quad (skip \;\|_f\; h0 \;;\; h0) \;.$$

Then $\mathbf{fc}.h0$ contains a branch $\langle c, t\rangle = \langle true, skip\rangle$, which satisfies

$$c \wedge wl.z.t.true \quad = \quad true \qquad \text{for every } z \in \mathbb{P}^H \;.$$

By definition (7), it follows that $weak.z.h0 = true$ for every $z \in \mathbb{P}^H$. We now use Theorem (16) with $v.0.h0 = false$ and $v.1.h0 = true$ to prove that $h0$ fairly terminates. This result suggests that the present formalization of weak predicative fairness is overly optimistic. (End of example)

Example 3. Let $\mathtt{x}$ be an integer program variable. Let $H = \{h1\}$ with $h1$ declared by

$$\mathbf{body}.h1 \quad =$$
$$(\mathtt{x} = 0 \rightarrow skip \;\|_f\; \mathtt{x} \neq 0 \rightarrow \mathtt{x} := \mathtt{x} + 1 \;;\; h1 \;\|_f\; \mathtt{x} \neq 0 \rightarrow \mathtt{x} := \mathtt{x} - 1 \;;\; h1) \;.$$

In this case the only stable predicates are *true*, *false*, $\mathtt{x} \geq 0$, $\mathtt{x} \leq 0$ and $\mathtt{x} = 0$. If function z is given by $z.h1 = (\mathtt{x} = 0)$, one can verify that

$$weak.z.h1 \quad = \quad (-1 \leq \mathtt{x} \leq 1) \;,$$

so that $alw.(weak.z) = z$. Now it follows from definition (9) that $h1$ fairly terminates only under precondition $\mathtt{x} = 0$. Notice that procedure $h1$ is almost equivalent to the stack implementation of procedure $h0$ of exercise 2, with x representing the stack size. (End of example)

Example 4. In this example we show that Theorem (18) indeed needs syntactic totality. Let $\mathtt{b}$ be a boolean program variable. Let $H = \{h0, h1\}$, declared by

$$\mathbf{body}.h0 \quad = \quad (h0 \;\|_f\; \mathtt{b} := \mathrm{false}) \;,$$
$$\mathbf{body}.h1 \quad = \quad (h0 \;;\; ?\mathtt{b}) \;.$$

In an example in Section 14.5, we have shown that $\mathbf{body}.h1$ is not syntactically total. We now show that

$$\neg(fair.weak.h1 \leq aterm.h1) \;.$$

In fact, we show that $fair.weak.h1 = true$ and $aterm.h1 = false$. The second assertion is proved in

$$\begin{aligned}
& aterm.h1 \\
= \quad & \neg wlp.h1.false \\
= \quad & \neg wlp.h0.(wlp.(?\mathtt{b}).false) \\
= \quad & \neg wlp.h0.(\neg \mathtt{b}) \\
= \quad & \neg true \\
= \quad & false \;.
\end{aligned}$$

The next thing is to determine the stable functions $z \in \mathbb{P}^H$. For $z \in \mathbb{P}^H$ we have

$$\begin{array}{ll} & wl.z.(\mathbf{body}.h1).true \\ = & wl.z.h0.(wl.z.(?\mathtt{b}).true) \\ = & wl.z.h0.true \\ = & z.h0\ , \end{array}$$

and also

$$\begin{array}{ll} & wl.z.(\mathbf{body}.h0).true \\ = & wl.z.h0.true \quad \wedge \quad wl.z.(\mathtt{b} := \mathrm{false}).true \\ = & z.h0 \quad \wedge \quad true \\ = & z.h0\ . \end{array}$$

It follows that

$$\begin{array}{ll} & z \text{ is stable} \\ \equiv & \{\text{definition } 14(3)\} \\ & [\,z.h1 \Rightarrow z.h0\,] \quad \wedge \quad [\,z.h0 \Rightarrow z.h0\,] \\ \equiv & \{\text{calculus}\} \\ & [\,z.h1 \Rightarrow z.h0\,]\ . \end{array}$$

The function *weak* is calculated in

$$\begin{array}{ll} & weak.z.h1 \\ = & \{(7);\text{ declaration without choice}\} \\ & wl.z.(\mathbf{body}.h1).true \\ = & \{\text{above calculation}\} \\ & z.h0\ , \end{array}$$

together with

$$\begin{array}{ll} & weak.z.h0 \\ = & \{(7);\text{ declaration with an unguarded fair choice}\} \\ & wl.z.h0.true \quad \vee \quad wl.z.(\mathtt{b} := \mathrm{false}).true \\ = & \{\text{second conjunct is } true\} \\ & true\ . \end{array}$$

It follows that $weak.z$ is stable for every function $z \in \mathbb{P}^H$, so that $alw \circ weak = weak$. It also follows that $weak.(weak.z).h = true$ for all $z \in \mathbb{P}^H$ and $h \in H$. This implies

$$fair.weak.h = true \qquad \text{for all } h \in H.$$

In particular, we have $fair.weak.h1 = true$, as announced. (End of example)

Example 5. Let $H = \{h0, h1\}$, declared by

$$\begin{array}{lll} \mathbf{body}.h0 & = & (\varepsilon \,[\!]_f\, h1)\ , \\ \mathbf{body}.h1 & = & h0\ . \end{array}$$

For a function $z \in \mathbb{P}^H$ we observe that

$$z \text{ is stable}$$
$$\equiv \quad \{\text{definition 14(3), and declaration}\}$$
$$[\, z.h0 \Rightarrow true \wedge z.h1 \,] \quad \wedge \quad [\, z.h1 \Rightarrow z.h0 \,]$$
$$\equiv \quad \{\text{calculus}\}$$
$$[\, z.h0 \equiv z.h1 \,] \; .$$

One easily verifies that both procedures need not terminate:

$$term.h = false \qquad \text{for both } h \in H.$$

We calculate

$$weak.term.h1$$
$$= \quad \{(7)\}$$
$$true \wedge wl.term.h0.true$$
$$= \quad \{14(0)\}$$
$$true \wedge term.h0 \wedge wlp.h0.true$$
$$= \quad \{\text{above calculation}\}$$
$$false \; .$$

By the characterization of stable functions obtained above, it follows that

$$alw.(weak.term) \leq term \; .$$

By definition (9), this implies that $fair.weak \leq term$, and hence, by formula (15), that $fair.weak = term$. The conclusion is that procedures $h0$ and $h1$ do not fairly terminate! Indeed, in the unique nonterminating execution path the choice for termination is enabled alternatingly, but not 'eventually at every procedure call'. (End of example)

15.5 The operational meaning

In the discussion in Section 15.1, the concept 'execution sequence' was used rather loosely. When investigating recursive procedures, we had better be more careful.

The operational meaning of fairness is based on the operational semantics. So, we use the configuration graph of general recursion, cf. Section 9.4. This is the set $X \times A^* \cup \{\infty\}$ with binary relation '$\rightarrow$' given by

$$\langle x, q\rangle \rightarrow \infty \quad \equiv$$
$$(\exists\, c \in S, r \in A^* :: q = c; r \wedge [\![c]\!].\infty.x) \quad \text{and}$$
$$\langle x, q\rangle \rightarrow \langle y, r\rangle \quad \equiv$$
$$(\exists\, c \in S :: q = c; r \wedge [\![c]\!].y.x)$$
$$\vee \quad (\exists\, h \in H, s \in \mathbf{body}.h, t \in A^* :: q = h; t \wedge r = s; t \wedge x = y) \; .$$

The elements of $X \times A^* \cup \{\infty\}$ are called *configurations*. An *execution sequence* is defined to be a finite or infinite sequence of configurations $u.i$ such that

$$u.i \to u.(i+1) \qquad \text{for all } i.$$

Relation $u \xrightarrow{*} v$ holds if and only if there is an execution sequence with $u.0 = u$ and $u.n = v$. Relation $u \xrightarrow{*} \infty$ means that there is an execution sequence that starts in u and ends in ∞ or is infinite.

An execution sequence is called *maximal* if and only if it is infinite, or ends in ∞ or in a configuration of the form $\langle x, \varepsilon \rangle$. Notice that there exist nonmaximal execution sequences that yet cannot be extended. Such a sequence ends in a configuration of the form $\langle x,\ c; r \rangle$ such that $\neg[\![c]\!].y.x$ for all $y \in X$. Usually, c is a guard $?b$ with $\neg b.x$.

In a maximal execution sequence $(i :: u.i)$, a term $u.i = \langle x,\ a; t \rangle$ with $a \in A$ is said to be *terminating* if and only if there is some $j > i$ with $u.j = \langle y, t \rangle$ for some state $y \in X$. If all terms of the sequence terminate, induction on the length of the initial string yields that the sequence is finite. Therefore, every infinite execution sequence has nonterminating terms. Since a tail of an infinite execution sequence is also an infinite execution sequence, every tail of an infinite execution sequence has nonterminating terms. This proves that every infinite execution sequence has infinitely many nonterminating terms.

If $u.i$ is a nonterminating term of an infinite execution sequence, then $u.i = \langle x, h; t \rangle$ for some $x \in X$, $h \in H$, $t \in A^*$. All subsequent terms of the sequence are of the form $\langle y, q; t \rangle$ with $q \neq \varepsilon$ and $\langle x, h \rangle \xrightarrow{*} \langle y, q \rangle$. In other words, the call of h diverges and command t is never reached. In that case, we speak of the *divergent procedure call* $\langle x, h \rangle$. In this way, we see that the nonterminating terms of an infinite execution sequence are associated to a list of nested divergent procedure calls.

We can now show that the formal definition of fairness has something to do with starvation of stable predicates.

(19) **Theorem.** Let $\langle x0, h0 \rangle$ be a procedure call with *fair*.$\psi.h0.x0$. For every infinite execution sequence starting in $\langle x0, h0 \rangle$ there is a stable function $z1 \in \mathbb{P}^H$ such that all divergent calls $\langle x, h \rangle$ of the sequence satisfy $\neg z1.h.x$ and that eventually all calls $\langle x, h \rangle$ satisfy $\psi.z1.h.x$.

Remark. In this abstract setting, predicate $\psi.z1$ represents the idea that $z1$ can be established. The theorem shows unfairness of the execution sequence in the sense that function $z1$ is subject to starvation. Notice, however, that we do not exclude the possibility that $z1.h.x$ holds for some terminating calls. (End of remark)

Proof. Let L be the set of the divergent calls $\langle x, h\rangle$ of the execution sequence. Let U be the subset of $\mathbb{P}^H$ given by

(20) $\quad z \in U \quad \equiv \quad z$ is stable $\quad \wedge \quad (\forall \langle x, h\rangle \in L :: \neg z.h.x)$.

Put $z1 = (\sup U) \in \mathbb{P}^H$. Function $z1$ is stable by Lemma 14(5). For every divergent call $\langle x, h\rangle$ of the sequence, we have

$$\begin{array}{ll} & z1.h.x \\ \equiv & \{\text{definition } z1\} \\ & (\sup z \in U :: z).h.x \\ \equiv & \{\text{calculus}\} \\ & (\exists z \in U :: z.h.x) \\ \equiv & \{(20)\} \\ & \text{false} . \end{array}$$

This proves

(21) $\quad (\forall \langle x, h\rangle \in L :: \neg z1.h.x)$.

In order to prove the existence of a divergent call $\langle x, h\rangle$ with $alw.(\psi.z1).h.x$, we observe that

$$\begin{array}{ll} & \neg(\exists \langle x, h\rangle \in L :: alw.(\psi.z1).h.x) \\ \equiv & \{\text{calculus}\} \\ & (\forall \langle x, h\rangle \in L :: \neg alw.(\psi.z1).h.x) \\ \equiv & \{(20) \text{ and } 14(7)(a)\} \\ & alw.(\psi.z1) \in U \\ \Rightarrow & \{\text{definition } z1\} \\ & alw.(\psi.z1) \leq z1 \\ \Rightarrow & \{(10)\} \\ & fair.\psi \leq z1 \\ \Rightarrow & \{fair.\psi.h0.x0 \text{ is given}\} \\ & z1.h0.x0 \\ \equiv & \{(21);\ \langle x0, h0\rangle \text{ is divergent}\} \\ & \text{false} . \end{array}$$

This proves the existence of a divergent call $\langle x1, h1\rangle \in L$ such that

$$alw.(\psi.z1).h1.x1 .$$

Since $alw.(\psi.z1)$ is stable, it follows from Theorem 14(4) that all procedure calls $\langle x, h\rangle$ after $\langle x1, h1\rangle$ satisfy $alw.(\psi.z1).h.x$, and hence also $(\psi.z1).h.x$. (End of proof)

Remark. In [Morris 1990] Section 5.1, an analogous property is given. Predicate $Q0$ of loc.cit. is the analogue of our function $z1$. It is a stable predicate, although he does not claim that. The proof of loc.cit. is based on transfinite induction. (End of remark)

15.6 A proposal for strong fairness

We now discuss a formalization of strong fairness as considered in Section 15.1. Inspired by [Morris 1990] Section 9, we use function *evt* of definition 14(24) to define $strong \in \mathbb{P}^H \to \mathbb{P}^H$ by

(22) $\quad strong.z.h \;=\; evt.(weak.z).h\ .$

By the description of *Evt* in Section 14.4, predicate *strong.z.h* says that a call of h induces (or is itself) a call k for which *weak.z.k* holds. It follows from formula 14(20) that

(23) $\quad [\,weak.z.h \;\Rightarrow\; strong.z.h\,] \qquad$ for all $z \in \mathbb{P}^H$ and $h \in H$.

Since *fair*.ψ is monotone in ψ, this implies that

(24) $\quad fair.weak \leq fair.strong\ .$

We might regard *fair.strong.h* as the condition that h fairly terminates with respect to strong fairness. A more precise interpretation is based on Theorem (19). In fact, let $\langle x0, h0\rangle$ be a call with *fair.strong.h0.x0*. Consider an infinite execution sequence starting in $\langle x0, h0\rangle$. By Theorem (19) there is a stable function $z1 \in \mathbb{P}^H$ such that all divergent calls $\langle x, h\rangle$ of the sequence satisfy *strong.z1.h.x*. Therefore, eventually every divergent call $\langle x, h\rangle$ induces a call $\langle y, k\rangle$ with *weak.z1.k.y*. This means that k has an enabled branch that establishes $z1$. Unfortunately, this does not mean that the divergence of call $\langle x, h\rangle$ is strongly p–unfair in the sense of 15.1. In fact, it may be that call $\langle y, k\rangle$ actually establishes $z1$, terminates, and is followed by another divergent call. This phenomenon is illustrated in the next example.

Example. Let $H = \{h0, h1\}$, declared by

$$\begin{array}{lcl} \mathbf{body}.h0 & = & (h1\ ;\ h0)\ , \\ \mathbf{body}.h1 & = & \varepsilon\ . \end{array}$$

It is clear that procedure $h0$ cannot terminate. Yet, for every function $z \in \mathbb{P}^H$, we have

$$\begin{array}{ll} & strong.z.h0 \\ = & \{(22)\} \\ & Evt.(weak.z).h0.false \\ \Leftarrow & \{14(20) \text{ and declaration}\} \\ & Evt.(weak.z).(h1\ ;\ h0).false \end{array}$$

$$= \quad \{14(22)\}$$
$$Evt.(weak.z).h1.(Evt.(weak.z).h0.false)$$
$$\Leftarrow \quad \{14(20) \text{ and declaration}\}$$
$$weak.z.h1$$
$$= \quad \{(7)\}$$
$$true \quad \wedge \quad wl.z.\varepsilon.true$$
$$= \quad \{14(0)\}$$
$$true\ .$$

By (23) and the last part of this computation, we also have $strong.z.h1 = true$. Therefore $strong.z.h = true$ for all z and all h. Using Theorem (16) with $v.n.h = (n > 0)$ for all $h \in H$, we get

$$fair.strong.h0 = true\ ,$$

so that $h0$ strongly terminates according to our formalism.

A similar example with simple recursion and a boolean program variable b is procedure h declared by

$$\mathbf{body}.h \quad = \quad (?\mathtt{b}\ ;\ \mathtt{b} := \neg\mathtt{b}\ [\!]\ ?\neg\mathtt{b}\ ;\ \mathtt{b} := \neg\mathtt{b}\ ;\ h\ ;\ h)\ .$$

Here we have a deterministic program that terminates if and only if initially b holds. According to our formalization, strongly fair termination holds regardless of the initial value of b. This can be proved by first showing that $[\,\mathtt{b} \Rightarrow weak.z.h\,]$ for every $z \in \mathbb{P}^H$, and subsequently that $[\,strong.z.h\,]$ for every $z \in \mathbb{P}^H$. (End of example)

Concluding Remark. The formal definitions of this chapter must be regarded as provisional or even tentative. We have therefore refrained from providing exercises.

CHAPTER 16

SOLUTIONS OF EXERCISES

Exercise 1.4.0. (a)

$$c; miracle \;\cong\; miracle$$
$$\equiv \quad \{(7), \text{ let } wg \text{ range over } wp,\ wlp \text{ and } p \text{ over } \mathbb{P}\}$$
$$(\forall\, wg, p :: wg.(c; miracle).p = wg.miracle.p)$$
$$\equiv \quad \{(13)\}$$
$$(\forall\, wg, p :: wg.c.(wg.miracle.p) = wg.miracle.p)$$
$$\equiv \quad \{(10)\}$$
$$(\forall\, wg :: wg.c.true = true)$$
$$\equiv \quad \{(2)\}$$
$$[\,wp.c.true\,] \wedge [\,wlp.c.true\,]$$
$$\equiv \quad \{\text{by (4), the lefthand conjunct implies the other one}\}$$
$$[\,wp.c.true\,]\ .$$

Exercise 2.3.0. (a) Clearly, t is an external variable threatened to be modified. Since t and y may change, we introduce specification constants T and Y and the postcondition Q : $\mathtt{t} = T \wedge y = Y$. The precondition $wp.(\mathbf{body}.h).Q$ is easily calculated. In this way we get the specification

$$\{\mathbf{ext}\ \mathtt{t!};\ \mathbf{all}\ T, Y \in integer\ ::$$
$$\mathbf{pre}\ P:\ y = T \wedge x + \mathtt{t} = Y,\ \mathbf{post}\ Q:\ \mathtt{t} = T \wedge y = Y\}\ .$$

The verification of the conditions (a), (b), (c) of (7) is immediate.

(b) Since program variable w is modified by the call, we assume that the call is $h(E, \mathtt{w})$ for some expression E. Rule (10) yields

$$\{\mathtt{w} = T \wedge E + \mathtt{t} = Y \wedge R\}\quad h(E, \mathtt{w})\quad \{\mathtt{t} = T \wedge \mathtt{w} = Y \wedge R\}$$

for all values Y and T and all predicates R with $Var.R \cap \{\mathtt{t}, \mathtt{w}\} = \emptyset$. In particular, choosing $T := X$ and $Y := 0$ and $R := true$, we get

$$\{\mathtt{w} = X \wedge E + \mathtt{t} = 0\}\quad h(E, \mathtt{w})\quad \{\mathtt{t} = X \wedge \mathtt{w} = 0\}\ .$$

This fits our aim when we take the actual parameter $E := -\mathtt{t}$.

Exercise 2.8.5. We introduce the abbreviation $q = wlp.L.(p \vee b)$ and observe that

$$\begin{array}{ll} & q \\ = & \{(15)\} \\ & wlp.(\mathbf{body}.L).(p \vee b) \\ = & \{(27) \text{ and calculus}\} \\ & (\neg b \Rightarrow p \vee b) \wedge (b \Rightarrow wlp.(c; L).(p \vee b)) \\ = & \{\text{calculus and definition of } q\} \\ & (p \vee b) \wedge (b \Rightarrow wlp.c.q) \\ \Rightarrow & \{\text{predicate calculus}\} \\ & p \vee (b \wedge wlp.c.q) \ . \end{array}$$

This proves $[q \Rightarrow p \vee (b \wedge wlp.c.q)]$. Since $[b \Rightarrow p \vee vf \geq 0]$, it follows that

$$[q \Rightarrow p \vee vf \geq 0] \ .$$

This may suggest the introduction of

$$R.n: \quad [q \Rightarrow p \vee vf \geq n] \quad \text{for } n \in \mathbb{N}.$$

Then we have $R.0$. The implication $R.n \Rightarrow R.(n+1)$ is proved in

$$\begin{array}{ll} & q \\ \Rightarrow & \{\text{above calculation}\} \\ & p \vee (b \wedge wlp.c.q) \\ \Rightarrow & \{R.n \text{ and monotony}\} \\ & p \vee (b \wedge wlp.c.(p \vee vf \geq n)) \\ \Rightarrow & \{\text{assumption}\} \\ & p \vee (p \vee vf > n) \\ \Rightarrow & \{\text{calculus}\} \\ & p \vee vf \geq n+1 \ . \end{array}$$

This proves that $R.n$ holds for all $n \in \mathbb{N}$. It remains to observe

$$\begin{array}{ll} & (\forall n \in \mathbb{N} :: R.n) \\ \equiv & [q \Rightarrow (\forall n :: p \vee vf \geq n)] \\ \equiv & [q \Rightarrow p \vee (\forall n :: vf \geq n)] \\ \equiv & [q \Rightarrow p \vee false] \\ \equiv & [q \Rightarrow p] \ . \end{array}$$

Exercise 3.5.0. (a) It suffices to observe that

$$\begin{array}{ll} & wp.L.false \\ = & \{2(14),\ 2(27) \text{ and calculus}\} \\ & (\neg b \Rightarrow false) \wedge (b \Rightarrow wp.c.(wp.L.false)) \end{array}$$

$$
\begin{aligned}
= &\ \ \{\text{calculus}\} \\
&\ b \wedge wp.c.(wp.L.\mathit{false}) \\
\Leftarrow &\ \ \{wp.c \text{ is monotone}\} \\
&\ b \wedge wp.c.\mathit{false} \\
= &\ \ \{\text{calculus}\} \\
&\ wp.(!b; c).\mathit{false}\ .
\end{aligned}
$$

(b) We use a proof by annotation, cf. Section 2.8:

$\{\mathtt{i} \geq 0\}$
while *true* **do** $\{vf = \mathtt{i}\}$
  $\{\mathtt{i} \geq 0 \wedge \mathit{true} \wedge \mathtt{i} \leq m\}$
  $?(\mathtt{i} \neq 0)$ $\{\mathtt{i} > 0 \wedge \mathtt{i} \leq m\}$
  $\mathtt{i} := \mathtt{i} - 1$ $\{\mathtt{i} \geq 0 \wedge \mathtt{i} < m \wedge m \geq 0\}$
od $\{\mathtt{i} \geq 0 \wedge \neg \mathit{true}\}$
$\{\mathit{false}\}$.

(c) In part (b) we proved that $[\,\mathtt{i} \geq 0 \Rightarrow wp.L.\mathit{false}\,]$. In the situation of part (b), one verifies that $wp.(!b; c).\mathit{false} = (\mathtt{i} = 0)$. Finally, we observe that $\mathtt{i} \geq 0$ does not implies $\mathtt{i} = 0$.

Exercise 4.1.4. It suffices to verify that for all $z \in W$

$$
\begin{aligned}
&\ z \leq (\inf w \in W : (\exists U \in Q :: w \in U) : w) \\
\equiv &\ \ \{(1)\} \\
&\ (\forall w \in W : (\exists U \in Q :: w \in U) : z \leq w) \\
\equiv &\ \ \{\text{trading}\} \\
&\ (\forall w \in W :: (\exists U \in Q :: w \in U) \Rightarrow z \leq w) \\
\equiv &\ \ \{p \Rightarrow q \equiv \neg p \vee q \text{ (twice) and De Morgan}\} \\
&\ (\forall w \in W :: (\forall U \in Q :: w \in U \Rightarrow z \leq w)) \\
\equiv &\ \ \{\text{interchange of quantifications}\} \\
&\ (\forall U \in Q :: (\forall w \in W :: w \in U \Rightarrow z \leq w)) \\
\equiv &\ \ \{(1)\} \\
&\ (\forall U \in Q :: z \leq (\inf U)) \\
\equiv &\ \ \{(1)\} \\
&\ z \leq (\inf U \in Q :: (\inf U))\ .
\end{aligned}
$$

Exercise 4.9.0. Let $W0$ be the subset of WLP given by

$$w \in W0 \quad \equiv \quad (\forall h \in H \cap C :: [p \Rightarrow w.h.p])\ .$$

Since $[p \Rightarrow wlp.a.p]$ for all $a \in S \cap C$, it follows that

$$[p \Rightarrow w.a.p] \quad \text{for all } w \in W0 \text{ and } a \in C.$$

Using definition (15), one can prove that

(*) $\qquad [p \Rightarrow w.c.p]$ for all $w \in W0$ and $c \in C^{\odot}$.

Since **body**.$h \in C^{\odot}$ for all $h \in H \cap C$, it follows that

$$[p \Rightarrow w.(\mathbf{body}.h).p] \quad \text{for all } w \in W0 \text{ and } h \in H \cap C.$$

Now Theorem (44) implies that $wlp \in W0$. By (*), this proves that

$$[p \Rightarrow wlp.c.p] \quad \text{for all } c \in C^{\odot}.$$

Exercise 5.1.4.

(a) $\quad ?p; c \sqsubseteq c; ?q$

$\equiv \quad$ {(1), let wg range over $\{wp, wlp\}$ and r over $\mathbb{P}$}

$\quad (\forall\, wg, r :: [\, wg.(?p; c).r \;\Rightarrow\; wg.(c; ?q).r\,])$

$\equiv \quad$ {calculus}

$\quad (\forall\, wg, r :: [\neg p \vee wg.c.r \;\Rightarrow\; wg.c.(q \Rightarrow r)\,])$

$\equiv \quad$ {$wg.c$ is monotone and $[r \Rightarrow (q \Rightarrow r)]$}

$\quad (\forall\, wg, r :: [\neg p \;\Rightarrow\; wg.c.(q \Rightarrow r)\,])$

$\equiv \quad$ {axiom 1(4); the term is monotone in r}

$\quad [\neg p \;\Rightarrow\; wp.c.(q \Rightarrow \mathit{false})\,])$

$\equiv \quad$ {calculus}

$\quad [p \;\vee\; wp.c.(\neg q)\,])$.

(b) $\quad c; ?p \sqsubseteq ?q; c$

$\equiv \quad$ {as above; first two steps}

(*) $\quad (\forall\, wg, r :: [\, wg.c.(p \Rightarrow r) \;\Rightarrow\; (q \Rightarrow wg.c.r)\,])$

$\equiv \quad$ {shunting}

$\quad (\forall\, wg, r :: [\, wg.c.(p \Rightarrow r) \wedge q \;\Rightarrow\; wg.c.r\,])$

$\Leftarrow \quad$ {calculus}

$\quad [q \Rightarrow wlp.c.p] \wedge (\forall\, wg, r :: [\, wg.c.(p \Rightarrow r) \wedge wlp.c.p \;\Rightarrow\; wg.c.r\,])$

$\equiv \quad$ {axiom 3(4) and exercise 3.3.1}

$\quad [q \Rightarrow wlp.c.p] \wedge (\forall\, wg, r :: [\, wg.c.((p \Rightarrow r) \wedge p) \;\Rightarrow\; wg.c.r\,])$

$\equiv \quad$ {$wg.c$ is monotone and $[(p \Rightarrow r) \wedge p \Rightarrow r]$}

$\quad [q \Rightarrow wlp.c.p]$.

The other implication is proved as follows. Formula (*) implies

$$[\, wlp.c.(p \Rightarrow p) \;\Rightarrow\; (q \Rightarrow wlp.c.p)\,] \;.$$

By formula 3(5), this equivales $[q \Rightarrow wlp.c.p]$.

Exercise 6.4.2. Consider predicate r defined by

$$r.y \equiv (\exists\, x \in X : [\![c]\!].y.x : p.x) \;.$$

For every predicate q we have

$$
\begin{array}{ll}
 & [r \Rightarrow q] \\
\equiv & \{\text{definition } r \text{ and } 1(2)\} \\
 & (\forall y :: (\exists x : [\![c]\!].y.x : p.x) \Rightarrow q.y) \\
\equiv & \{\text{calculus}\} \\
 & (\forall y :: (\forall x : [\![c]\!].y.x : p.x \Rightarrow q.y)) \\
\equiv & \{\text{interchange}\} \\
 & (\forall x :: (\forall y : [\![c]\!].y.x : p.x \Rightarrow q.y)) \\
\equiv & \{\text{calculus}\} \\
 & (\forall x :: p.x \Rightarrow (\forall y : [\![c]\!].y.x : q.y)) \\
\equiv & \{(1) \text{ and } (15)\} \\
 & (\forall x :: p.x \Rightarrow wlp.c.q.x) \\
\equiv & \{1(2)\} \\
 & [p \Rightarrow wlp.c.q] \\
\equiv & \{5(10)\} \\
 & [sp.c.p \Rightarrow q]\ .
\end{array}
$$

This implies that $r = sp.c.p$.

Exercise 8.2.0. (a) The set R is sup–closed in MT since for every subset U of MT we have

$$
\begin{array}{ll}
 & (\sup U) \in R \\
\equiv & \{\text{definition of } R\} \\
 & (\sup U) \circ e \le g \circ (\sup U) \\
\equiv & \{4(2), \text{ let } p \text{ range over } \mathbb{P}\} \\
 & (\forall p :: (\sup U).(e.p) \le g.((\sup U).p)) \\
\equiv & \{4(3) \text{ and } 4(0), \text{ let } u \text{ range over } U\} \\
 & (\forall p, u :: u.(e.p) \le g.((\sup U).p)) \\
\equiv & \{\text{monotony of } g\} \\
 & (\forall p, u :: u.(e.p) \le g.(u.p)) \\
\equiv & \{\text{definition of } R\} \\
 & U \subset R\ .
\end{array}
$$

The second assertion now follows from Theorem (4)(c).

(b) By Theorem (9)(a,f), it suffices to prove that R is closed under functional composition:

$$
\begin{array}{ll}
 & f, h \in R \\
\equiv & \{\text{definition of } R\} \\
 & f \circ e \le g \circ f \quad \wedge \quad h \circ e \le g \circ h \\
\Rightarrow & \{4(7)(d)\}
\end{array}
$$

$$f \circ e \circ h \leq g \circ f \circ h \;\wedge\; f \circ h \circ e \leq f \circ g \circ h$$
$\Rightarrow$ $\{g \leq e$ and 4(7)(d)$\}$
$$f \circ h \circ e \leq f \circ g \circ h \leq f \circ e \circ h \leq g \circ f \circ h$$
$\Rightarrow$ {definition of R}
$$f \circ h \in R\ .$$

(c) By Theorem (9)(a,g), it suffices to prove that R is closed under finite infima: for any finite subset U of MT we have

$(\inf U) \in R$
$\equiv$ {definition of R}
$(\forall p :: (\inf u \in U :: u.(e.p)) \leq g.(\inf u \in U :: u.p))$
$\equiv$ {g commutes with finite infima}
$(\forall p :: (\inf u \in U :: u.(e.p)) \leq (\inf u \in U :: g.(u.p)))$
$\Leftarrow$ {monotony}
$(\forall p, u :: u.(e.p) \leq g.(u.p))$
$\equiv$ {definition of R}
$U \subset R\ .$

Exercise 11.3.1. Let E be the set of pairs of commands

$$\langle g\ ;\ \mathrm{v} := k * \mathrm{v} \quad , \quad \mathrm{v} := k\ ;\ h\rangle\ .$$

By rule (5), it suffices to prove $E \subset (\approx)$. This is proved by means of rule (6). Since

$$\mathit{abort}\ ;\ \mathrm{v} := k * \mathrm{v} \;\cong\; \mathit{abort} \;\cong\; \mathrm{v} := k\ ;\ \mathit{abort}\ ,$$

we have $\mathbf{abort}^{\odot}.q \cong \mathbf{abort}^{\odot}.r$ for all pairs $\langle q, r\rangle \in E$. By (4)(a), the commands g, h, $\mathrm{v} := k$ and $\mathrm{v} := k * \mathrm{v}$ all belong to *Lia*. Since $(\mathrm{v} := k * \mathrm{v}) \in S^{\odot}$, it follows from (4)(d) that $(g\,;\,\mathrm{v} := k * \mathrm{v}) \in$ *Lia*. Since $\mathrm{v} := k$ is a deterministic simple command, we have $(\mathrm{v} := k) \in$ *Sy.Muc* by Theorem 8(20)(a). By (4)(d) it follows that $(\mathrm{v} := k\ ;\ h) \in$ *Lia*. This proves the first condition of rule (6).

For every congruence $(\sim)$ on $A^{\odot}$ that contains $E \cup (\approx)$, we have

$\mathbf{body}^{\odot}.(g\ ;\ \mathrm{v} := k * \mathrm{v})$
$=$ {declaration g}
$(c\ ;\ \mathrm{v} := 1 \,[\!]\, ([\!]\, i \in I :: d.i\ ;\ g\ ;\ \mathrm{v} := i * \mathrm{v}))\ ;\ \mathrm{v} := k * \mathrm{v}$
$\approx$ $\{\mathrm{v} := 1\ ;\ \mathrm{v} := k * \mathrm{v} \;\cong\; \mathrm{v} := k\ ;$
$\quad \mathrm{v} := i * \mathrm{v}\ ;\ \mathrm{v} := k * \mathrm{v} \;\cong\; \mathrm{v} := k * i * \mathrm{v}$; now use (7)$\}$
$c\ ;\ \mathrm{v} := k \,[\!]\, ([\!]\, i \in I :: d.i\ ;\ g\ ;\ \mathrm{v} := k * i * \mathrm{v})$
$\sim$ $\{E \subset (\sim)$ and $\sim$ is a congruence$\}$
$c\ ;\ \mathrm{v} := k \,[\!]\, ([\!]\, i \in I :: d.i\ ;\ \mathrm{v} := k * i\ ;\ h)$
$\approx$ $\{\mathrm{v} := k\ ;\ \mathrm{v} := \mathrm{v} * i \;\cong\; \mathrm{v} := k * i$; use (7)$\}$
$c\ ;\ \mathrm{v} := k \,[\!]\, ([\!]\, i \in I :: d.i\ ;\ \mathrm{v} := k\ ;\ \mathrm{v} := \mathrm{v} * i\ ;\ h)$

$\approx$ {c and $d.i$ commute with $\mathbf{v} := k$, and (7); declaration of h}
$\mathbf{body}^{\odot}.(\mathbf{v} := k \,;\, h)$.

Now rule (6) yields $E \subset (\approx)$.

Exercise 11.3.4. In order to show that the rule proposed is applicable, we observe

$\mathbf{abort}^{\odot}.L \cong \mathbf{abort}^{\odot}.M \quad \wedge \quad L, M \in Lia$
$\equiv$ {(0), 10(0) and (4)(a)}
$?\neg b \,[\!]\, ?b \,;\, c \,;\, abort \quad \cong \quad ?\neg b \,[\!]\, ?b \,;\, abort$
$\equiv$ {use choice of c}
true .

For every congruence $(\sim)$ that contains $E \cup (\approx)$, we have

$\mathbf{body}^{\odot}.L \sim \mathbf{body}^{\odot}.M$
$\equiv$ {10(0)}
$\mathbf{body}.L \sim \mathbf{body}.M$
$\equiv$ {$\sim$ is a congruence that contains $\approx$, and $\mathbf{body}.h \cong h$ for all h}
$L \sim M$
$\equiv$ {$\sim$ contains E}
true .

The invalid rule would imply that $L \cong M$. We have

$$L \;=\; \mathbf{while}\ \mathrm{i} \neq 0\ \mathbf{do}\ \mathrm{i} := \mathrm{i} - 1\ \mathbf{od}\ ,$$
$$M \;=\; \mathbf{while}\ \mathrm{i} \neq 0\ \mathbf{do}\ \varepsilon\ \mathbf{od}\ .$$

Using the techniques of Chapter 2, one can easily prove that $wp.L.true = (\mathrm{i} \geq 0)$ and $wp.M.true = (\mathrm{i} = 0)$. So, L and M are semantically different. Therefore, the proposed rule is not valid.

Exercise 13.4.0. For any relation E on commands we have

$(\forall \langle q, r\rangle \in E :: \mathbf{abort}^{\odot}.q \sqsubseteq \mathbf{abort}^{\odot}.r)$
$\equiv$ {(15)}
$(\sup \emptyset) \in Wg_0.E \quad \wedge \quad (\inf \emptyset) \in Wg_1.E$
$\Leftarrow$ {$\emptyset$ is a chain, see Section 7.2}
$Wg_0.E$ is sup–decked and $Wg_1.E$ is inf–decked
$\Leftarrow$ {Section 13.2}
E is safe
$\Leftarrow$ {Theorem (12)}
$E = (\ll)$.

Since $(\ll)$ is a preorder, we have $q \ll q$ for all commands q. So, for the second question it suffices to exhibit a command q with $q \notin Lia$. This has been done in

Section 11.7.

Exercise 14.1.3. (a) First use Hoare's Induction Rule to prove that $wlp.h.false = true$, i.e. that h is guaranteed not to terminate. By (0), it follows that

(*) $\qquad wl.z.h.p = z.h \quad$ for all $p \in \mathbb{P}$.

Now z, given by $z.h = (\mathrm{v} > i)$, is stable because of

$$
\begin{aligned}
& (wl.z)^0.(\mathbf{body}.h).true \\
= \quad & \{\text{declaration } h\} \\
& (wl.z)^0.(\mathrm{v} := \mathrm{v}+1\ ;\ h\ ;\ \mathrm{v} := \mathrm{v}-2\ ;\ h).true \\
= \quad & \{\text{use (*) with } p := (wl.z)^0.(\mathrm{v} := \mathrm{v}-2\ ;\ h).true\} \\
& (wl.z)^0.(\mathrm{v} := \mathrm{v}+1).(z.h) \\
= \quad & \{4(25) \text{ and definition } z\} \\
& ws_0.(\mathrm{v} := \mathrm{v}+1).(\mathrm{v} > i) \\
= \quad & \{\text{assignment}\} \\
& \mathrm{v}+1 > i \\
\Leftarrow \quad & \{\text{definition } z\} \\
& z.h\ .
\end{aligned}
$$

(b)

$$
\begin{aligned}
& (wl.z)^0.(\mathbf{body}.h).true \\
= \quad & \{\text{declaration } h\} \\
& (wl.z)^0.(skip\ \|\ \mathrm{v} := \mathrm{v}+1\ ;\ h\ ;\ \mathrm{v} := \mathrm{v}-2\ ;\ h).true \\
= \quad & \{(wl.z)^0 \text{ is a homomorphism that extends } wl.z\} \\
& (wl.z)^0.skip.true \\
& \wedge\ (wl.z)^0.(\mathrm{v} := \mathrm{v}+1\ ;\ h\ ;\ \mathrm{v} := \mathrm{v}-2).(wl.z.h.true) \\
= \quad & \{(wl.z)^0|S = ws_0 \text{ and } (0)\} \\
& true \wedge (wl.z)^0.(\mathrm{v} := \mathrm{v}+1\ ;\ h\ ;\ \mathrm{v} := \mathrm{v}-2).(z.h \wedge wlp.h.true) \\
= \quad & \{\text{calculus, definition of } z \text{ and } 3(5)\} \\
& (wl.z)^0.(\mathrm{v} := \mathrm{v}+1\ ;\ h\ ;\ \mathrm{v} := \mathrm{v}-2).(\mathrm{v} > i) \\
= \quad & \{(wl.z)^0|S = ws_0\} \\
& (wl.z)^0.(\mathrm{v} := \mathrm{v}+1\ ;\ h).(\mathrm{v}-2 > i) \\
= \quad & \{(0) \text{ and calculus}\} \\
& ws_0.(\mathrm{v} := \mathrm{v}+1).(z.h \wedge wlp.h.(\mathrm{v} > i+2)) \\
= \quad & \{\text{exercise 5.7.0}\} \\
& ws_0.(\mathrm{v} := \mathrm{v}+1).(z.h \wedge false) \\
= \quad & \{(wl.z)^0|S = ws_0\} \\
& false\ .
\end{aligned}
$$

Clearly, $z.h$ does not imply $false$. Therefore, z is not stable.

Exercise 14.2.0.

$wl.z$ is a fixpoint of D_0

$\equiv$ {let h range over H and p over $\mathbb{P}$; use 4(26)}

$(\forall h, p :: wl.z.h.p = (wl.z)^0.(\mathbf{body}.h).p)$

$\equiv$ {(0) and (1)}

$(\forall h, p :: z.h \wedge wlp.h.p = (wl.z)^0.(\mathbf{body}.h).true \wedge wlp.(\mathbf{body}.h).p)$

$\equiv$ {(10) and 4(19)}

$(\forall h, p :: z.h \wedge wlp.h.p = unf.z.h \wedge wlp.h.p)$

$\equiv$ {$\Leftarrow$: easy; $\Rightarrow$: use $p := true$ and 3(5)}

$(\forall h :: z.h = unf.z.h)$

$\equiv$ {equality of functions}

z is a fixpoint of unf.

REFERENCES

K.R. Apt [1981]: Ten years of Hoare's logic. A survey – Part 1. ACM Trans. Program. Languages and Systems **3** (1981) 431–483.

K.R. Apt, G.D. Plotkin [1986]: Countable nondeterminism and random assignment. J. ACM **33** (1986) 724–767.

R.J.R. Back [1988]: A calculus of refinements for program derivations. Acta Informatica **25** (1988) 593–624.

R.J.R. Back, J. von Wright [1989a]: A lattice–theoretical basis for a specification language. In: J.L.A. van de Snepscheut (ed.): Mathematics of Program Construction, Lecture Notes in Computer Science 375 (Springer, Berlin, 1989) pp. 139–156.

R.J.R. Back, J. von Wright [1989b]: Combining angels, demons and miracles in program specifications. Åbo Akademi A86, Turku Finland, 1989. To appear in Theoretical Computer Science.

R.J.R. Back, J. von Wright [1990]: Duality in specification languages: a lattice–theoretical approach. Acta Informatica **27** (1990) 583–625.

R.C. Backhouse [1986]: Program Construction and Verification (Prentice–Hall International, 1986).

J.W. de Bakker [1980]: Mathematical Theory of Program Correctness (Prentice–Hall, 1980).

J.W. de Bakker, L.G.L.T. Meertens [1975]: On the completeness of the inductive assertion method. J. Comput. Syst. Sci. **11** (1975) 323–357.

J.W. de Bakker, W.P. de Roever [1973]: A calculus for recursive program schemes. In: M. Nivat (ed.): Automata, Languages and Programming 1972 (North Holland, 1973) pp. 167–196.

M. Barr, C. Wells [1990]: Category Theory for Computing Science (Prentice Hall International, 1990).

K.M. Chandy, J. Misra [1988]: Parallel Program Design, A Foundation (Addison–Wesley, 1988).

E.W. Dijkstra [1975]: Guarded commands, nondeterminacy and formal derivation of programs. Commun. ACM **18** (1975) 453–457.

E.W. Dijkstra [1976]: A Discipline of Programming (Prentice–Hall, 1976).

E.W. Dijkstra (ed.) [1990]: Formal Development of Programs and Proofs. University of Texas at Austin Year of Programming Series (Addison–Wesley, 1990).

E.W. Dijkstra, C.S. Scholten [1990]: Predicate Calculus and Program Semantics (Springer V, 1990).

N. Francez [1986]: Fairness (Springer V, 1986).

J.H. Gallier [1987]: Logic for Computer Science. Foundations of automatic theorem proving. (Wiley & Sons 1987).

D. Gries [1981]: The Science of Programming (Springer V, 1981).

D. Harel [1984]: Dynamic logic. In: D. Gabbay, F. Guenthner (eds.): Handbook of Philosophical Logic, Vol. 2 (Reidel, 1984) pp. 497–604.

E.C.R. Hehner [1979]: **do** Considered **od** : a contribution to programming calculus. Acta Informatica **11** (1979) 287–304.

E.R.C. Hehner [1984]: Predicative programming, Part 1. Commun. ACM **27** (1984) 134–143.

E.R.C. Hehner [1992]: A Practical Theory of Programming. Forthcoming.

W.H. Hesselink [1988]: Interpretations of recursion under unbounded nondeterminacy. Theor. Comp. Sci. **59** (1988) 211–234.

W.H. Hesselink [1989a]: Initialisation with a final value, an exercise in program transformation. In: J.L.A. van de Snepscheut (ed.): Mathematics of Program Construction, Lecture Notes in Computer Science 375 (Springer V, 1989) pp. 273–280.

W.H. Hesselink [1989b]: Processes and formalisms for unbounded choice. Tech. Rep. CS 8917, Groningen University, 1989. To appear in Theoretical Computer Science.

W.H. Hesselink [1990]: Command algebras, recursion and program transformation. Formal Aspects Comput. **2** (1990) 60–104.

C.A.R. Hoare [1969]: An axiomatic basis for computer programming. Comm. ACM **12** (1969) 576–583.

C.A.R. Hoare [1971]: Procedures and parameters: an axiomatic approach. In: E. Engeler (ed.): Symposium on Semantics of Algorithmic Languages, Lecture Notes in Mathematics 188 (Springer V, 1971) pp. 102–116.

C.A.R. Hoare [1989]: Notes on an approach to category theory for computer scientists. In: M. Broy (ed.) Constructive Methods in Computing Science NATO ASI Series F 55 (Springer V, 1989) pp. 245–305.

K. Jensen, N. Wirth [1985]: Pascal User Manual and Report, third edition. Springer V. 1985.

R.M. Karp [1959]: Some applications of logical syntax to digital computer programming. Thesis, Harvard University, 1959.

D. Lehmann, A. Pnueli, J. Stavi [1981]: Impartiality, justice and fairness: the ethics of concurrent termination. In: Proc. Internat. Conf. on Automata, Languages and Programming, Lecture Notes in Computer Science 115 (Springer V, 1981) pp. 264–277.

J.J. Lukkien [1991]: Parallel program design and generalized weakest preconditions. Thesis Groningen 1991.

Z. Manna [1974]: Mathematical Theory of Computation (McGraw–Hill 1974).

Z. Manna, A. Pnueli [1974]: Axiomatic approach to total correctness of programs. Acta Informatica **3** (1974) 253–262.

Z. Manna, J. Vuillemin [1972]: Fixpoint approach to the theory of computation. In: M. Nivat (ed.): Automata, Languages and Programming 1972. (North Holland, 1973) pp. 273–292.

A.J. Martin [1983]: A general proof rule for procedures in predicate transformer semantics. Acta Informatica **20** (1983) 301–313.

J. McCarthy [1980]: Circumscription – a form of non-monotonic reasoning. Artif. Intell. **13** (1980) 27–39.

C. Morgan [1990]: Programming from Specifications. (Prentice Hall, 1990)

C. Morgan, P.H.B. Gardiner [1990]: Data refinement by calculation. Acta Informatica **27** (1990) 481–503.

J.M. Morris [1987]: A theoretical basis for stepwise refinement and the programming calculus. Sci. Comp. Program. **9** (1987) 287–306.

J.M. Morris [1990]: Temporal predicate transformers and fair termination. Acta Informatica **27** (1990) 287–313.

G. Nelson [1989]: A generalization of Dijkstra's calculus. ACM Trans. Program. Languages and Systems, **11** (1989) 517–561.

D. Park [1979]: On the semantics of fair parallelism. In: D. Bjørner (ed.): Abstract Software Specifications, Lecture Notes in Computer Science 86, Proceedings, Copenhagen 1979 (Springer V, 1980) pp. 504–526.

W.P. de Roever [1976]: Dijkstra's predicate transformer, non-determinism, recursion, and termination. In: Mathematical Foundations of Computer Science 1976, Lecture Notes in Computer Science 45 (Springer V, 1976) pp. 472–481.

J.P. Queille, J. Sifakis [1983]: Fairness and related properties in transition systems – a temporal logic to deal with fairness. Acta Informatica **19** (1983) 195–220.

A. Tarski [1955]: A lattice theoretical fixpoint theorem and its applications. Pacific J. Math. **5** (1955) 285–309.

A.M. Turing [1949]: On checking a large routine. In: Report of a Conference on High–Speed Automatic Calculating Machines. University Mathematical Laboratory, Cambridge, 1949, pp. 67–69.

J. von Wright [1990]: A lattice–theoretical basis for program refinement. Thesis, Åbo Akademi, Turku, Finland, 1990

INDEX OF CONCEPTS AND IDENTIFIERS

Entries are indexed by section numbers. In most cases we only provide the defining occurrences.